Critical Multicultural Conversations

Critical Education and Ethics

Editors

Barry Kanpol, *Indiana University – Purdue University Fort Wayne*
Fred Yeo, *Southeast Missouri State University*

Critical Multicultural Conversations

edited by

Greg S. Goodman and Karen Carey
California State University, Fresno

HAMPTON PRESS, INC.
CRESSKILL, NEW JERSEY

Printed in the United States of America

Library of Congress Cataloging-in-Publication Data

Critical multicultural conversations / edited by Karen Carey and Greg Goodman
       p.cm.-- (Critical education and ethics)
   Includes bibliographical references and index.
   ISBN 1-57273-572-4 -- ISBN 1-57273-573-2 (pbk.)
     1. Multicultural education--United States. 2. Critical pedagogy--United States.
   I. Carey, Karen T., 1952 - II. Goodman, Greg S., 1949- III. Series.

LC1099.3.C75 2004
370.11'5--dc22   2003067764

Cover photograph by Gustavo Alberto Garcia Vaca—www.chamanvision.com

Hampton Press, Inc.
23 Broadway
Cresskill, NJ 07626

This work is dedicated in memory of Nate Smith (August 31, 1911 – December 28, 2001). Nate's political and community activism was powered by a passion for social justice. One of the original Gray Panthers, Nate's name and memory is revered for decades of organizing for the support of Boston's poor and under-represented.

This book is also dedicated to Colonel Rick Husband, who was the commander of NASA's Space Shuttle Columbia. On February 1, 2003, the Columbia was lost during reentry into the Earth's atmosphere. Colonel Husband received his Master of Science in mechanical engineering at California State University, Fresno in 1990. Colonel Husband was an inspiration to many at CSU, Fresno, and his achievements will not be forgotten.

CONTENTS

ACKNOWLEDGMENTS

Many individuals have contributed to the completion of this book. Foremost, we would like to thank Shirley Steinberg for her unyielding commitment to this book's publication. Shirley's advocacy for the fundamental principles of Critical Theory helped to buoy these authors during the years of process editors and writers endure en route to book completion and publication.

We, also thank Peter McLaren for his visionary leadership and teaching. Peter was the professor for many of the writers presented in this volume. Turning from professor to mentor and example, Peter saw this book's potential and encouraged his students to write for the furthering of critical pedagogy's position within the canon of multicultural education.

All of the contributors are indebted to Barry Kanpol for his astute reading of this work and his provision of editorial expertise. Barry's contributions to the advance of critical pedagogy are legend, and his support for our contribution to the field is appreciated by all of our writers.

We thank the California State University, Fresno and the University of California, Davis' Joint Doctoral Program in Educational Leadership for the opportunity to bring together almost all of the writers presented herein. Inspired by Peter McLaren and by many other esteemed faculty such as Doug Minnis, Sharon Brown-Welty, Paul Shaker, Susan Trace, Finnian McGinn, and Phyllis Kuehn, these writers represent the best of the outcomes of an Educational Leadership doctoral program. The faculty and graduates have joined together to create a text worthy of the preparation of students of education throughout the United States.

Thanks, too, to Barbara Morton for her expertise and many hours of editorial exercise. And, in the end, our appreciation is heartfelt for our partners, Andy Goodman and Allan Cohen. Through their continuous support, the journey from start to finish was made much more enjoyable.

PREFACE

At the time of this writing, on the eve of a massive U.S. military assault on Iraq, it hardly seems a precipitous moment to be writing a preface on the merits of diversity and multicultural education. On the other hand, the time could not be more urgent.

As I sat down to write this preface, I was preoccupied with thoughts about the present state of the union. I will only hit on a few points that immediately come to mind: We have a corporate media that treats corrupt government officials with kid gloves, but there is no public outcry; we learn matter-of-factly that the contracts for fighting Iraqi oil well fires have already been given to a subsidiary of Halliburton, the corporation once run by Dick Cheney, but again there is no public outcry; we learn that the supposed evidence of Saddam's nuclear program was based on hastily forged documents, but still there is no public outcry; and we seem to have conveniently forgotten (after the horror of September 11, 2001) or don't seem to care any more that investigations into the alleged connections between the Bush administration and the recent financial scandals involving Enron and other major U.S. corporations have all but fizzled. Faced with a compliant press, the Bush administration is pushing the country to the edge of a political precipice.

At the current historical conjuncture we in the United States are faced with the actions of an unelected President of the United States. He is the selected front-man of an oil cartel junta who has successfully discredited representative democracy and judicial impartiality and world opinion. He has also amassed the most powerful invasion force in world history that has begun to unleash hell against a nation of 22 million people who happen to be ruled by a murderous and malevolent dictator. We have Congressional Democrats who are so terrified of being branded unpatriotic that they pander to the whims of the administration's hawks like blubbering quislings. (Bush hijo always looks bigger when you are on your knees.) There is reason to be concerned that our presidential oil mafia is threatening to turn Iraq into, in the words of John Powers, a "game preserve for American corporations;" however, there is little outcry against the rolling back of our constitutional rights in order to protect us from those who might choose to retaliate against us within our own borders. When we are told that Bush believes he is fighting the biblical struggle between good and evil, placing the United States incontrovertibly on what he believes is the inviolate side of virtue, we look for the outrage from our country's clerics and religious leaders but search far and wide to find any public condemnations. I could go on about attempts by the current administration to destroy Medicaid, the stacking of the courts with antichoice judges, and the stealing of money from the poor to give to the rich but, well, that seems pretty much to be politics as usual in the history of many U.S. administrations. What do we make of the supposed free press in this country when the government can be exposed for spying on members of the U.N. Security Council—an event that became a worldwide scandal—and yet we can't seem to find reports of this anywhere in the majority of the U.S. presses? (Solomon, 2003). This is hardly surprising. Take Fox News: A recent advertisement for Fox News Channel showcased the following words of Roger Ailes, Chairman, Fox News: "America Guarantees a Free Press . . . Freedom Relies on a Fair Press. . . ." Ailes, former chief strategist for Nixon, Reagan, and Bush, works for Australian billionaire Rupert Murdoch. Every one of the newspapers owned by Murdoch's News Associates vigorously supports the war on Iraq, to which *The Nation* responds: "Compared with Murdoch, Mao Zedong, who said, "Let a hundred flowers bloom," was a free-speech fanatic" (2002, p. 7).

How can we create a democratic and diverse society when the media pander wildly to those who are filled with collective delusions and who plump for the status quo: Let's blame the French for not getting us worldwide support for the invasion of Iraq; let's blame the Security Council; the U.N. is irrelevant when it comes to what's good for the Homeland and besides, it's anti-American and socialist. I've heard a lot of this kind of sentiment expressed while driving home from the campus in the evening and listening with curiosity and alarm to late-night Christian radio commentary. The self-identified untutored citizens who are proud of never having read a nonfiction book and who regularly tune into FOX News are showing their cards like never before. Their stereotypical view of people of color (especially Arabs these days), their America Firstism and tongue-flicking jingoism, and their fraternity-gone-wild cheerleading for American values has helped to make historical amnesia a precondition for nurturing U.S. citizenship and made it an unchallengeable source of moral authority in international relations.

Where there is hope for this country is in the people who have been part of a worldwide public outcry against the U.S. war machine and its drive towards the oilfield of Iraq. They have taken to the streets in protests the size and intensity of which have not been seen since the days of the Vietnam War. We cannot overlook the valiant efforts of the antiglobalization and antiwar movements in this and in other countries or those who are defending what civil rights we have left here in the Homeland. The burgeoning opposition to the authoritarian populism and military Keynesianism as currently practiced by the United States is truly heartening.

Although the majority of American citizens dearly want to believe that the invasion of Iraq is actually a rescue operation to free a country from an evil dictator and to destroy his weapons of mass destruction, it's not all that easy in the face of opposing viewpoints. Yet one will rarely find those opposing viewpoints expressed in the corporate media. Well-founded and reasoned claims against war are ridiculed in the corporate media, if in fact they are even given a hearing. (Nobody talks about how the United States provided Saddam Hussein with the ingredients for his deadly arsenal and turned the other way when he gassed Iranian soldiers and Kurds). When I travel to Latin America, invariably I am asked about the impact of Noam Chomsky upon the U.S. public. My answer is simple: there is little impact because one of the greatest spokespersons on American foreign policy is rarely ever seen on national media. We are truly living in Orwell's 1984 nightmare scenario.

Isn't it time that we, as educators, took stock of the kind of literacy we want our students to acquire in the process of their formation as citizens? As the great Brazilian educator, Paulo Freire (1998), warned: To read the word and the world today absolutely demands challenging the hegemony of the status quo knowledges and opinions manufactured and circulated by the corporate media. This is what I have called the process of critical patriotism. This, of course, is precisely the struggle that progressive and radical educators have waged for many decades. And the fact that earlier victories are in the process of being rolled back should not be cause for giving up the fight. In fact, it is a signal to us that we need to fight harder.

As with any struggle, the struggle for multicultural diversity can become co-opted or domesticated by well-intentioned progressives. One of the central concerns that I have been addressing over the last several years is that multiculturalism has lost its connection to wider class and social struggles and has debarred itself from serious consideration as an ally of the left.

Greg Goodman and Karen Carey both recognize many of the shortcomings of multicultural education, but also its strengths and potential for educational transformation. They have brought together an impressive group of educators to move beyond the precincts of mainstream multiculturalism and to take the fight against racism and exclusion directly into the classroom. The authors whom they have brought together in *Critical Multicultural Conversations* have had considerable experience working in the areas of bilingual education, multicultural education, students with special needs, school leadership, and standards for teachers. Whereas much of the literature in multicultural education addresses theoretical implications for rethinking diversity and student empowerment in the classroom, the essays in *Critical Multicultural Conversations* are written, for the most part, from the perspective of classroom teachers, administrators, and policy makers. All the contributors work within the critical tradition, and as such are less concerned with breaking new theoretical ground than with establishing multicultural education from the ground up and making it a reality to be lived, and not just preached from the pages.

Goodman and Carey's set of authors recognize that calls for diversity do not necessarily add up to a serious challenge to the status quo. Each in his or her own way, the authors are aware that challenging the status quo means challenging the epistemological assumptions that underwrite mainstream educational theory and practice.

Challenging relations of power and privilege that have been sedimented into racist and patriarchal systems of classification and that support existing capitalist social relations of exploitation is not an easy task, especially at this moment of resurgent racism against people of Middle Eastern descent and a retreat from civil liberties and individual protection under the Constitution. This is why *Critical Multicultural Conversations* becomes such an important intervention at this moment in time.

An active engagement with Greg Goodman and Karen Carey's volume will help educators, administrators, and community activists challenge status quo conceptions of mainstream multiculturalism and lay the groundwork for the development of a critical multiculturalism that takes the issue of democracy and diversity seriously. There is no more important task for educators at this current moment in world history.

Peter McLaren
Los Angeles, 2003

REFERENCES

Freire, P. (1998). *The pedagogy of hope.* New York: Continuum.
Nation Notes. *The Nation*, March 31, 2002, p. 7.
Solomon, N. (2003, november 17). Cracking the media walls. *These Times*, pp. 2-27.

FOREWORD

A little more than a year ago I pulled my Buick, the last of agricultural mud crumbling off its underbody, into the parking lot at Fresno State University. A few minutes early for a day-long workshop for the scholars of these papers, I closed my eyes and reassembled the previous day when I was in Cantua Creek, a hamlet 50 miles west of Fresno made up of 60 or so homes, a single post office, and the school, the center of all activities. Cantua Creek is removed from even the most rudimentary notion of town or city life—no stores or gas stations, no stoplights. The single stop sign can be ignored, as there is only the occasional vehicle—usually a monstrous tractor—to hog the narrow road. I had been invited by Mario Cobarruvias to talk with the kids, all Spanish-speaking. I had traveled through an occasional cloudburst 160 miles from my home in Berkeley to arrive on time for my presentations. Cantua Creek was, by far, the smallest town I'd visited in order to spread the word that reading was not only good for you but also fun. I was prepared to tell them it is like taking vitamins for the brain!

Cantua Creek. I addressed the children, going from room to room with my simple supply of stories, jokes, chants, and single song—"Venga a Ver Mi Rancho." They were all smiles and I was all smiles. During lunch select students from the Home Economics class had prepared bowtie pasta with Bolognese sauce for me. There were flowers on the table, cloth napkins, and—why not?—candles flickering! The kids, girls and boys, ages twelve and thirteen, wore aprons they had sewn themselves. And look! Place cards for the four special guests that included administrators from the county office. Was an author ever so honored as when a young student placed under his nose a plate of homemade cookies?

I was then joined by Jessie de la Cruz, the subject of my young-adult biography, and she told stories about living and working in Cantua Creek during the 1930s. To the children—and some of the younger teachers and staff—the 1930s may as well have been 1492! Jessie, adorned in her UFW earrings swinging with each slow step and Viva La Causa pin on the lapel of her jacket, strode

along the hallways to visit other classrooms, the eyes of these children following us, as we were new to them. I played up my visiting author role and jumped
on the school bus that was taking kids to play soccer against a school in
Tranquility, fifteen miles away. I cheered them on until the bus, coughing
smoke, pulled away.

School was dismissed at 3:00, but the day was not done for Jessie and me.
The day had been truly packed! Earlier that morning the entire school had
watched Tranquility High perform a scene from my play "Novio Boy" in the
cafeteria. We headed there again for our session speaking to parents, some of
whom had come in from the fields. However, with a half-hour to ourselves, we
drove to a row of abandoned farm worker houses—"houses" is not the right
word, as they were one-room structures without plumping or electricity. I asked,
"Did you live in one of those?" Jessie shook her head; she said that she lived in
a tent. She was looking for the place where her family had pitched their tent. "I
think it's here," she said, pointing to a tree. Then she corrected herself as I
drove slowly down the rain-soaked road where I had picked up the mud that
clung under my car. "No, no, it's here." But I could tell that she was unsure,
though she was certain that the work was as brutal as when she first dragged a
sack—a "socko" in Spanglish—in 1936 when she was seven years old.

But that was yesterday. Today I rested my eyes, sighed, and got out of my
car with the image of Cantua Creek on the back of my eyelids. I sighed from a
fatigue that disappeared when I was greeted by these professors. They were a
welcoming and bright bunch, and truly curious about me, a writer from their
backyard, namely Fresno, and a graduate of Fresno State in 1974. They were
the kind of people you would like to have as colleagues in a university, colleagues that I couldn't find when I was teaching. Greg Goodman, the facilitator,
actually greeted me outside the door of the Alumni House, which resembles a
colonial mansion that Colonel Sanders might have built once he came into his
fortune.

What did I talk about? I spoke about the nuts-and-bolts of poetry and essay
writing and gave my own testimony of what is occurring in public schools, plus
anecdotes about my writing life, my successful books and those others that sit in
the darkness of a drawer as manuscripts never to be published. I recall a serious
tone among these scholars to get this text of multicultural and gender perspectives written. I recall a roundtable explanation of their aims. Of course, because
I'm not a scholar, I feigned that I understood everything, although I hadn't used
a footnote since taking Victorian Literature (at Fresno State, by the way) in
1973. In a way, I could understand their heady scholarship. I understood that
any time scholars embark on written articles—especially ones that take risky
stands, such as these—there is a nervousness, if not an occasional doubt, and
plenty of plain old frustration. One jazz legend, when asked what he felt when
he was composing, said, "If you're not nervous, then you're not paying attention." These scholars were paying rapt attention. I sensed their nervousness,
though, and was keenly aware that every one of them was prepared to get it

done. And so they have in this large and impressive study. Here is a balance of scholarship and humanity in the writing, and true stories from the trenches.

I write for both adults and young people, but there is not a day that goes by that I'm not thinking of the children in our schools. I'm certain it's true for these scholars. There were ten of us sitting around a table on a Saturday when the sun was eclipsed by the morning fog but ready to break through. Every one of us could have been some place else—at home, in the foothills surrounding Fresno, out on the tennis courts. But we weren't. We were there at the Alumni House, sitting so close that we could been have holding hands.

We are all pro-children, pro-education. Each scholar has testimony worth hearing. My task is to welcome the reader of this valuable anthology. Thus, I begin with my longish testimony to both children and schools in what I will call "Author for a Day: Glitter and Rainbows." The essay is about how I discovered that besides trying to build up a canon of young-adult literature featuring Latino youth as protagonists I also must conduct myself in a noble manner. I must be willing to reach out and—literally—shake hands. In short, I'm a functionary, meaning that I have to go about California and the southwest telling children that it's OK to pick up a book, to enjoy school, to make something of one's self. But before you discover for yourself the scholarly studies regarding multicultural instruction, I tell you how I began to know children.

After the 1990 publication of Baseball in April, my first book for young readers, I began to get invitations to come and wear the cocked hat of Author for a Day, especially at schools where Mexican American children warmed almost every chair. I felt good, if not wholly excited, because I wanted to know the readers I'd heard from—Raquel, Dulce, Armando, Fortino, and Joel the Gangster, chavalitos who wrote me the sweet letters that rained glitter and contained crayoned rainbows on lined paper. The letters arrived like clouds from schools in Fresno, Porterville, Sanger, Huron, Shafter, no-nonsense schools in the great San Joaquin Valley. At one such school, for instance, the vice principal had to weigh quite heavily his decision to bring Gary Soto as Author for a Day or buy three NFL-authentic footballs. He went for the footballs and perhaps he had a winning season. I'll never know.

I was in love with my readers, brown faces shadowing my own characters with names like their own. I could see them turning the page, a fistful of sunflower seeds in their laps. Now I could see them up front. I had done many books signings but was never so happy as when a little girl came up and, hands pressed together sweetly, said, "I want to be a writer too!" I gave her a free book and bit my tongue when I started to say, "Sweetie, don't do that to yourself. Go into engineering!"

A year later a second young-adult book came out, Taking Sides, which had on the cover a boy going up for a basketball lay-up. Like my first book, whose cover had boys in a pick-up truck wearing baseball caps, it hinted at a sports story. So, when I went to Shafter, my young reader assumed that I had played minor league ball and given pro basketball a try. They were surprised at my average height, the gray marching through my hair, and my arms that were not strong enough to move the podium without the help of the librarian. Nevertheless, during recess, they expected me to play baseball with them. Teams were made up, and with fifteen on each side, the field was clotted with more kids than dandelions. There were 3-second basemen, for instance, and I was one of them, a tiny glove dangling from the end of my wimpy arm. Luckily, the one pop-up that drifted my way I was able to catch. I was all teeth, happy that I hadn't disappointed them. I popped my fist in my glove and yelled, "Orale!"

But before recess ended, just as I was getting into the game and chattering louder than any of them, I managed to misjudge a grounder that popped against my chest. In a panic I gathered the ball quickly and let it fly from my hand to first base. It sailed like a dirty bird, scattering three girls watching from the sidelines. One of the girls was my best customer—she had bought two books during the school fair. Later, after two more periods of creative reading and goofy stories, I, Author for a Day, was led out to play basketball. For the first time in my life, I was chosen first. After all, hadn't I written a basketball novel? He has to be good, they thought.

Following two feeble shots the kids caught on that I was no good. In one drive toward the hoop, when I was open and beckoning for the ball, my teammate looked me straight in the eyes, and I could see that she wanted to pass me the ball but knew better. She feigned a pass to me but shot it to a small kid with unlaced shoes. Right there, with black on my palms and twin moons of sweat under my arms, I understood my position from their eyes: a good writer but what a hack on the court.

On another more serious school visit, I was asked by a teacher to meet with a parent whose son had run away from home several days before. I met the tearful mother in the hallway, and we walked onto the schoolyard. Just as I started trying to comfort her with some inept words, we spotted the boy on the far end of the school grounds. When we started walking toward him, he vanished, continuing the emotional game of tag that so upset his teachers and parents. I suggested that we get into my car and look for him, the town being very small. Surely we could find him. We drove up and down the streets, the mother telling me repeatedly that everything was OK at home, he was not being beaten, he was eating enough, that the town was a hellhole but he was much loved. We drove until the mother stopped talking. It was clear to both of us that the town was not small enough to find a boy who doesn't want to be found.

The peak of these surrealistic author days occurred at Huron Elementary, where they held, among other festivities, a school contest to draw Gary Soto's face. This occurred on the evening of the Gary Soto Parade in which approximately 800 celebrants marched—800 from a town of only 4,000!

We were celebrating the première of my little film "The Bike," which featured actors from Huron, a town that, except for three families, is entirely Mexican or Mexican American. The cafeteria was noisy. There were small babies, big babies, school children, sweethearts, vendors, grandparents, and the mayor proclaiming good wishes to raza!

The film also featured my uncle, "El Shorty," a foundry worker for 20 years. He was asked to judge the Gary Soto portraits. We walked along one side of the cafeteria chuckling at the 100-plus portraits. Uncle Shorty kept saying "Qué feo," meaning "how ugly" I was. My uncle was laughing. I was laughing. The portraits showed me with big teeth, crooked glasses, spiky hair, big ears, square head—all the body parts of a happy-go-lucky Frankenstein. The pictures were full of love and enough talent to suggest that the human features, lopsided as they were, added up to me.

Ribbons were awarded to the winners. A bicycle was auctioned off. Speeches were given and children half-listened with nachos in their mouths.

Finally the movie was shown to applause and laughter, not entirely because it was funny (it is), but because they recognized their friends in the film. When the lights came on, I was shocked to see the paper cups, staggered chairs, puddles of soda, candy wrappers, sweaters and jackets, and popcorn like snow on the cafeteria floor—the calamity of a town entertaining itself as best it could.

I was surprised when children tugged at my sleeve and held up their wrists, asking for autographs. I played along, wondering if Woody Allen would run from such attention. I signed my name on their wrists and grew weary.

Later, as Author for a Day, I had to stack chairs and collect my wits in order to later be funny at the cast party in my honor. I received my check and then gave back some of it by picking up the dinner tab.

The letters still arrive, still like clouds. When I open them, glitter rains on my table, and the first-grade rainbows fill my eyes with something like love.

Gary Soto

Young People's Ambassador
California Rural Legal Assistance
& the United Farm Workers of America

INTRODUCTION

THE RECONQUEST

There are languages buried in the earth.
Languages that unite us
In deepening breaths.
Recently, the trees of our voices have been cut
And buried
Between cement and mirrors.
Within, far within us,
Are the roots of these words,
That in time,
Will form jungles through the air.

Gustavo Alberto Garcia Vaca

The writers of *Critical Multicultural Conversations* join a large family of authors in the wide, multifarious domain of multicultural education. The growth of interest in diversity or multiculturalism flows from changes in thinking about social order as represented by the power or dominance of certain social groups. This domination is expressly defined as hegemony. According to Kincheloe and Steinberg (1997), "hegemony involves the maintenance of domination not through force but through the winning of the consent of those being dominated" (p. 112) to remain in subordinated positions. Critical multicultural writers reflect upon the failed promise of free and equal opportunities for all persons living within a democratic society and work to stimulate the realization of the dream of true freedom (Bourdieu, 1993; Fraser, 1997; Freire, 1970, 1997; Giroux, 1992; Kincheloe & Steinberg, 1997; McLaren 1997).

1

This revolution in thinking through postmodern, Marxist, post-Marxist, and critical multicultural perspectives has been driven by the questioning of a group of individuals exasperated by the ethics of a world that supported fascism, Nazism, and divisive, immoral politics (Gramsci, 1988; Habermas, 1984; Horkheimer & Adorno, 1972). Continuing a post–World War II dialogue initiated by Martin Heidegger and followed by Theodor Adorno and Max Horkheimer, Jurgen Habermas questioned the dominant Western thinking known as Modernity (White, 1995). Pre-eminent among the concepts of Habermas was the concept of universality (1984). According to Warren (1995), this notion, sometimes also called "radical democracy," specifies that all people share a right to equal, "self-development and self-realization" (p. 167). Ironically, this recent postmodern desire for a "radical democracy" was not a later 20th-century creation. These philosophic beliefs can be traced to Jean Jacques Rousseau, John Stuart Mill, Thomas Jefferson, and Ralph Waldo Emerson. Jefferson's intent, as well as the purpose of all of the "founding fathers" of the American Republic, was to physically and intellectually escape the tyranny and oppression from religious and political persecution that the English imposed upon their people. These notions were radical in the 1700s, but they should not be considered so today.

The history of the American experience has been reflective of the warring forces of good and evil in relation to the fundamental issues of living in a democracy and what this means (Novak, 2002). This competition between winning free rights and the enslavement or persecution of the victims of American hubris can be documented with many examples. As examples of both sides of this fight, woman's suffrage and the winning of equal rights under the law was a victory of the early 20th century, and, conversely, the attempted genocide of the Native American community stands, with slavery, as one of the biggest disgraces of the American conscience.

In more recent times within the United States, and especially since the passage of civil rights legislation in 1964, there has been a steadily growing movement to increase the work of purportedly democratic institutions, such as schools, to translate the rhetoric of equality into the practice of equal access to a free and appropriate public education. With the passing of the Americans with Disabilities Act of 1990, these rights of nondiscrimination were extended to include all Americans and to provide access to all other public and private institutions. This access extends beyond the mere physical boundaries that formerly excluded individuals to now include all essential and fundamental activities associated with living within a free society such as learning.

In concert with the courageous and liberatory work of the last 40 years by such prominent leaders as Martin Luther King, Coretta King, John Kennedy, and Simon Wiesenthal (to name just a few), a large number of gifted scholars have put their shoulder to the task of articulating pathways to social transformation (Bucher, 1999; Comer, 1980; DeVillar, Faltis, & Cummins, 1994; Fraser, 1997; Ignatiev & Garvey, 1996; Giroux, 1997; hooks, 1989; Kincheloe &

Steinberg, 1997; McLaren, 1997; Mouffe, 1988; Shohat & Stam, 1994). These writers work to inform educators eager to develop methodologies to fulfill the mandate to teach all students. As a result, these writers have contributed to the creation of a strong foundation for the further continuation of the development of educational opportunities for all students.

The arguments for equality are not lightly proffered. The clear implication of not changing the pedagogy that perpetuates hegemony and continues to work to oppress second-language learners, women, gay/lesbian/bisexual persons, minorities, and all other underrepresented individuals may very well cause the ultimate destruction of this society. James Fraser (1997) states this eloquently:

> A society worth living in must, in the long run, be a society that is truly built on the strengths and contributions of all of its citizens, in which the range of cultures contributes to the building of a new whole that is richer than even the best that any one part has to offer. But the building of that kind of culture demands that all citizens see each other as people who have important elements to contribute. (p. 183)

Where *Critical Multicultural Conversations* breaks rank with most texts written to inform multicultural education is that its authors seek to translate research and critical theoretical perspectives into workable or transmittable programs. We write to give teachers, administrators, and school site workers (all educators) some specific tools to inform the emancipatory work (praxis) of multicultural education. To add inspiration and to bring soul to the work, we have included current pieces of literature to spirit our pedagogical writing. Were we to leave out the spirit and soul of this work, we would risk stultifing the process and remain trapped in a traditional, textual representation. We write for the people, and we want to share the joy of the process. The joy is in feeling the love of shared connections of real meaning and deep understanding (Freire, 1970). This is the value of developing multicultural education on a revolutionary level (McLaren, 1997). This book is not for those wishing to stand on the sidelines or to give only rhetoric to the process. This book is for people who want to work hard and make change occur.

We write, too, to express our commitment to this process of building multicultural communities. We believe that this begins with the effort of each person. The achievement of truly multicultural communities will be accomplished only after what has been situated as minority positions become truly democratic, majority representations. This text gives you something you can do, and it works to support the feelings that will inspire you to teach everyone in your class or school. We speak to beginning teachers, counselors, psychologists, and administrators: You bring new energy and ideas to your schools. We want you to be informed as to how you can make your students' experiences engaging, emancipatory, and exciting.

The writers in this text connect to the philosophic position described as critical pedagogy. Critical pedagogy is the contribution and result of 30 years of writing and discussion inspired by the mentor, Paulo Freire. Freire's feelings of compassion and love for the whole of the people lead to the development of the liberatory and transformational educational philosophy known as critical pedagogy. Pedagogy, the essential function of the practice of teaching, is critical (of the utmost importance) because of its opposition to oppression. Peter McLaren (2000), in his biography of Freire, states, "To a greater extent than any other educator of this century, Freire was able to develop a pedagogy of resistance to oppression. More than this, he lived what he taught. His life is the story of courage, hardship, perseverance, and an unyielding belief in the power of love" (p. 147). In his seminal work, *Pedagogy of the Oppressed*, Freire observed that not only the oppressors attack the downtrodden. Freire (1970) states, "Self-deprecation is another characteristic of the oppressed, which derives from their internalization of the opinion the oppressors hold of them. So often do they hear that they are good for nothing, know nothing and are incapable of learning anything—that they are sick, lazy, and unproductive—that in the end they become convinced of their own unfitness" (p. 45). Freire's work has inspired the writing of many notable educators such as Barry Kanpol, Sonia Nieto, Peter McLaren, Henry Giroux, James Fraser, Shirley Steinberg, Joe Kincheloe, and Donald Macedo to name just a few.

Critical theorists write to support multiculturalism, feminism, gay, lesbian, bisexual, and transgendered individuals (gblt), and other groups of ideologically connected individuals suppressed by the dominant culture. Critical theorists believe that all individuals in the society are entitled to full participation in the process of living freely and democratically. Sadly, these notions are resisted by forces desirous of the perpetuation of hegemony and by a white conservative majority. Groups and individuals supporting an archaic insistence that all others deny their "color" and "melt" into white identity continue to contribute to the oppression of difference. In support of difference, critical educators wish to validate individual identity and see this cultural re-norming as a necessary and important component of democratic and socially conscious schools. According to Audre Lorde (1984), "Difference must not merely be tolerated, but seen as a fund of necessary polarities between which our creativity can spark like a dialectic" (pp. 111-112).

Whiteness, in the sense with which we discuss it, is not the skin color white. The white to which we refer has to do with attitudes and beliefs deeply embedded within the white society. Whiteness is ubiquitously enmeshed throughout the American cultural and political landscape. Peter McLaren (1997) defines this position eloquently:

> Whiteness constitutes and demarcates ideas, feelings, knowledge, social practices, cultural formations, and systems of intelligibility that are identified with or attributed to white people and that are invested in by white peo-

ple as "white". Whiteness is also a refusal to acknowledge how white people are implicated in certain social relations of privilege and relations of domination and subordination. Whiteness, then, can be considered as a form of social amnesia associated with modes of subjectivity within particular social sites considered to be normative. (p. 267)

We are not suggesting the establishment of a reverse racism. We are calling for a re-examination of the ways that we conduct ourselves within the context of our society, and in this case specifically within schools, to build the inclusion of all into our pedagogical foundation.

For schools to convert from institutions of white cultural reproduction to sites of multicultural liberation, all teachers need to welcome the diversity surrounding them and work to eliminate the subversive subjugation of covert racist practices. This is an extension beyond tolerance of difference to an active inclusion of the voices of the students and the families they represent in the process of building respect for diversity. Only when the majority of the school's population is in agreement with praxis (everyday working process of liberation) of critical pedagogy, will we truly be in a state of affirmation of the difference and a celebration of each other's liberation. As Sonia Nieto (1996) states, "It means developing multicultural settings in which all students feel reflected and visible" (p. 356).

As the reader will note in the chapters ahead, this is not an easy process. This is *the* challenge of the 21st century. How we resolve the transformation of our culture into a viable cultural home representative of all diversity will determine whether or not our democracy survives. Changing the schools and the society in which they operate involves a major shift in the thinking and power relations that have historically operated to maintain social positions. We all enjoy the benefit of diversity's fruits: the dances, music, food, and festivals. Now we must work to make the way for what Ella Shohat and Robert Stam (1994) call "shared social desires and identifications" (p. 49). Clearly, the mandate for today's educator is to work to create transformations of both the individuals and the culture within which they live. For you, the teacher, this means creating a classroom that is safe for each individual and home for all!

One of my greatest teaching challenges as a white male is to identify and to mitigate the negative implication of the power imbalance inherent in the student/teacher relationship coupled with the white racial issues. The dual issues of racism and sexism are imbedded within the sociopolitical landscape, and they are nowhere more readily apparent than within a classroom setting. In school, the additional characterization as the teacher/grader/evaluator looms large over the students' potential for success or an outcome of failure. As an educator, this problem of being white and male has caused me to examine my own sense of self as "an other" from culturally different individuals.

In my classroom, as I have worked to address the issues of racism and oppression within our society, I almost always sense a defensiveness from my white students. For white students oppressed by poverty and familial discon-

nection with success because of substance abuse, mental illness, or other difficult issues, there is a deafness to these issues of multiculturalism. The issues
are personalized as another roadblock for their success. Now these white students feel that they have to fight even harder for their place. These identifications with loss of status are hard to accept. Although no one will stand before
the class to defend whiteness and or the racism it implies, there is a strong feeling of resistance on the part of white students to constructively engage in conversations about race. This is especially true within the topic of white privilege.
Oppressed white students have to really stretch their imagination to understand
this problem.

There is no denying that the world has changed demographically; however,
regarding the social position of the underrepresented, it is safe to say that white
dismantling of hegemony is not going to be easily proffered. Examples such as
California's racist Proposition 187 (to expel from school and deny health services to children of illegal immigrants) and Proposition 209 (the end of affirma-
tive action) are but two glaring examples of the strength and ubiquity of the
white majority's desire to maintain exclusionary practice.

According to noted psychologists David and Derald Wing Sue (1999),
"being a White person in this society means chronic exposure to ethnocentric
monoculturalism as manifested in White Supremacy. It is difficult, if not impossible, for anyone not to inherit the racial biases, prejudices, misinformation,
deficit portrayals, and stereotypes of their forebears. To believe that we are
somehow immune from inheriting such aspects of White supremacy is to be
arrogant, naïve, or self-deceived" (p. 145). The unintentional racism and its
harmful consequences are the primary advisory in the development of trust
essential for successful teacher/student relationships. As Herb Kohl (1994)
states in his beautiful book *"I Won't Learn from You,"* "to agree to learn from a
stranger who does not respect your integrity (I read this to mean race, sexual
preference, ability/disability) causes a major loss of self" (p. 6). No learning
occurs in classrooms containing exclusionary cultural values such as white curriculum or any single culture identification.

Standing before my classes, I now ask my students, "Why would a white
male stand before you and argue against the perpetuation of white male privilege?" The answer is that I relate. My father's parents were penniless, Ukrainian
immigrants to the United States in 1917. They left their homeland to escape the
poverty of Ukraine and their persecution as Jews. As a continuing part of the
Diaspora (the scattering of the Jewish people across the globe), my grandparents found each other, fell in love, moved to northern New Hampshire (a climate similar to Ukraine), and raised thirteen children. There, in remote northern
New Hampshire, they continued the traditions of a conservative Jewish family
and celebrated the rituals of their religion within the confines of their home.

Although Jews, for the most part, have white skin, their minority identifications are clearly intact. Although the Holocaust continues in modern memory, I
am convinced that there are genes within Jews that mark them as minorities.

Being only one-half of one percent of the world's total population, Jews are the metaphor for minorities. Although I can hide my Jewish identity in my whiteness and behind a veil of silence about my culture, I cannot escape the feelings of personal isolation and minority alienation. This is especially true when I'm confronted by large images of National Christian majority politics or other, even small, exclusionary activities such as the Christian Club praying around the flag outside my school office window. These realities maintain my connections and feelings of brother/sisterhood with all who have been oppressed and those who continue to be victims of racism.

Finally, the challenge for all of us as a society is to find the universality (Habermas, 1984), the overarching common denominator that will bring us together for the future of our planet. The problem is not one of giving up our identities, nor is it a question of learning all there is to know about every culture. Multicultural understanding is a continuing of the conversations that bring us together, not a cookbook or a simple linear equation. The challenge of the integration of diverse points of view is one of self-examination and openness to new ideas, differing cultural perspectives, and possible inter-identifications between all people. To this end, this book is about conversations between fourteen different writers and their diverse audience: you. You can experience the feelings these writers bring to the work and you can learn, from their perspectives, the challenges that you'll face. We hope you are inspired. As Vaca suggests in the opening poem, *The Reconquest*, the roots of the languages that unite us are buried within ourselves. Our work is to enliven, foster, and enrich those conversations in our daily practice as educators of tomorrow's citizens.

REFERENCES

Bourdieu, P. (1993). *The field of cultural reproduction*. New York: Columbia University Press.

Bucher, R. D. (1999). *Diversity consciousness*. Upper Saddle River, NJ: Prentice Hall.

Comer, J. P. (1980). *School power: Implications of an intervention project*. New York: Free Press.

DeVillar, R. A., Faltis, C. J., & Cummins, J. P. (1994). *Cultural diversity in schools: From rhetoric to practice*. Albany: State University of New York Press.

Fraser, J. (1997). Love and history in the work of Paulo Freire. In P. Freire (Ed.), *Mentoring the mentor: A critical dialogue with Paulo Freire*. New York: Peter Lang Publishing.

Freire, P. (1970). *Pedagogy of the oppressed*. New York: Continuum Press.

Freire, P. (1997). *Mentoring the mentor: A critical dialogue with Paulo Freire*. New York: Peter Lang Publishing.

Giroux, H. (1992). *Border crossings: Cultural workers and the politics of education*. New York: Routledge.

Giroux, H. (1997). *Pedagogy and the politics of hope: Theory, culture, and schooling.* Boulder, CO: Westview.

Gramsci, A. (1988). *An Antonio Gramsci reader.* New York: Schocken Books.

Habermas, J. (1984). *The theory of communicative action, Vol. 1.* Boston: Beacon Press.

hooks, b. (1989). *Talking back.* Boston: South End Press.

Horkheimer, M., & Adorno. T. W. (1972). *Dialectic of enlightenment* (John Cumming, Trans.). New York: Seabury Press.

Ignatiev, N., & Garvey, J. (1996). *Race traitor.* New York: Routledge.

Kincheloe, J., & Steinberg, S. (1997). *Changing multiculturalism.* Buckingham, England: Open University Press.

Kohl, H. (1994). *I won't learn from you. And other thoughts on creative maladjustment.* New York: The New Press.

Lorde, A. (1984). *Sister outsider.* Freedom, CA: The Crossing Press.

McLaren, P. (1997). *Revolutionary multiculturalism: Pedagogies of dissent for the new millennium.* Boulder, CO: Westview.

McLaren, P. (2000). *Che Guevarra, Paulo Freire, and the pedagogy of revolution.* Lanham, MD: Rowman & Littlefield.

Mouffe, C. (1988). Radical democracy: Modern or postmodern? In A. Ross (Ed.), *Universal abandon? The politics of postmodernism* (pp. 31-45). Minneapolis: University of Minnesota Press.

Nieto, S. (1996). *Affirming diversity: The sociopolitical context of multicultural education.* New York: Longman.

Novak, B. (2002, Fall). Humanizing democracy: Matthew Arnold's nineteenth-century call for a common, higher, educative pursuit of happiness and its relevance to twenty-first century democratic life. *American Educational Research Journal, 39*(3), 593-637.

Shohat, E., & Stam, R. (1994). *Unthinking Eurocentrism: Multiculturalism and the media.* New York: Routledge.

Sue, D. W., & Sue, D. (1999*). Counseling the culturally different: Theory and practice.* New York: John Wiley.

Warren, M. E. (1995). The self in a discursive democracy. In S. K. White (Ed.), *The Cambridge companion to Habermas.* Cambridge, England: Cambridge University Press.

White, S. K. (1995). Reason, modernity, and democracy. In S. K. White (Ed.), *The Cambridge companion to Habermas.* Cambridge, England: University Press.

CHAPTER ONE

Multicultural Education

A Blueprint for Educators

Mahmoud F. Suleiman

California State University, Bakersfield

AMERICA

The gold of her promise
*   has never been mined*
Her borders of justice
*   not clearly defined*
Her crops of abundance
*   the fruit and the grain*
Have not fed the hungry
*   nor eased that deep pain*
Her proud declarations
*   are leaves on the wind*
Her southern exposure
*   black death did befriend*

Discover this country
*   dead centuries cry*
Erect noble tablets
*   where none can decry*
"She kills her bright future
*   and rapes for a soul*
Then entraps her children
*   with legends untrue"*
I beg youDiscover this country.

Maya Angelou

"America," from *Oh Pray My Wings Are Gonna Fit Me Well* by Maya Angelou, copyright ©1975 by Maya Angelou. Used by permission of Random House, Inc.

The United States' universal culture is based on the diversity of various micro cultures that interact meaningfully within the overarching framework of democracy. Yet, very often history tells us that much more needs to be done to ensure a harmonious interaction among diverse groups and cultures. Social and educational institutions tend to be the laboratories for testing the maxims upon which the U.S. culture is based. In modern times, schools have been characterized as both the change agents for a pluralistic society and institutions of cultural reproduction.

Undoubtedly, the culturally diverse nature of U.S. society is dynamic and evolving. Within this context, the classroom may be seen as a microcosm that symbolizes these dynamic changes and represents a concrete "slice of life" in the democracy we live in. Students in today's classrooms represent a wide range of linguistic, sociocultural, and ethnic variables comprising the culture of schools. Because the premise of the pluralistic democratic society is to value the diversity that exists in all aspects of life, it is worthwhile to revisit the role of educators in terms of the diverse classroom and the unique needs of its participants.

Ironically, there are those who argue that living in a democracy gives individuals the freedom to be ignorant, or, at least unquestioning, with respect to the intellectual rigors of maintaining cultural identities representative of diversity. However, throughout its history, the United States has "demanded assimilation of 'mainstream values' from all who reached its shores" (Daly & O'Dowd, 1992, p. 179). Although a great number of children have benefited from the U.S. public educational system's attempts to teach democratic principles, there still exists a denial of "societal benefits to vast numbers of Americans based on characteristics as arbitrary as ethnicity, gender, and/or class" (Daly & O'Dowd, 1992, p. 179). This is, of course, due to the monocultural stratification embedded in the culture of public education (Banks, 1995). In particular, professional education preparation programs including teaching, counseling, school psychology, and administration have failed to adequately prepare educators to meet the challenges of maintaining a true democracy through valuing pluralism.

Because of this deficit, it is imperative to look closely at the ingredients of successful professional education preparation programs that value differences and affirm the diversity of all learners (Suleiman, 1997, 1999). Rather than place the blame on students or teachers, it is more fruitful to confront these challenges by incorporating a more comprehensive, and thus more democratic, approach to educational training. Such an approach has to have the potential to help educators in order to facilitate the process of change and emancipation.

Based on the premise and promise of multicultural education, this chapter capitalizes on diversity within a global context. Multicultural education takes the position that diversity is a natural and healthy phenomenon in democratic societies. As such, multicultural education seeks to embrace unity through diversity and to dismantle any manmade barriers that negatively affect human dignity. In particular, it seeks to inculcate needed professional values for the promotion of pluralistic schools. In this model, prospective educators ought to be prepared to work within a multicultural educational framework. This chapter focuses on the issues relevant to professional educational preparation to promote adequate training through enhancing each individual's sensitivity to the cultural, linguistic, and cognitive characteristics of diverse learners as they relate to both learning and living as a responsible citizen. The discussion provides both theoretical and practical implications for professional educators to fully equip themselves to become more effective with all learners in multicultural settings.

HISTORICAL REVIEW

Given the history of diversity in the U.S. educational institutions, the debate has always focused on the validity of such assimilationist sociological accounts as the melting pot theory. Because this theory has always failed to affirm the diversity in the American society, the search for solutions led educators and researchers to revisit cultural pluralism in an attempt to achieve equity and social justice in various institutions such as schools. According to Daly and O'Dowd (1992), and reaffirmed by Banks (1994), the seeds for multicultural movements were planted in the early 1930s. At this time, efforts to promote sensitivity to the differences brought by students in the classroom culminated in the creation of alternatives to assimilationist approaches to education such as the American Council on Education (ACE), the Anti-Defamation League (ADL), and the National Education Association (NEA), among others. The main function of those organizations was to develop a more meaningful approach to intergroup relations and to provide support for diverse groups in order to prevent prejudice and discrimination from plaguing society. These associations also recognized the potential for schools and teachers to facilitate change conducive to the promotion of social justice and harmony.

Although major accomplishments of these alternatives (such as ethnic studies) were evident in promoting the value of positive human relations as they pertain to schooling, those reform efforts have largely failed to become institutionalized (Daly & O'Dowd, 1992; Ogbu, 1995; Suleiman, 1995, 1997). It appears that mainstream educators have failed to internalize a multicultural ideology. This failure to change reflects the misunderstanding of intergroup educational reforms and their contributions to the goal of the American educational system (Banks, 1994, 1995).

At the same time as the dismantling of segregation in the wake of the 1954 Brown decision, the postmodern multicultural movement started to gain momentum. Ethnic pride was reinforced by several constitutional amendments contributing to enhancing diversity among people of color and affirming their metaphysical-spiritual and intellectual presence within public institutions.

Examples such as the 1964 Civil Rights Act, the 1967 Bilingual Education Act, and the 1974 Equal Education Act contributed to the proliferation of voices for social justice and equity. In particular, the purpose of this litigation was to ensure equal rights for all participants in the schools. As a result, multicultural concepts started to become more broadly infused within schools, despite the movement's limited effect upon racist strongholds.

The scope of multicultural education in the public educational institutions such as schools and universities initially took the form of highlighting contributions of diverse groups to the American civilization. Federal money was allocated to prepare teachers and faculty to develop multicultural awareness. Moreover, the demographic changes continued to demand more to be done to develop a "greater understanding of the contributions that the various cultures could make to an increasingly pluralistic society" (Daly & O'Dowd, 1992, p. 183). Multicultural education continued to be born out of urgent need, given the complex sociopolitical contexts that allowed inequity, discrimination, prejudice, and other social ills that plagued American public schools (Nieto, 2000). In short, multicultural education was born out of the need to revitalize the American democracy, to facilitate the desired changes initiated by the civil right's movement, and to celebrate the diversity of all citizens in the pluralistic society (Grant, 1995).

Accordingly, "if change were to occur in the nation's schools, it was obvious that teacher-preparation institutions would have to assume a leadership role in developing programs that would enable prospective teachers to become sensitive to issues of multicultural, nonsexist education in the classroom" (Daly & O'Dowd, 1992, p. 184). If the diversity of the American society were to be affirmed and celebrated, prospective educators would need to acquire the skills and competencies that help them meet the cognitive, linguistic, and social needs conducive to learning in the diverse classroom (Banks, 1994; Chisholm, 1994; Gay, 1995).

AN EMPOWERING FRAMEWORK FOR EDUCATORS

Multicultural educator preparation is a concept that encompasses an array of sociological, sociolinguistic, sociocultural, psychological, philosophical, and pedagogical elements (Bennett, 1999; Garza & Barnes, 1989; Grant, 1995; Ovando & Collier, 1998; Suleiman, 1997; Suleiman & Moore, 1997a). These components are inherent in the basic premise of multicultural education and its promising educational consequences.

In order to provide a philosophical foundation for effective schooling, it is worthwhile to look into the definition of multicultural education that must be incorporated within professional educational programs. Because multicultural education is a continuing process, it is important to identify its promises in translating the ideals of democracy and actualizing its desired educational goals by instilling the values, skills, and competencies in its educators.

According to Suzuki (1984), multicultural education is defined as a multidisciplinary educational program that provides multiple learning environments matching the academic, social, and linguistic needs of students. These needs may vary widely due to differences in race, sex, ethnicity, or sociolinguistic backgrounds of the students and educators. In addition to enhancing the development of their basic academic skills, the multicultural education programs should help students develop a better understanding of their own backgrounds and those of other groups that compose our society. Through this process, the program needs to help students learn to respect and appreciate cultural diversity, overcome ethnocentric and prejudicial attitudes, and understand the sociohistorical, economic, and psychological factors that have produced the contemporary conditions of inequality, alienation, and ethnic polarization. Within the overarching framework of democracy, multicultural education should also foster students' and educators' ability to critically analyze curriculum and to make intelligent decisions about real-life problems and issues through a process of democratic, dialogical inquiry. Finally, multicultural education should help conceptualize a vision of a better society and give students the necessary knowledge, understanding, and skills to enable them to move society toward greater equality of freedom, the eradication of degrading poverty and dehumanizing dependency, and the development of a meaningful identity for all people.

Multicultural education is a comprehensive educational approach that aims to multiply learning opportunities for all participants and celebrate the cultural diversity represented in various educational and social institutions. In particular, it permeates the curriculum and teaching methods, including the socialization and interactional processes among diverse participants in the culture of schools. Furthermore, the content and methodology of multicultural education must be founded on a democratic philosophical base that reflects a clear understanding of cultural pluralism and its sociopolitical implications in educational settings. The theoretical and pedagogical foci of multicultural approaches are centered on integration of multicultural education into not only a specific unit or course, but into all content areas in a systematic and vastly expansive manner. According to multiculturalists, to promote civic values and instill social justice in a pluralistic society, agents of change must construct the relevant knowledge, create novel equitable pedagogical practices, and celebrate diversity in educational institutions (Banks, 1995; Grant, 1995).

Providing what deficit theories cannot offer, multicultural education affirms individuals' rights and encourages active participation of diverse groups through a democratic dialogical process (Nieto, 2000). In particular, it affirms its responsibility to prepare educators in order that they may assist all children, adolescents, and adults to understand the significance of cultural heritage in their personal development and participation in democracy. It assumes that (a) ethnic heritage is part of each person's endowment, (b) language exerts a powerful effect on development of attitudes and skills, and (c) culture influences identity and learning.

In addition, multicultural education is a democratic collaborative process that is both affectively and cognitively developed. To enhance democratic values through teacher education programs, the mere incorporation of content is not sufficient in and of itself; through the understanding and true empathy of what cultural pluralism and democracy are, we can accomplish the goals of multicultural education. As far as schools are concerned, these goals are set for students, whereas others are set for educators. They are also inherent in the multicultural framework for schooling in democratic institutions.

GOALS FOR EMPOWERING STUDENTS AND EDUCATORS

The goals of multicultural education are as comprehensive as its premises. Suffice to mention the set of goals pertaining to students and teachers. The understanding of these goals is necessary for implementation, because we cannot afford more lip service in the educational arena; what is needed is an educational reform that is carried out by committed education leaders who understand the needs of their students on the one hand, and their role as educators in meeting these needs, on the other.

Goals for Students

As many critical educators agree, students of color have been victimized as scapegoats in the public schools (Banks, 1995). This victimization entailed blaming their diversity (e.g., ethnicity, language, etc.) as the main reason for their failure (Deyhle, 1992), and the resulting institutionalized racism ranged from segregating and tracking students to having lower expectations of them for achievement and success (Nieto, 2000). In an attempt to empower all students, multicultural education challenges us to revisit the conditions inherent in the culture of schools that explain the failure of students. In other words, it maintains that the educational system has not succeeded in reaching out to the students by adapting to their needs. Accordingly, multicultural educational solutions, based on rich diversity, provide all students with ample opportunity to:

1. Develop positive attitudes towards others of diverse backgrounds;

2. Acquire knowledge and skills in order to appreciate diversity;

3. Eradicate negative stereotypical images fostered by ethnocentrism;

4. Bridge the gap of differences through understanding and empathy;

5. Develop historical understanding of their multiethnic society;

6. Develop democratic skills and pluralistic civic values;

7. Appreciate the dynamic societal changes in the democracy;

8. Develop awareness of the world of reality around them;

9. Explore realistic demographic and cultural variables that affect all society.

In addition to providing the opportunity for students to celebrate and enjoy their educational and civic right, educators must ensure that these goals are implemented. The implementation of these goals must be measured not only by acquiring the prescribed knowledge about the American society, but also through the actions reflected in the interactional patterns of students in the culture of schools and society at large.

Goals for Pre-Service Educators

Like students, educators have been blamed for the failure to meet the challenge of diversity in the classroom. Although educators' attitudes, idiosyncrasies, biases, prejudices, and perceptions do influence the success of their students (Bennett, 1999; Ladson-Billings, 1994, 1995; Nieto, 2000), it is unwise to use educators alone as scapegoats in an attempt to explain school failure. Generally, educators tend to be the product of the teacher-preparation programs they were in. If these programs lack adequate ingredients for preparing prospective educators, then these individuals will reflect the inadequacy of the preparation process. Multicultural education, therefore, is also a source of empowerment for educators. To do so, multicultural programs have a set of goals for teachers that are equally important. Accordingly, prospective teachers and educators must:

1. Know, understand, and appreciate different experiences and contributions of minorities and other ethnic groups in American society;

2. Show a thorough understanding of the nature of the pluralistic society, the conflict in American society, and the basic causes of institutional racism, sexism, and social inequality;

3. Develop a sound rationale of multicultural education through a philosophical base that incorporates pedagogical principles that can be transferred to curricular areas;

4. Enhance optimal academic and social development of students through the knowledge and process that include sociocultural factors that influence the learning process;

5. Understand students' attitudes, values, and other motivational forces that affect their performance;

6. Acquire knowledge in multicultural pedagogy and instruction to augment the spirit of democracy in classrooms so that professional learning can occur for both teachers and students;

7. Learn effective classroom management and mediation techniques that benefit students of diverse sociocultural backgrounds; and

8. Utilize multicultural materials that are sensitive and relevant to students' sociocultural backgrounds to maximize their academic achievement.

These goals form the blueprint that shapes the process of preparing educators for today's classrooms, and they provide an outline for implementing the key elements to achieve congruence between teaching and learning. Most importantly, these goals can only be achieved through a collaborative approach. All of the school's citizens, from classroom employees to the school board members, need to actively work to support the individual students and the diversity they represent.

A Call for Action

To integrate various multicultural aspects in the educational process within the proposed conceptual framework, a number of guidelines that facilitate the fulfillment of the objectives of the democratic educational opportunities for diverse settings should be considered. Banks (1994) conceptualizes that multicultural education is multidimensional in nature; it consists of five interconnected dimensions: "(a) content integration, (b) the knowledge construction process, (c) prejudice reduction, (d) an equity pedagogy, and (e) an empowering school culture and social structure" (p. 4). One of the most fundamental dimensions of multicultural education is the knowledge construction process, because it relates to "the extent to which teachers help students to understand, investigate and determine how the implicit cultural assumptions, frames of references, perspective, and biases within a discipline influence the ways in which knowledge is constructed within it" (Banks, 1994, p. 5).

These dimensions have important implications for educators. Because of the need to maintain a dynamic balance between all cultures within the school, it is necessary to empower all students and teachers to be prepared to co-exist within diverse settings. Furthermore, understanding students' and teachers' characteristics, feelings, attitudes, and experiences can help the programs in attaining the desired educational goals (Garcia, 1991; Gay, 1995; Nieto, 2000). In this way, educators will be able to develop more democratic values and attitudes within themselves and their students so that they may become more active participants in our pluralistic society.

Based on this approach, educators in multicultural schools should take into consideration the following guidelines:

1. *Confronting prejudices and biases.* Maintaining a positive attitude toward all students and believing that all students want to learn and succeed are major prerequisites for effective multicultural learning and teaching. One should not view others through incongruent cultural filters that might result in prejudice and bias. Most importantly, the best education is an outgrowth of empathy. By being a good listener and interactive observer, one can develop an increased ethnic consciousness among the members of different groups and help depolarize interethnic hostility and conflict within the classroom and the greater school environment.

Garza and Barnes (1989) suggest that multicultural education involves providing "opportunities to validate and accept their own cultures as a basis for the acceptance of other cultures" (p. 7). Thus, future educators must be trained to value diversity represented in their unique interactional patterns. They should promote a profound understanding of the self through the understanding of others and vice versa. In fact, each individual is unique and incorporates a set of subcultures.

2. *Studying the history of the American educational system from a critical multicultural and pluralistic perspective.* Historical issues have valid implications for understanding conditions of inequity and social injustice. It must be borne in mind that history ought to be studied in an informative way. For example, blame cannot be placed on whites as the main cause of injustice against people of color; rather, students should seriously engage in reflecting upon past events as they relate to the present and future of the society. In addition, they should deal with the social and historical realities of American society to help students gain a better understanding of the causes of oppression and inequality and of the ways in which these social problems might be eliminated (Banks, 1994; Bennett, 1999; Suleiman 1999; Suleiman & Moore, 1997b). Students should see themselves in the curriculum as valued members of the multicultural society. Textbooks, literature, and materials must be free from any misinformation and bias, nor should they perpetuate prejudicial and negative stereotypical images about the groups they represent. The effective implementation of multicultural education must be

approached as a long-term process. Providing the best education for all requires us to utilize multicultural resources in the local community and increase the active involvement of concerned participants for the education of all or our students (Bennett, 1999; Cortés, 1990).

3. *Educators should be prepared to become multicultural brokers in the pluralistic school community.* Gay (1995) maintains that a cultural broker "is one who thoroughly understands the different cultural systems, is able to interpret cultural symbols from one frame of reference to another, can mediate cultural incompatibilities, and knows how to build bridges or establish linkages across cultures that facilitate the instructional process" (p. 37). To do so, many skills and objectives "should form the substantive core of all teachers of teacher preparation programs" (Gay, 1995, p. 37). Thus, programs need to help prospective educators construct the adequate knowledge first; then impart the change process through action and mediation; and incorporate equitable pedagogical practices (Banks, 1995; Gay, 1995; Grant & Gomez, 1996; King, 1995; Nieto, 2000).

    In addition, prospective educators should be an integral part of a community network. Educators should be trained to work collaboratively with clinicians, nurses, parents, administrators, community leaders, and all participants in the social and educational institutions. Because continuity among these institutions should be maintained to best meet the social and educational needs of all students, prospective educators should be afforded the opportunity to play their role in various social networks.

4. *Prospective educators should be trained to individualize instruction.* This allows prospective educators to provide compatible learning methods that are bound by the unique sociocultural aspects that affect achievement in diverse classrooms. A sound multicultural pedagogy should be based on "culturally correct" learning methods and curricula that incorporate sensitivity, empathy, relevance, and effectiveness. Through the use of culturally sensitive materials and techniques, students' academic achievement in all areas will increase. Once educators effectively demonstrate a careful understanding of the learning situation, their students' motivation will be increased. Most importantly, culturally relevant curriculum and instructional techniques should relate personally and experientially to the cognitive, academic, social, and linguistic abilities of their students. As these vary from one student to another, educators should be encouraged to individualize the teaching methods and use a variety of teaching aids to address different modalities of learning.

Sameness in teaching for all will guarantee educational inequity for many (Cortés, 1990).

Until prospective educators attain a meaningful level of multicultural competency, they may not be able to work effectively in diverse settings. Gay (1995) argues that "no one should be allowed to graduate from a teacher (professional educator) certification program or be licensed to teach without being well grounded in how the dynamic of cultural conditioning operates in the teaching and learning" (p. 37). A professional education training model based on multicultural democratic principles can guide and empower prospective educators as they select the subject matter content relevant to their students' identity. Also, this model allows participants to set pertinent educational goals and objectives conducive to students' attitudes and motivation. Multicultural education helps educators acquire skills and knowledge needed to meet their individual civic responsibilities. Providing a rationale for multicultural education also gives educators the support they need in facing pressures and questions from colleagues, community, and students.

Once university preparation programs train educators to give credence to all students' cultures and their contributions to humanity through multicultural curricular activities and instructional strategies, the desired promising educational outcomes will follow. Enhancing students' self concept, augmenting their motivation, affirming our society's democratic pluralism, and appreciating cultural diversity are all natural outgrowths of a well-grounded, critical multicultural pedagogy.

CONCLUSION

The growing diversity of the society is largely reflected in the U.S. public schools and inevitably affects the educational processes. Undoubtedly, educational reform efforts in preparing educators for the 21st century require a drastic step in pluralizing teacher education so that prospective teachers keep up with the evolving educational demands in today's technological and knowledge-based society. Unless we immerse future educators in the realm of multiculturalism and its pedagogical praxis, we will continue to alienate language-minority children and deprive mainstream students of benefiting from multiple learning opportunities. Because the diverse classrooms pose a challenge for prospective educators, professional preparation programs should infuse multiculturalism into all avenues of learning/teaching situations. This includes preparing all future educators to become more competent in the ever-changing, diverse global society. Thus, future educators should be provided with the opportunity to utilize multicultural curricular and teaching practices and to incorporate relevant experiential activities that nourish knowledge acquisition so they will truly know and value the merits of diversity in today's multicultural society.

REFERENCES

Banks, J. (1994). *An introduction to multicultural education.* Boston: Allyn & Bacon.

Banks, J. (1995). Multicultural education: Historical development, dimensions, and practice. In J. Banks & C. Banks (Eds.), *Handbook of research on multicultural education.* New York:Macmillan.

Bennett, C. (1999). *Comprehensive multicultural education: Theory and practice* (4th ed.). Boston: Allyn & Bacon.

Chisholm, I. M. (1994). Preparing teachers for multicultural classrooms. *The Journal of Educational Issues of Language Minority Students, 14,* 43-67.

Cortés, C. (1990). E pluribus unum: Out of many one. *California Perspectives, 1,* 13-16.

Daly, N., & O'Dowd, D. (1992). Teacher education programs. In C. Diaz (Ed.), *Multicultural education for the 21st century.* Washington, DC: NEA School Restructuring Series.

Deyhle, D. (1992). Constructing failure and maintaining cultural identity: Navajo and Ute school leavers. *Journal of American Indian Education, 31*(2), 24-47.

Garcia, E. (1991). *Education of linguistically and culturally diverse students: Effective instructional practices.* Santa Cruz: National Center for Research on Cultural Diversity and Second Language Learning, University of California.

Garza, S., & Barnes, C. (1989). Competencies for bilingual multicultural teachers. *The Journal of Educational Issues of Language Minority Students, 5,* 1-25.

Gay, G. (1995). Building cultural bridges: A bold proposal for teacher education. In F. Schultz (Ed.), *Multicultural education* (2nd ed.). Guilford, CT: Dushkin Publishing Group.

Grant, C. (Ed.). (1995). *Educating for diversity: An anthology of voices.* Boston:Allyn & Bacon.

Grant, C. A., & Gomez, M. L. (Eds.). (1996). *Making schooling multicultural: Campus and classroom.* Englewood Cliffs, NJ:Prentice-Hall.

King, J. (1995). Cross-centered knowledge: Black studies, curriculum transformation, and social action. In J. Banks & C. Banks (Eds.), *Handbook of research on multicultural education.* New York: Macmillan.

Ladson-Billings, G. (1994). Who will teach our children: Preparing teachers to successfully teach African American students. In E. Hollins, J. King, & W. Hayman (Eds.), *Teaching diverse populations: Formulating a knowledge base.* Albany: State University of New York Press.

Ladson-Billings, G. (1995). Multicultural teacher education: Research, practice and policy. In J. A. Banks & C. A. Banks (Eds.), *Handbook of research on multicultural education* (pp. 747-761). New York:Macmillan.

Nieto, S. (2000). *Affirming diversity: The sociopolitical context of multicultural education* (3rd ed.). New York: Longman.

Ogbu, J. (1995). Understanding cultural diversity and learning. In J. Banks & C. Banks (Eds.), *Handbook of research on multicultural education.* New York: Macmillan Publishing.

Ovando, C. J., & Collier, V. P. (1998). *Bilingual and ESL classrooms: Teaching in multicultural contexts* (2nd ed.). New York: McGraw-Hill.

Suleiman, M. (1995, December). *The art of communicating multiculturally: Implications for teachers.* Paper presented at the Annual Speech Association Conference of Puerto Rico, San Juan. (Also available through ERIC Clearing House on Urban Education)

Suleiman, M. (1997). Valuing children through values education: An agenda for the new millennium. *The Journal of the Kansas Association for Supervision and Curriculum Development, 14*(3), 67-88.

Suleiman, M. (1999). Field experiences in diverse settings: Implications for teacher empowerment. *National Social Science Perspectives Journal, 13*(1), 153-160.

Suleiman, M., & Moore, R. (1997a). Defining teachers' roles through leadership paradigms: Implications for effective teaching. *National Social Science Perspectives Journal, 11*(2), 111-118.

Suleiman, M., & Moore, R. (1997b). *Instilling civic and democratic values in all students: A multicultural perspective.* ERIC Clearinghouse on Urban Education.

Suzuki, B. H. (1984). Curriculum transformation for multicultural education. *Education and Urban Society, 16*, 294-322.

CHAPTER TWO

Problem Posing

Freire's Transformational Method in ESL

Bin Bin Jiang

International Language Institute
University of the Incarnate Word, San Antonio

WISDOM

I studied it and it taught me nothing.
I learned it and soon forgot everything else:
Having forgotten, I was burdened with knowledge—
The insupportable knowledge of nothing.

How sweet my life would be, if I were wise!
Wisdom is well known
When it is no longer seen or thought of.
Only then is understanding bearable.

Thomas Merton

"Wisdom" By Tomas Merton, from THE COLLECTED POEMS OF THOMAS MERTON, copyright ©1957 by The Abbey of Gethsemani. Used by permission of New Directions Publishing Corporation.

Of those who have longed for a change in education that supports all people, no one stands above the icon of multicultural education: Paulo Freire. Known widely for his first work, *Pedagogy of the Oppressed* (1970), Paulo Freire is regarded as the father of critical pedagogy. Born on September 19, 1921 and raised in northeastern Brazil, Freire grew up in a poor but loving and support- ive family (McLaren, 2000). Continuing his education to include both a law degree and a doctorate in education, Paulo Freire's emergence as the mentor of the pedagogy of love has been the inspiration of postmodern educators throughout the world. Freire is also revered as the creator of adult literacy pro- grams that have included as many as 24,000 cultural circles committed to assist approximately two million illiterate Brazilian workers in a national literacy program.

Beyond Freire's affect upon his homeland Brazil, his thinking and writing have reached millions throughout the world. According to McLaren (2000), "A courageous scholar, social activist, and cultural worker who was admired for his integrity and humility, Freire became internationally renowned for developing an anti-imperialist and anti-capitalist literary praxis employed by progressive educators throughout the world" (p. 142). Freire criticized education for being a "credit banking," factorylike system and advocated loving, liberating education- al practices based upon dialogues between teachers and learners. The purpose of these dialogues was to produce personal transformation and liberation of the learner (Fraser, 1997). In Freire's (1970) own words, "If I do not love the world—if I do not love life—if I do not love people—I cannot enter into dia- logue" (p. 71).

This chapter describes a year-long transformational learning and teaching experience with a class of 30 low, beginning-level English as a Second Language (ESL) students. This program's pedagogy was based upon the methodology and philosophy of Paulo Freire (1970). Of special interest was the problem-posing approach that Freire developed to help teach literacy to the poor and illiterate in his native Brazil in the late 1950s. In order to transform the con- ventional banking system of education, Freire started a new institutional culture he called "culture circles" to contradict the traditional passive concept of schools (Freire, 1971, 1973). In the culture circles, coordinators replaced the traditional teachers, dialogue replaced lectures, group participants replaced the students, and codified learning units replaced alienating syllabi (Freire & Macedo, 1998). Freire used culture circles to challenge participants to think crit- ically about their lives, social issues, and to present their reflections with pic- tures through the form of dialogue.

Culture circles later evolved into literacy classes with carefully chosen pic- tures (stories, songs, etc.) and generative words that presented emotionally and socially problematic issues in participants' lives. The dialogue based on each picture and generative word awakened participants' consciousness of the funda- mental causes of the problems and how they could take action to effect change (Shor, 1980). At the same time, participants in Freire's literacy programs were empowered with reading and writing skills essential to engaging themselves in social and political processes, such as gaining the vote. According to Freire (1998):

> Problem-posing education, as a humanist and liberating praxis, posits as fundamental that the people subjected to domination must fight for their emancipation. To that end, it enables teachers and students to become subjects of the educational process by overcoming authoritarianism and an alienating intellectualism; it also enables people to overcome their false perception of reality. The world—no longer something to be described with deceptive words—becomes the object of their transforming action by men and women which results in their humanization. (p.76)

To achieve this goal, Freire advocates a dialogical approach in which every member of the community—teacher/student, administrator/teacher, health educator/community member—become co-learners in the liberation process. "In this way, the problem-posing educator constantly re-forms his reflections in the reflection of the students. The students—no longer docile listeners—are now critical co-investigators in dialogue with the teacher" (Freire, 1998, p. 75). Critical thinking begins with the understanding of the fundamental reason for one's status (socioeconomic, cultural, political, etc.) in society. Further, critical thinking develops into decision making and action taking that can change one's life and immediate environment. As a result, authentic knowledge, evolving from the interaction of reflection and action occurs when people engage in transforming action (Freire, 1985). A problem-posing methodology includes three components: (a) listening, or investigating the issues or generative themes of the community; (b) dialogue, or codifying issues into discussion starters for critical thinking; and (c) action, or strategizing the changes students envision following their reflection.

Problem posing is applicable to refugee and immigrant English as a Second Language (ESL) students in particular because most of these students come from backgrounds that are similar to the participants in Freire's literacy programs—low socioeconomic status with limited or no access to education in their home countries. After coming to the United States, many of them have experienced emotional and social barriers in learning English, culture shock, lack of self-confidence, homesickness, and a sense of loss and vulnerability in the new environment. ESL students of all ages carry pedagogically similar characteristics. My research focused upon a class of adult learners from extraordinarily diverse backgrounds. The 30 students I worked with in the beginning, low-level ESL class, the second-lowest level of seven levels of ESL classes in a valley adult school located in the heart of the largest agricultural region in California, had the same problematic realities.

Most of the students in the class were involuntary immigrants (Ogbu & Matute-Bianchi, 1986) whose length of stay in the United States varied from

Ethnicity	Male	Female	Total
Ethiopian	1	1	2 (6.7)[1]
Hispanic	2	6	8 (26.7)
Hmong	6	8	14 (46.6)
Laotian	0	4	4 (13.3)
Mien	0	2	2 (6.7)
Total	9 (30)	21 (70)	30(100)

[1]Percentages are within parentheses; total is greater than 100 because of rounding.

four months to fifteen years and included five ethnic groups: 67 percent Southeast Asian refugees (including Hmong, Laotian, and Mien) from the Vietnam War over two decades ago, 27 percent Hispanic, and 6 percent Ethiopian. All students except one were married and had three to fifteen children in their respective families.

In this particular class, women accounted for 70 percent of the students, and Asian women comprised 67 percent of all women in the class. Students' ages ranged from 20 to 60; their age distribution is presented below. Hence, 73 percent of the students were between 20 and 40 years old. The age span, however, was even greater, as 17 percent of the students were at least 51 years old.

The formal education level of 80 percent of the students was exceptionally low by United States' standards, ranging from no formal schooling to some form of elementary schooling, and, by this same standard, generally low for all the students in the class. Most of them (90%) received financial assistance through GAIN, a program that provided enrolled students with stipends and employment assistance. These students were poorly motivated and had low self-esteem. They received six hours of daily instruction, three in my class and three in a vocational ESL class.

Age Range	Total
20-30	12 (40)[1]
31-40	10 (33)
41-50	3 (10)
51-60	5 (17)

[1]Percentages are within parenthesis

There were nine different languages spoken in the class, none of which I could understand or use to communicate. While facing the challenges in this adult ESL class, I was taking a graduate class in research methods at a local university. The professor of the course, Dr. Yvonne Freeman, was an expert on bilingual education and ESL methodology. She was also a firm believer and a strong advocate of Paulo Freire's critical pedagogy. I was introduced to Paulo Freire's liberatory education theories in her previous classes. With the encouragement and guidance of Dr. Freeman, I decided to apply problem-posing methodology in my own classroom as an action research project. Throughout the semester, the whole class, consisting of experienced K-12 teachers, also provided insightful feedback and suggestions to support me in this action learning endeavor.

In the following pages, I present some of the activities that my students and I created and participated in as colearners as we explored together the path of learning survival English, which helped them to become critical thinkers and action takers in their own personal and family lives as well as their immediate community—our classroom. Each activity included the three components of problem posing and created the spiraling effect that evolved into another activity consistent with the principles of problem posing: thematic learning.

COMMUNITY BUILDING

In the beginning of the year, the class was silent and the students demonstrated a lack of motivation and interest in learning English. Many of them looked sad and even unhealthy. Consequently, the attendance rate was not very high. The only thing they used to say to me was "Sorry, teacher, I don't know." What they said was true in respect of their knowledge of English. However, they did communicate among themselves in their own cultural and linguistic circles using their native languages that I did not understand. Since I fortunately had a multilingual aide in the classroom, I asked her to translate the themes of the student conversations. I also talked to the students individually to inquire about the reasons for their absences, their families, and their concerns. The aide had been with the students the year before I came and knew most of them well, so she also provided important information regarding their backgrounds and their problems to help me understand the students' situations. In sum, the low socioeconomic status and the low level of my students' education, the psychological factors of past traumatic experiences, language shock, and culture shock caused my students to demonstrate high levels of stress and lack of motivation in learning English.

To surmount the social and psychological barriers that adult learners may encounter, Schumann (1978b, p. 106) suggested ". . . finding language instructors who have a deep understanding and acceptance of the learner's inadequacies, anxieties, and insecurities . . . [to] enable the learner to overcome the trauma of language shock and culture shock." The SLA theories and ESL methodology that I had learned in my graduate TESOL classes and my personal experiences living in the United States helped me to understand some of the needs of my own students. They needed support and understanding in a community setting in which they could share their experiences, their worries, and concerns from their life experiences. Thus, I proposed a culture sharing time in the class. I started with sharing my own culture and life by bringing pictures of my family, and artifacts from my country. I told the class about myself, why I came to the United States, and my family in China. The students did not understand everything I said, but they saw the pictures of my family, my country, and my culture.

This was the ice breaker. Students began to ask me questions with the help of the multilingual aide because they saw similarities between my life and theirs–away from native land and family, adjusting to a new culture, speaking a different tongue. After that day, they began to see me in a new light—someone they could trust and care about. I asked them to bring in things they valued from their own cultures and families to share with the class. One Hmong woman brought a whole set of clothes that she made for her daughter to wear for the New Year. With the help of the aide in the class, she explained how they were made and when they were to be worn. A pregnant Lao woman brought the socks and hat she had knitted in Lao style for the expected baby. The Ethiopian students brought their traditional clothing to the class and one of them told about his thirteen-year experience in the army in his country. One of my Hispanic students brought a saddle, horse reins, a lasso from Mexico, a cowboy hat, and a Mexican blanket to share with the class. He showed the class how to use the saddle, reins, and lasso. A Lao woman dressed up in traditional clothes and sang a native song to the class. One Hmong student who used to be silent brought in two musical instruments, explained in Hmong that he made one of them, and played for the class. Everyone enjoyed the music he played, and he became more active in class.

Each sharing presented a natural opportunity for all the class members to participate in learning about an individual student and his or her life story. The students related culture and history, which resulted in dialogues and discussions about the Vietnam War, the death of family members, the refugee camps in Thailand, the depression and confusion stemming from living in United States culture, children growing up in the United States not knowing their cultural heritage, and disrespecting parents. The culture sharing was similar to the cultural circles in Freire's problem posing that provided opportunities for the participants to become consciously aware of their experiences and realities before they could make changes.

This culture sharing helped the class members to have more pride in their culture and increased their self-esteem and self-confidence. It also motivated students to learn English in order to share with others, which resulted in a higher attendance rate. At the same time, they also learned to appreciate other cultures as well. With the help of visual aids, they understood more clearly the content of the discussion and participated in it through verbal and even body language. Culture sharing contributed to the development of a positive environment of a community of learners. The sharing time also helped them to know one another better, which, in turn, helped students to feel they were all part of a large family. They learned to greet each other in one another's native languages as a sign of appreciation of all the cultures represented in the community. This sensitivity helped students to feel more comfortable in sharing personal experiences and caring about one another.

When the pregnant Laotian women gave birth to a baby girl, one of the class members announced it to the class. Other class members then explained that she was a divorced woman with two children in the United States and her ex-husband, the father of the baby girl, was in Thailand. Because of the class sympathy and care for the baby and the mother, they decided to donate some money and bought presents for the baby, along with a congratulation card to the mother signed by everyone wishing both of them happiness and good luck. The woman was deeply moved and later brought her baby girl to class to share with us her joy and to express her appreciation.

This culture sharing activity was also a valuable experience for me. I learned about the lives, history, and oppression that my students had experienced in their contexts, which helped me to see more themes for future learning units. As a participant and co-learner in the culture sharing conversations, my respect and understanding for each of the class members grew as they opened up to our class community by sharing their beautiful cultural traditions, their struggles through war and hardships, and their talents and knowledge about parts of the world that I did not know. They broadened my perspective on how social, cultural, and historical factors could affect individual learners and helped me to understand them in multiple dimensions (DeVillar, 1994, pp. 50-51).

COLLABORATIVE GROUP WORK

Because of my interest in students' sharing of their cultures, their stories, and their talents, I took pictures of all the activities we had in class and brought the photos to class. The students were excited to see themselves in the pictures. In order to celebrate and keep these wonderful memories, we decided to put the pictures on the bulletin board. Then I thought it would be even more meaningful if the students could document their own activities. However, they were just beginning learners of English, and it would be too challenging for them to work on their own. According to the social learning principle of Vygotsky (1962, 1978), students working together can gain access to new areas of learning potential beyond those they are able to accomplish alone. In other words, effective, long-term learning takes place when learners engage in meaningful activities, work in dyads or small groups, take an active role in the learning process, collaborate with one another, and exercise choice during their activities. As students collaborate, they learn to externalize their thoughts in order to communicate with each other, to solve problems, and to construct concepts–thus learning (Freeman & Freeman, 1994, p. 56). In order to facilitate such learning, teachers become mediators, helping students through their interaction to reach higher levels of proficiency. Vygotsky refers to the distance between the individual level of students and the potential level students can reach in collaborative interaction as the Zone of Proximal Development.

Learning to function in groups also helps students to function in society: "In communities of learners, students appear to learn how to coordinate with, support, and lead others, to become responsible and organized in their management of their own learning, and to be able to build on their previous interest to learn in new areas and to sustain motivation to learn" (Rogoff, Matusov, & White, 1996, p. 410). In other words, "Learning must be an active, social, discovery process, guided by the teacher, rather than a transmission process controlled by the teacher. . . " and "A learner is a thinker and an engaged participant; each role informs and transforms the other" (DeVillar, 1999, p. 45).

Using these principles, I arranged the students into several groups. As members of the class community, they were willing to help each other in their collaborative group work. Each student contributed what he or she could to the writing within their particular group. For example, one person would take the role of scribe and editor; others helped with the vocabulary or assisted with the spelling of a word; and others would assist with the structures of the sentences. Still others helped with the layout, for example, by determining where to integrate the photographs with the writing. Then, each group shared its text-and-image work with the class before placing the individual project on the bulletin board. The level of pride exhibited by students with respect to their projects was very high.

This activity, using the pictures (or the codes) from the culture sharing, continued with the theme, but was transformed into more dialogue and action through the collaborative group work of learning to write about themselves and their actions and read each others' writings. By working together to learn to read and write in English, they took active steps towards overcoming their language difficulties and towards making positive changes in their own lives.

JOURNAL WRITING

As my students developed more self-esteem and motivation in learning English in the four modes (listening, speaking, reading, and writing), they became more active in class activities, helped one another in their group projects, and took an active role in deciding what they wanted to learn and how they were going to learn, including negotiating the types and ways that learning activities were designed and presented. The students enjoyed the weekly cultural sharing time so much that we gradually changed it to the first daily activity, which students shared experiences in their family and community with the class to start our everyday class. However, some students could not understand everything that was being shared due to lack of vocabulary or listening proficiency; they suggested that I write what the class shared on the board so that they could copy and share the writing with their families. This started our class journal in which we integrated listening, speaking, reading, and writing within one activity.

The journal writing often related to the students' daily lives or to current events. Before writing, the students first shared their experiences with the class orally. Afterwards, the class collectively discussed and negotiated the vocabulary, form, and content of the entry to be entered into the classroom journal. During this process, the students received assistance from me and from the aide, who provided scaffolding regarding the vocabulary and grammatical structure needed. After completing the entry, they practiced reading their journal out loud, and they received assistance in their pronunciation and in clarifying the meaning of new words. The daily journals provided authentic reading material for not only the class members, but also for some of the family members. Because the content was about their family members or their community, some of the children of the class members became more interested in reading and writing.

When we learned about emergency procedures and reviewed words such as ambulance and accident, one of the students shared a story about his brother. His brother had eaten poisonous mushrooms, and the family had to call an ambulance. I wrote the story on the overhead, and the students practiced reading it. This was another example of relating learning to authentic life experiences. My students found it very interesting, meaningful, and enjoyable.

This activity was one of the favorite activities—for both the students and myself–as it engaged the whole class in a writing project to produce a collective journal and evolved through different students' input over time. This practice adhered to the principle that students needed to be immersed in literature of all kinds to help them progress in writing to become more proficient writers "through exposure to books and print . . ." (Weaver, 1994, p. 98).

SIMULATIONS

Cummins' (1981) notion of context-embedded instruction as "interpersonal involvement in a shared reality that reduces the need for explicit linguistic elaboration of the message" (p. 11) is essential to beginning ESL classes. The instructor can use pictures, realia, activities modeled by the teacher, books that have rich illustrations, and the language aide to provide meaningful instruction. In the specific adult L2 situation described here, communication was facilitated through: (a) use of appropriate reading materials with pictures, (b) slower and shorter utterances in instruction, and (c) the help of a multilingual aide.

In order to make learning more meaningful and authentic to the students, our curriculum closely related the students' learning to their daily lives (Freeman & Freeman, 1998). Learning to use the telephone is important to the students for both emergency use and everyday living. In one unit that dealt with emergency procedures, the students practiced conversations in the classroom with real telephones and engaged in conversational role-playing situations. For example, the students practiced how to make emergency calls to the hospital and doctor in case the Laotian woman in the class, who was pregnant, went into labor. Students learned to listen to directions and to report emergencies. At the same time, they learned how to report concerns, such as informing school personnel of their children's absence due to illness.

When students studied the unit on shopping, they engaged, singly and through group projects, in making up menus, comparing prices for various foods from ads in the local newspaper, and composing related shopping lists. Each group then presented to the rest of the class, saying what they wanted to prepare, what they needed to buy, and where they had decided to purchase the items. Later, when we had potluck lunches, students were able to explain how to make the food they had brought and provide the name of the dish. In order to make some of these themes more comprehensible to students, we simulated a grocery store within the classroom with cash registers, canned foods, counters, and price tags. Students played various roles.

These simulation activities provided students with useful tools to become more independent and active in dealing with daily living situations that were very frustrating to them before because they did not know how to communicate with the school about their children's sickness, report family emergencies, or even converse with the clerks at grocery stores. With the improvement of their English literacy, they gained more confidence in themselves and were willing to take more risks in learning to read and write in English.

READING AND WRITING PROJECTS

A meaningful way in which to introduce and develop students' writing is through immersion in literature of all kinds. The first book we read together in class was called *What a Wonderful World*. It demonstrated the beauty of the world with beautiful pictures and simple verses. The students enjoyed reading along with me. This reading naturally led us into the discussion of their homeland and their writing about their homeland. Their work amazed me; it contained words with codes they knew—pictures of their homes, rivers, farm animals, trees, and flowers that represented their lives and their stories. At the same time, I also realized how much help they needed in order to become literate in English (as most of their writings consisted of only words or phrases) so that they could share their stories and have their voices heard. It taught me again that their lives comprised the best themes for learning to read and write.

Because the students were interested in learning to write about themselves and their family members, another writing project the class did was a letter that each member wrote to a pen pal about him/herself and his/her family. We also read simple biographies before we started the writing project. The aide and I wrote about ourselves and our families as models for the students. This writing was relevant and meaningful to everyone and the results were fascinating. To many of the class members, this was the first time that they shared information about their families and histories with others in writing, which was a milestone to them. It was the evidence of the beginning of their transformation from illiteracy to literacy. The class members shared their letters in our class with one another and later put them on our bulletin board as a form of our class publication.

The bulletin board also attracted students and teachers from other classes to visit and read every issue of our class publications—from artifacts from different cultures, the pictures of their culture sharing activities with brief descriptions of each, to letters and longer writings about heroes and presidents in their own countries. The students and teachers were fascinated by the exciting events taking place in our class, which also motivated other teachers to change some of their class activities and collaborate with us in planning special events together. Our classroom community had positive influences on our surroundings that promoted the changes in a larger community—the branch site of the adult school.

As the students developed their literacy skills, they were not only able to share their work with a larger community, but they also demonstrated more critical themes in their writing content and creative format (Freire, 1994). They learned the different types of writing styles used in journal writing, letter writing, and note writing. For instance, during the latter half of the school year, students began to write in their journal about their weekends, their spring vacation about special events. One Hmong student seemed to be learning English very slowly until he played Hmong music to the class and was encouraged by other students. One weekend, he witnessed a killing incident near his apartment. With the help of his children, he wrote about the incident and shared his writing with the class, to everyone's surprise. This journal evoked discussions on gang violence in the local community, which led to the topic of how to keep their own children from the gang influence and how to watch out for one another in their own neighborhood. This example also illustrated the unlimited potential motivated learners could have in sharing experiences of their lives (even if negative) that could be transformed into actions that would change their lives.

One of the students had a car accident and was injured and taken to the hospital one afternoon. He is Ethiopian, and because he often volunteered for class activities and helped the other students, he was considered a class leader. When the class heard about his accident, they were very sad and concerned. I seized this opportunity to ask each of my students to make a sympathy card to wish him well. Some of them used their own language, and the aide helped them to translate. Most of them also drew pictures, such as happy faces, to cheer him up. He was very grateful for the support and wrote a thank you letter to the class. This was an opportunity for everyone to express in writing their care and concern for another member in the class community, and they did beautifully in creating their own cards.

In the month of Lincoln's and Washington s birthdays we read biographical stories about these American presidents. The students learned how these presidents contributed to important events in American history. They also asked a lot of questions about the information contained in the books. The knowledge they gained helped them to pass the citizenship test. We also celebrated President's Day as a class with a group project in which students wrote about famous presidents or heroes from their native cultures. They drew pictures of the person and wrote about his or her life and contributions to that particular country.

This project was more challenging to my students than the previous projects had been because it involved new vocabulary, especially words relating to specific historical terms and events. However, with the help of their group members, the aide, myself, and sometimes their family members, we succeeded in completing the project. We put these writing projects on display on the classroom bulletin board. This display attracted students' and other teachers' attention from more advanced classes. This achievement, in turn, made my students feel proud about the fact that they could write something that was of so much interest even to the higher level students. This was in a sense a community publication and showed the importance publication plays in building students' self-esteem (Freeman & Freeman, 1994).

INSTRUCTIONAL AIDE'S ROLE

As indicated earlier, the multilingual aide's assistance in the classroom made the learning more effective. The instructional aide was a very important agent in the classroom as first-language support was one of the essential scaffolding elements that the beginning learners needed. The multilingual aide—who spoke Hmong, Lao, Mien, and English—and the instructor, together served to model collaborative teamwork. The aide also provided demonstrations and gave short summaries of stories and activities in the above primary languages. These actions greatly helped students to better understand instructions and content. I also requested that the aide ask students for feedback on what they did and did not like about certain activities and suggestions about how I could better meet students' needs. The daily collaboration between the aide and myself in the classroom also provided a role model for the students in their collaborative activities.

OUTCOME OF THE CLASS

Students enjoyed the class and developed higher self-esteem and a higher degree of self-confidence. They also developed positive attitudes towards learning and a higher motivation to continue on to the next level of education. Their relationship with their children improved as they shared their books and projects with their children and sometimes received linguistic support from them. This also appeared to motivate their children's learning at school. In addition, they took more charge of their own learning by participating in the curriculum development of the course.

In reflecting upon my students' growth in their reading and writing, I can see definite progress in both. At first they were reluctant to try to read storybooks. However, with my encouragement and their increasing interest, they began to take books home and some even asked their children to translate the stories into their own language so that they could understand the stories better and could help their classmates to understand more. Later, students borrowed books to take home to read to their own children. Some students loved some of the books so much that they copied them to read at home.

Gradually my students developed good reading habits, which helped them to increase their vocabulary and helped them in their writing; many borrowed books to take home to read. The class later also established a shared reading time in which everyone read together. In addition, students chose their own books to read silently when they finished their assignments. One indication of my students' progress was that most of them were able to read the instructions in the textbook and other students' journals on their own towards the end of the school year.

There were also extended outcomes in the following years. For example, some passed the citizenship test, some went on to get high school equivalency, some went on to community college, some students were able to find jobs, and a few went into business. For example, the Ethiopian student who had a car accident successfully started his own business within three years.

CONCLUSION

Building a classroom community of culturally diverse adult learners provides a safe and risk-free environment in which students are comfortable learning and are willing to help each other. Using student life experiences as codes in teaching makes learning authentic and interesting, thereby helping the students learn more effectively. Through sharing and discussions about the students' experiences, they become more critically aware of the problems in their lives and work collaboratively to improve or solve their problems–to actively engage in the learning of reading and writing in English and to make more positive steps in changing their own reality as well as that of their immediate community–both family and classroom. (Shor, 1980, p. 48)

When students come across difficulties in learning, encouragement is always important and context-embedded instruction makes learning more comprehensible, lowering the affective filter of the students. Last but not the least, collaborative group work provides scaffolding for the students, especially for the less advanced students, so that they can learn from each other. Freirean educators also believe that lessons should be learner centered and should have immediate meaning and purpose for the learner, and that learning takes place in social interaction. Learners, themselves, are the ones who actually construct knowledge, thus becoming empowered through a collaborative learning process.

REFERENCES

Cummins, J. (1981). The role of primary language development in promoting education success for language minority students. In Office for Bilingual Bicultural Education (Ed.), *Schooling and language minority students: A theoretical framework* (pp. 3-49). Los Angeles: Evaluation, Dissemination and Assessment Center (California State University).

DeVillar, R. A. (1994). The rhetoric and practice of cultural diversity in U.S. schools: Socialization, resocialization, and quality schooling. In C. J. Faltis, R. A. DeVillar, & J. P. Cummins (Eds.), *Cultural diversity in schools: From rhetoric to practice* (pp. 25-56). Albany: State University of New York Press.

DeVillar, R. A. (1999). Developing critical literacy through technology in U.S. schools: Reflections and projections. In J.V. Tinajero & R.A. DeVillar (Eds.). *The power of two languages: Effective dual language use across the curriculum* (Millenium Edition). New York: McGraw-Hill.

Fraser, J. (1997). The work of Paulo Freire. In P. Freire (Ed.), *Mentoring the mentor: A critical dialogue with Paulo Freire.* New York: Peter Lang.

Freeman, D. E., & Freeman, Y. S. (1994). *Between worlds: Access to second language acquisition.* Portsmouth, NH: Heinemann.

Freeman, D. E., & Freeman, Y. S. (1998). *ESL/EFL teaching: Principles of success.* Portsmouth, NH: Heinemann.

Freire, A. M. A., & Macedo, P. (Eds.). (1998). *The Paulo Freire reader.* New York: Continuum.

Freire, P. (1970). *Pedagogy of the oppressed.* New York: Seabury.

Freire, P. (1971). To the coordinator of a culture circle. *Convergence, 4*(1), 61-62.

Freire, P. (1973). *Education for critical consciousness.* New York: Seabury.

Freire, P. (1985). *Politics of education.* South Hadley, MA: Bergin and Garvey.

Freire, P. (1994). *Pedagogy of hope.* New York: Continuum.

Freire, P. (1998). The banking concept of education. In A.M.A. Freire & D. Macedo (Eds.), *The Paulo Freire reader.* New York: Continuum.

McLaren, P. (2000). *Che Gueverra and Paulo Freire: The pedagogy of revolution.* Lanham, MD: Rowman & Littlefield.

Merton, T. (1967). *Selected poems of Thomas Merton.* New York: New Directions.

Ogbu, J. U., & Matute-Bianchi, M.U. (1986). Understanding sociocultural factors: Knowledge, identity, and school adjustment. In Office for Bilingual Bicultural Education (Ed.), *Beyond language: Social and cultural factors in schooling language minority students* (pp. 73-142). Los Angeles: Evaluation, Dissemination and Assessment Center.

Rogoff, B., Matusov, E., & White, C. (1996). Models of teaching and learning: Participation in a community of learners. In D.R. Olson & N. Torrance (Eds.), *The handbook of education and human development.* Oxford: Blackwell.

Schumann, J. (1978b). *The pidginization process: A model for second language acquisition.* Rowley, MA: Newbury House.

Shor, I. (1980). *Critical teaching and everyday life.* Chicago: University of Chicago Press.

Vygotsky, L. (1962). *Thought and language* (Eugenia Hanfmann and Gertrude Vakar, Trans.). Cambridge, MA: MIT Press.

Vygotsky, L. (1978). *Mind in society: The development of higher psychological processes.* Cambridge, MA: Harvard University Press.

Weaver, C. (1994). *Reading process and practice.* Portsmouth, NH: Heinemann.

CHAPTER THREE

Finding Pride and the Struggle for Freedom to Assemble

The Case of Queer Youth in U.S. Schools

Mary L. Gray

University of California, San Diego

FOR EACH OF YOU

Be who you are and will be
Learn to cherish
that boisterous Black Angel that drives you
up one day and down another
protecting the place where your power rises
running like hot blood
from the same source as your pain.

When you are hungry
learn to eat
whatever sustains you
until morning
but do not be misled by details
simply because you live them.

"For Each of You", from CHOSEN POEMS: OLD AND NEW by Audre Lorde. © 1982, 1976, 1974, 1973, 1970, 1968 by Audre Lorde. Used by permission of W.W. Norton & Company, Inc.

Do not let your head deny
your hands
any memory of what passes through them
nor your eyes nor your heart
everything can be used
except what is wasteful
(you will need to remember this when you are accused of destruction).
Even when they are dangerous
examine the heart of those machines
which you hate
before you discard them
but do not mourn their lack of power
lest you be condemned to relieve them.

If you do not learn to hate
you will never be lonely
enough to love easily
nor will you always be brave
although it does not grow any easier.

Do not pretend to convenient beliefs
even when they are righteous
you will never be able to defend your city
while shouting

Remember our sun
is not the most noteworthy star
only the nearest.

Respect whatever pain you bring back
from your dreaming
but do not look for new gods
in the sea
nor in any part of the rainbow.

Each time you love
love as deeply
as if it were
forever
only nothing is eternal.

Speak proudly to your children
where ever you may find them
tell them
you are the offspring of slaves
and your mother was
a princess in darkness.

Audre Lorde (1970)

WHY PRIDE IS HARD TO COME BY FOR QUEER YOUTH IN U.S. SCHOOLS

Taking pride in one's deeds and words is considered something of a needed step in the growth of self-esteem. Whether in work, relationships, or appearance, pride becomes an expression of our acceptance and appreciation for the talents we possess and a reflection perhaps of the acknowledgement—and endorsement—we receive from others. Educators often appeal to pride to motivate students to care about themselves, their schools, and their work. It is common to hear educators speak of "school pride" in relation to successful athletic programs and academic honors; they "take pride" in their students' achievements and this feeds students' desires to further excel. However, school accolades are always tempered by the need for agreement with and acceptance from the broader community. As a result, local political debates over community values have a substantial impact on the development of pride for and among lesbian, gay, bisexual, and transgender (lgbt) youth in educational communities. This chapter attempts to outline why pride among lgbt youth is painfully elusive; I will highlight the struggles in educational environments that pit youth against adults and progressive social justice efforts against the mores of a predominantly homophobic and heterosexist society. Using narratives from lgbt youth describing their experiences in school settings, I hope to challenge readers to consider what is at stake in the case of lgbt youth and the ways in which these stakes intersect with the challenges faced by other socially marginalized youth.

Let me begin by defining a few terms. The collection of narratives used in this essay are part of a larger project attempting to bring youth voices to the forefront of the discussion around what it means to be queer in the United States today (Gray, 1999). I use the term "queer" to refer to youth who readily and politically identify as gay, lesbian, bisexual, transgender, or questioning of the heterosexual norm of this society. "Youth" has a rather fluid meaning in the lgbt community. Depending on when someone "comes out" to themselves or others, the category "youth" may fit someone in their preteens to late 20s. For the purpose of this discussion, I am referring to folks eighteen years old and younger when I speak of youth. Their voices make it clear that questioning and queer youth are on the frontlines of the battle to define what it means to be queer and what rights are afforded lgbt individuals. Rather than see lgbt youth concerns as somehow isolated and incidental, we must recognize the ways in which young people are placed in the center of the cultural debates revolving around sexuality and other forms of discrimination. We must also validate the need for educators to lead the way in creating safe and open discussions for these debates that acknowledge the existence of lgbt youth in their midst.

It's an interesting paradox that in order for queer folks to be directly engaged in addressing issues of bigotry, even to address and counter the ques-

tioning of our right to exist, we must make a public act of asserting ourselves—
outing ourselves. This is never a solitary event. It is a performance we enact
everyday. Being "out" or rather experiencing exposure could come easily
enough. There have been (and in most states still are) acts of law and surveil-
lance focused on rooting out "immoral homosexual acts"—tracking the homosexual has been a modern American obsession from McCarthy to Falwell. And
for a queer person, the simple reading of someone's glance—flirting with someone—has meant risking so much more than a polite (or not so polite) rebuff; it
has meant exposure or at least suspicion and the compromising of one's heterosexual appearances and privileges. The mere acts of holding a partner's hand in
public and taking part in a public political demonstration for same-sex domestic
partnership rights carry the possibility of hostility and violence (for a discussion
of anti-lgbt hate crimes see Conaty, 1996; D'Augelli, 1992; Haider-Markel,
2000; see Friend, 1993, Rey & Gibson, 1997; Rivers & D'Augelli, 2001 for a
specific discussion of violence in schools). Simply put, being out takes pride—a
belief that what one is doing deserves not just acknowledgment but appreciation
and respect. Queer Pride—that secure sense that it is perfectly acceptable and
healthy to question and challenge society's constructions of gender or to have
an interest in someone regardless of his or her gender—comes from a volatile
struggle that is far from won.

What are some of the specific factors that make this sense of pride fleeting?
Certainly, the pathologizing of homosexuality by the medical community has
played a significant role. Additionally, the conservative Religious Right has
rhetorically taken on homosexuality as an emblem of what is morally eroded in
the United States (Herman, 2000; Rofes, 1997). To put it concisely, pride is difficult to come by for queer folks because at this moment we are still predominantly—both socially and politically—unacceptable. Yet, we exist and in growing numbers at increasingly younger ages; lgbt people are refusing to relinquish
their rights to public acceptance because of their sexual and gender differences
(Herdt, 2001).

It is critical to note that a certain amount of pride has been garnered and culled
from our legal system over the past decade. Winning legal protection has become
a key strategy for gaining legitimacy. But, again, this has led to an interesting
paradox: Pride remains the privilege of the socially legitimate. This requires lgbt
people to conform political strategies to the task of uniformly saying, "I'm just
like all of you, but with a little difference and that difference is a private matter
that I pledge to keep quiet so as not to offend." Youth have a very different relationship of access to this politically negotiated pride. Queer and questioning
youth have no legitimizing legal system to directly access, and therefore must rely
on adult allies in the battle to define lgbt political and cultural priorities. Often
times, these adult allies are hard to come by. Adult allies—queer and straight
alike—are often accused of "recruiting youth into the homosexual lifestyle."

Because of this misperception, educators mentoring lgbt youth have been
the targets of harassment by their communities and school districts (Jordan,

Vaughan, & Woodworth, 1997). Several state measures in the past two decades have focused specifically on blocking lgbt teachers from employment, only serving to make lgbt teachers less willing to reach out to queer and questioning youth (Button, Rienzo, & Wald, 2000). These sociopolitical circumstances have kept adults at bay or least limited in what they can do to offer support to youth questioning their sexuality (Rofes, 1989).

Additionally, if the marginal acceptance of queerness has been paid for (by adults) in promises to remain quiet and look like everyone else, youth are less interested in paying this price. Why? Simply put, youth are so utterly silenced in their daily lives, they gain no ground by promises of silence and assimilation. In many less urban places, they are literally too disconnected from their local lgbt communities to find solace or connection outside their school communities (Gray, in progress; Sears, 1991). Where adults' claims to be like everyone else may have currency, for youth such claims wear thin at a time when defining oneself—distinguishing a sense of identity—is a critical part of their daily struggle to become self-confident individuals (Rotheram-Borus & Langabeer, 2001). In many parts of their lives, youth face assumptions that invalidate their ability to "know anything," least of all their sexual or gender identity. Queer and questioning youth are more often than not characterized as confused about their sexuality/gender, as though these categories "clear up" naturally once you've reached adulthood. To present themselves as no different than their peers denies the everyday realities of lgbt youth experiences. They cannot bring their sweethearts to the homecoming game or dance without risking physical harm. They cannot form social or political organizations without out-of-the-ordinary scrutiny and intervention from their school administrations. They cannot easily find one another in a crowd without marking themselves, declaring themselves proudly to be lgbt or questioning youth. For queer adults, refuge from the pressures to assimilate into a straight world can be sought in a bar or in the privacy of their home. Most lgbt youth do not have a physical space in which they can safely be proud of who they are and share their lives with peers. Often their own home can be as dangerous a place to be queer as their school campus or the local recreation center (Savin-Williams, 2001). Ironically, as much danger as there is in drawing attention to their difference, the realities of youth experiences suggest that blending in with their straight peers has just as many costs. Most significantly, their sense of self-esteem can pay the heaviest toll (Remafedi, Farrow et al., 1994).

We must also consider the environment in which lgbt youth wage their wars to "have pride" and to be "out." Their primary battles are fought daily in the schools, not the legislature. And while youth struggle with their desire for connection to peers and a larger community, they are still surrounded by hostility to who they even "think" they are or appear to be. Any effort to be out and proud jeopardizes their safety in most U.S. school environments (McLaren, 1995).

In the following excerpts, lgbt youth describe their experiences in school. Their voices are sometimes eloquent, sometimes rough, but their honesty and reflective thoughtfulness offer perspectives we rarely see or hear. Young queers face daily heterosexism and harassment in predominantly hostile school environments. Schools tend to represent everything young people are expected to model as they are groomed to take their place in society as fully participating adults. Kathryn Herr (1997) notes it is the "role of societal institutions, such as schools, to promote the pervasive ideology" (p. 52). Gender roles and (hetero) sexuality are cemented through the molding experiences of school dances, high school parties, and the like. There is arguably no stronger bastion of conformity and ramrodding of mainstream normality than high school, where all youth are expected to get decent grades, find their first love, and move on to the responsibilities of adulthood in a quiet, orderly fashion. This environment is violently antagonistic towards anyone—queer or otherwise—dabbling with the norm, pushing against what one is expected to be. It is here that social pressures to fit in and seem straight are at their thickest for most queer youth and most often framed as something individual youth should deal with in private. Herr (1997) argues against seeing the struggles of lgbt youth as the "personal problem" of a few young people. Analyzing a young lesbian's narratives about the hostility she experienced in schools that eventually led to her dropping out, Herr concludes that schools must see the homophobic environments of schools as a "school and societal issue as well as a personal one for professionals working in schools" (p. 63).

It is not surprising that several of the young people in this selection describe their school experiences with rage and frustration. And, yet, several of them were able to turn a bad situation into a learning experience for those around them (and make it out alive and in one piece in the process). It is a sad comment on our current school system that an overwhelming number of the young people represented here describe their school experiences as no less than a living nightmare.

Anthony's Story

I go to school in Hayward. It's strictly hell. They're so close-minded. Right now, some of my closest friends know I'm gay. You know, they're not all so afraid. They're just like, "we know this." I mean, all the reactions I've gotten have been "we know this, Anthony" you know? They know me already. I am a queen.

A lot of people pick on me at school and pick fights with me. At school, I've had "fag" spray painted on my locker, gay porn pinned to my locker, and death threats on my locker, too. I had three boys suspended the other day for harassing me, saying they're trying to pick fights with me, calling me a faggot, a queer, and all that stuff. I finally just got pissed and I was about to fight 'em, but I said, "look, you want me to show you what a real queer can do?" So I went to the principal's office and told her. They were there threatening to beat me up after school if they got suspended. Well, the principal's just like, "we'll see who's gonna threaten who." I was so happy.

Other faculty members at school are supportive. Both of the principals know I'm gay. My music teacher knows I'm gay because I'm in choir. And the counselor knows I'm gay. It's pretty cool they're accepting, you know. This is the first time they ever really had a gay young person go to their school at age 14. It blows their minds. They're really cool there.

I think there are some kids at school that may be gay or lesbian, but they don't want to come out in school. I think we need to have a gay group in our school. Basically, I'm almost completely out at school. I mean, I am such a queen you cannot miss me, okay? But, I'm sick and tired of everybody asking, Are you gay? Are you a faggot? Are you a queer? I'm like, "shut up!" I'm sick and tired of all these questions.

Adam's Story

I started off in kindergarten in an expensive private school. What amused me was that the computer skills I learned there got me through all of my middle school computer classes, which I think says something very interesting. As of first grade, I went to public school, where I discovered that school was a Bad Thing. I never really socialized well—I was too open, all emotion and trust and no defense. I daydreamed, I stuttered, and in general, I didn't get along well with other children.

High school was torture, pure and simple. I've always been sort of effeminate, and every day felt like a struggle to hide what I was thinking from everyone else. I really don't know how I survived it all. It wasn't simply my sexuality, of course, but that was what was primarily on my mind. My high school, Lee High, was full of stereotypical rednecks, and "fag" was VERY commonly used, though never to my face. I remember sitting in class and quickly looking down at my papers every time someone said "gay" or "fag" because I was afraid people would see the expression of surprise or pain on my face and figure it out. At that point, of course, life would be over. To make matters worse, all my friends were scattered across the five high schools in the city, so I had few people to turn to for support.

The terrible headaches I got as a kid became less frequent when my Senior year began, but I was restless and unsatisfied with school. It occurred to me that few well-adjusted gay men would stay in my hometown of Huntsville, Alabama, for long, and that I wasn't likely to find anyone there. Classes weren't challenging me, and the homophobia at my school was making me miserable. I mean, I was doing well, winning writing awards, running the newspaper and literary magazine, but I felt like my time in Huntsville was over.

That's when I discovered Simon's Rock. Three hundred students; intense and personal academics; extremely liberal (I'd heard there was NO homophobia); and it rescued students out of high school, not requiring a diploma. Best of all, it was in the North. So I did one of the scariest things I've ever done next to coming out, and applied. I got accepted, dropped out of high school halfway through my senior year and flew off to Massachusetts to go to college.

Alan's Story

I didn't really have a good environment in high school to come out. The thing that got me to come out was that in my peer counseling group, we dealt with ten subjects, and one of the subjects was sexuality. When I was a junior, I was out to maybe two people in my high school. And that's when we first discussed that issue. A lot of the peer counselors that I was with would discuss the issue but they really wouldn't take it seriously, and constantly told fag jokes and everything in front of everyone. And here I am, the little closet fag, sitting here listening to this. It really made me feel bad. So, I decided at that point, I would start to speak out as pro-gay, even though I wasn't identifying as gay and I wasn't out at the time. When we were discussing the issue, I made a huge speech about it, and I think that affected a lot of people, knowing that it mattered to some people. I think their general impression was "oh, it doesn't matter, because people really aren't gay." What I think teachers could do is just make gay people visible and not be afraid of that.

When I was in history class, I'd be learning all this history, and I almost felt like it didn't even apply to me, because I didn't relate to it, it wasn't about my people, these people hadn't been through the same experiences that I had, this was someone else's history. I still learned it and everything, but there would be times when I'd know a certain person in history was gay, and they'd make them out to be straight in this history book. That really bothered me a lot, it made the kind of people that I could relate to invisible, so I couldn't relate at all. What I really did like was when teachers would bring up the fact that this author is gay or whatever, and we would discuss it. When homosexuality would be talked about in an objective way and not looked down upon, it made me feel as if I could approach that teacher. We had the first gay city council member elected in San Diego, and not one of my teachers talked about it. The only reason I knew was because I was down in Hillcrest, the gay area in San Diego and the news was everywhere. Schools need teachers that present a gay positive image; teachers that don't let kids get away with calling each other fags in class; teachers that don't hesitate to talk about gay issues. Treat homophobia just like you would racism. Racism is not accepted any longer, and homophobia shouldn't be either. I didn't approach any of my teachers about being gay until I didn't care any more.

I had some liberal teachers. I came out to a lot of my teachers before I came out to the school. I really hold it against some of them that they told me not to come out. I only had two teachers encourage me to come out, and I told them that that was what I wanted to do. I don't think I'll ever forget one teacher in particular, my AP English teacher, Mr. Dennis Wymbs. I told him that I was gay and that I was seriously thinking about coming out, and he said it was a bad idea, that I shouldn't do it. And this is for you: Fuck you, Mr. Wymbs! I'm out! I did it and I lived through it. You suck.

When I came out in high school, it was kinda weird because I was, like, a good student. I got good to okay grades, I was really involved. I played the tuba, and was tuba section leader for two years, I was in peer counseling for two years, I was a group leader in peer counseling, I did all the rights things. So, when I came out, it was like, "how can this guy that does all the right things be gay?" And I had been asking myself the same question for a long time.

As soon as I came out to one of my classes as a class project, about 15 minutes after the class was over, we had a break, and by my next class everyone knew, they'd heard. It was the hottest piece of gossip around. It was pretty wild. My school was a large school, probably about 2,600, 2,800, something like that. It was so strange that everyone knew.

Initially, people were kind of in shock, and so I didn't get much reaction. But once it started to sink into people, I started to get more reactions. I would either get support from someone or I would be called names. I was the only out person in my high school at that point. I remember walking down the hall being called "Tinkerbell" and "fairy" and "faggot" and all that kind of stuff. It got really bad, to the point where I had to be escorted from class to class because people would follow me. At lunchtime, I would go sit in a room just to eat my lunch by myself, and people would open the door just to look at me, like I was some sort of spectacle to them. I would get threats of violence and spit on.

I wanted to go to prom with a guy really badly, just to show everybody that I could, but my boyfriend already had a date with a girl. So I went into San Diego's Gay Youth Alliance and asked everybody "who wants to go to prom?" I ended up going with this guy I didn't even know who went to San Diego State. By the time prom happened, we had met three times. I only saw him once again after that.

Going to prom with a guy caused a lot of problems because people didn't like the idea of me "ruining" their prom by coming with a guy. But I did it anyway and I got death threats before I went to prom, pretty much from the entire LaCrosse team, the football team, and the wrestling team. I had a meeting with the principal of my high school about it. I just said, "Look, I'm getting all these threats." And he said, "We'll take care of it." We thought we were gonna have police protection when we went, but we didn't. It was fine, though. We had a great time. I doubled with a lesbian couple, one of whom went to my school. It was so liberating to stand there, slow dancing with a guy in front of all of these people that I had grown up with. People were staring at us with their jaws on the floor in disbelief. I would just smile at them. The photographers gave us funny looks when we went to get our pictures taken. It was really neat to know that I was the first one at my school to do this. It was my own little revolution and I was proud to be able to stand up for myself and not let other people's opinions and threats stop me from doing what I wanted to do so badly. It was absolutely incredible. I'd do it again in a second.

Dawn's Story

I was very sensitive to everything that went on at school, I had a totally messed up sense of reality. I felt like everyone was gonna hate me, I took everything very, very personally. High school was very abusive because of that. All the "faggot" and "dyke" comments affected me a lot, and I felt really helpless because I didn't have any other options until I started going to a support group. That group totally changed things. When I saw happy gay people, functioning gay people, youth that were like talking about sex and their significant others in normal terms, like girlfriend, boyfriend and like normal things, I could relate. They go out and go dancing, and they go out to dinner, and they hold hands in the street. That was really amazing.

So I went through, I don't know, about several months of just combating and dealing with it all, getting into gay culture, getting into having gay friends, being out, wearing buttons, pins or symbols. Then I got pride happy. And I told everybody. I have everything. It started to be a really big thing. I started coming out to other family members. My sister obviously knew. During that time, I lost contact with my stepdad and basically with my stepbrother. And so, even to this day, they're not real clear. What was an interesting coincidence is, after the summer that I started going to support group, and I started really coming out and telling people, it was also the summer that I decided to leave high school, after my sophomore year.

I decided that intellectually I was ready to leave; it was pointless for me to be in high school. And I had no friends really, besides my two best friends, who were in fact leaving high school. It was totally pointless for me to stay there. I also realized that I had spent this entire summer working through all my internalized homophobia shit—I mean, not all of it because I'm not even done now—but working through it—and I was gonna go back into this incredibly abusive environment, where I would either have to sacrifice myself or put myself on the front lines and be fired at all the time. That was really hard for me to deal with, so I didn't. I decided that there was no way that I could compromise myself and go back to high school. So I left. Just like that. In about two days, I left.

I went to junior college, and I found that it was much easier to come out in junior college. People were generally either apathetic or accepting. They just honestly didn't give a shit very often. I've only had one person explicitly attack me or threaten me. I come out in basically every class that I'm in. I was doing speeches on it, writing papers on it, discussing it when it would come up in a classroom or when something relevant to it came up. And, I never really got any problems. I mean, I might get some weird looks, but it was never a problem. And I'd only have to see them for an hour and walk off campus. They really didn't care about me, and that was really conducive to dealing with coming out.

What was cool about leaving high school, though, was I got to totally reevaluate my entire life and my social scene. I structured basically my entire social scene on my support group and on the people in that group and of that family, you might say my gay family, the coffee shop scene. I got to structure my entire social scene so when I went into friendships, even if they were straight people, it was on the table right from the beginning. I didn't have to come out to that many people. I just kind of said, "Oh, well, this is me, and if you can't deal with it, then I don't want to be your friend. And if you can, I'd love to have you around."

Paige's Story

A couple of kids at my high school got suspended because they had a sticker on their car that said "Stop AIDS, Stop Fags." They were kicked out for a week, I think . . . maybe three days or something. But their suspension by my principal was definitely the result of pressure from a teacher by the name of Jan Willoughby; she was a very progressive teacher in my high school. Earlier, my principal actually had to go through sensitivity training for a comment he made at a Los Gatos Lions Club speech. He said that the Golden Gate Bridge connected jungle land and fairy land. I don't know the whole joke, but it was pretty bad. He also said other things about how women shouldn't jog because they'll bruise their eyes. So, sensitivity wasn't really a strong point for him.

There are no out teachers at Los Gatos High. I know of one queer person there, but she's still not out. She's still there, though. I know of one other person who's also queer, and she's definitely not out and definitely not going to be any time soon. Unfortunately, she will never do it, I mean, because I think there's probably a good chance that she would either be demoted or somehow lose her job. I think it's completely appropriate for a teacher to be out at school. I think it lends a support network to some of the kids who might look for someone, you know, to talk to. Although, I think it's the teacher's personal decision, you know.

I think a lesbian would definitely be more accepted than a gay man being an out teacher from the students. I think, in general, that's pretty true. In my town, it seems to be. I'm sure there'd be the normal little fly of rumors around and about, and a couple of people, a couple of the jocks going "dyke, dyke," you know, and shit like that. But really, aside from the consequences of the administration who might feel they're doing the best things for the kids if they fire the teacher, I think the student body would be pretty okay about it. I'm sure there'd be a lot under their breath. Apathy perhaps.

It was almost summer, right before school had ended, so I was still 15. I went to lunch with four of my close friends and I just put it out on the table that I was bi—here it is. That's how I've learned to live my life, I think. Anyhow, three of them were supportive, and one was kinda like, "Oh, okay, that's cool," that type of thing. About a week later, I think the whole school knew. I don't know for sure, but I know it had definitely been passed along the grapevine.

Then my scooter was banged up. It was bent up and "dyke" was written on the side of it. I quit that day. I mean, I'd had a lot of troubles and personal problems before that. I didn't like high school. That was just kinda like the icing on the cake. I just felt like shit; I cried. I don't think there's any other way to describe it, I felt almost violated. That might be a strong term, considering the guy who did it never came anywhere near me. I totally knew who did it though. He obviously didn't even have the balls to face me. The guy's just an asshole. It's not even worth dealing with him 'cause he's such a dick.

I did bring it to the attention of the vice principal by the name of Patty Hughes. You know, she said, "It's just graffiti, it doesn't mean anything, it wasn't directed at anyone special, I'm sure it wasn't directed at you." And just wrote it off as graffiti, and school security took a picture of it and said they'd try to find out who did it.

At that time in high school, I was kind of tired of everyone, and I knew that I was beyond that. Those four girls who were my friends in high school were about the only four people I ever talked to on a regular basis. I had a lot of older friends who went to DeAnza College, and I spent a lot of time with them. I realized high school was so not for me. When you can't tell someone in confidence something like that and the whole school knows, I don't know. It had just been building up the last semester. Little things, like teachers who were just really, really, really rude to me. I had a biology teacher, Mr. McDonald, who told our whole class that we would be nothing. That was one of the reasons I dropped out. He made that whole year a living hell for me. Just recently, I went down to my old high school and I showed them my report card because I got a 3.7 on my first set of college grades. Oh, I felt so good! Dropping out of high school was the best thing I ever did.

Lisa's Story

To give you an idea about the high school I went to, there were only a few minority students at my school: three black girls, they were all sisters. We had two Mexican girls, sisters. We had one half-Japanese girl. Not a lot of diversity and open minds there.

After I came out at my Senior Boat Cruise, I did presentations on gay youth in different classrooms where I got permission to speak. I got a pretty good response with the teachers I asked, because I knew them pretty well, and they were some of my favorite teachers. I asked my favorite teachers first. I went in and I did these presentations, and I learned a lot of different skills. Being able to do class discussions and teach people and just basically answer questions in a manner that's acceptable, can teach you a lot. There were people who asked all different kinds of questions. Some of the freshmen were brave and asked questions, and the people who acted up were brave and asked me a lot of questions. There were questions like, "Did I believe in God?" "What were my beliefs in God?" "How could I do this if I knew it was wrong?" "How do lesbians have sex?" and that sorta thing. For the answer to that last question, we would write "homo" and "hetero" on the board and draw a line down the middle. Then we'd say, "okay, name some of the things straight people do, I'll write it down, and then I'll write down if gay people do that." That's how the Pacific Center—a local gay support organization—does it.

We started doing the presentations in about February. And, I did about eight presentations. And it's a three-day presentation. The format kinda goes: first, we give a background study out. Or actually, first we give a survey on the first day. We give a background study. Then we answer any questions that people have that they put on a survey we hand out. And then the second day we have a video, and then we have discussion afterwards. The second day we also pass out some short stories, have 'em read 'em, and then the next day we have a discussion. We finally came up with this little role playing thing. It was very effective in certain classes. What we'd do is we'd have two volunteers. One person, we'd flip a coin to make it fair, one person had to be gay, had to be closeted, they couldn't come out during the skit. The other person was gonna tell a gay joke. The gay joke was one that I'd heard in a chemistry class the year before. The joke was, "What does gay stand for? Got AIDS yet." So this person got to kinda feel what it was like. And, then afterwards we'd discuss, how you think this person's feeling, what could they do, what do you think they should do. The first class I did was a senior class, it was an English class. All my friends were in this class. I knew practically everybody. And one of my best friends comes up and she says, "I didn't really understand it before. I accepted it, but now since I've heard your presentation I understand it. I kinda was thinking about it the other day, and I got it, you know. I just understood it, you know."

And after one of my presentations, I had a student come up and come out to me. I was happy that she came out. She was asking for some more information. So, I told her, "I'll take you to the new youth group." So the day we were supposed to go, she couldn't do it, or whatever. Like, a week later or something, I said, "Well, you want to go to a movie in the Castro, I'll show you around there." And so, we went to The Castro and we saw "Bar Girls." I really liked that movie. It was funny. I laughed the whole way through it. She knew I had a girlfriend at the time, and she got the wrong idea, and she kinda grabbed my hand on the way out of the theater. And I'm, like, "ohhh, damn!"

I was pretty sure that some of the other people I went to high school with were queer. I saw one friend of mine who I played softball with and soccer with in the gay bar, JR's, one evening. And I've seen her since at things like the AIDS Walk. Her girlfriend plays in my softball league, so I see her just about every week now. We don't really talk about school that much. We kinda just talk about what's going on now. It was never, like, we went through the formal acknowledgment of each other as queer. It was just kind of like the nodding of, "yeah, you're queer, I'm queer too." We didn't come out to each other in high school. I hadn't come out at the time she graduated. She graduated when I was a sophomore. I always suspected about her, wondered. And then I saw her in the local queer dance club, and it was, like, "aahh!" The light went on.

Matt's Story

I remember walking down the hall and having people say things and spit on me. I was spit on like three times all through my high school life and I didn't think that happened to anybody else. The first time it happened, somebody spit on my face, right in front of two of my best friends. I didn't do anything about it, I just stood there. And actually, that made him look like an utter, utter fool. Everybody was just looking at him. I never really got in that many fights in high school, amazingly. A lot of straight guys would flirt with me in high school, which was really annoying.

My school was divided halfway down the middle: People who absolutely loved me and people who absolutely hated me. A lot of people by then had gotten to know who I was and really liked my character, really liked who I was. Other people who didn't know me, didn't want to get to know me, totally hated me. Sometimes they didn't even have to say anything. It was just the way they talked about me, it was the way they looked at me even sometimes, and acted around me. Some people wouldn't even drink from the water fountain after I had been there. Other people would actually say things.

We moved away from Pawnee, and moved to a place called Davenport, where I ended up dropping out of school completely. My mom had told me that I couldn't graduate from Pawnee. In Pawnee, I had been stalked by this particular person, and I had informed teachers and stuff like that. Only one teacher would help me. I told the principal about it. He didn't do anything until the boy came to school with a gun. They found the gun at lunchtime, meaning that the boy had an opportunity to kill me from the time he got to school until lunchtime.

When I moved to Davenport, I started realizing there were certain people at the school who were really, really obsessed with giving me shit. So I dropped out of that high school too and I went to a neighboring town's high school. That was going really good. I had friends there. One person in particular was gay and out, and he was a really good friend of mine. And then it started happening again. One particular person just picked me out and was really, really giving me problems, and he found out where I lived. So then I dropped out of high school there, and I never went back. I stayed home in my room for close to two years, didn't do anything.

These narratives paint a picture familiar to many queer adults raised and educated in the United States. As much as we may wish to block from our minds the intensity of animosity towards difference that permeates U.S. high school experiences, we need only turn towards an event like Columbine High and its ghostly contagion to see its violent expression. When I heard the news of the shooting, one of the first things that went through my mind was "I hope those kids weren't queer." I'm not certain if my concern was the blow it would serve to queer youth political organizing or a sadness that things were getting even worse—this bad for queer kids that they'd feel no other recourse but to gun down those who tormented them.

Within days of the shooting, stories circulated that the two young men who had shot their classmates were suspected of being gay. The rumor was fueled by Rev. Jerry Falwell's claim that the youth involved were gay—as though this was evidence of the moral and pathological deterioration behind the shootings. It's logical that such a rumor would start; certainly in schools, being different is quickly associated with being queer, both literally and figuratively. The taunts most commonly hurled at those youth who are different are "faggot" and "dyke." Arguably, nothing carries greater impact or insult than these words among youth.

In our national efforts to understand how a Columbine could have happened, the greatest attention is paid to issues of gun control and parental involvement in the lives of youth. The situation is complicated and I'm not suggesting that less attention should be paid to either of these issues. But, I am arguing that the experiences of harassment and torment queer and questioning youth face in school environments cuts to the heart of something that for the most part is being overlooked. In our effort to understand the kind of violence embodied in the Columbine shootings, we are unwilling or unable as a society to face the degree to which we endorse the violent oppression and suppression of difference.

Working with queer youth—listening to their experiences—gives us the clearest picture of the overt antagonism and aggressive intolerance that exists institutionally, socially, and culturally in the United States today. This aggression is a visible marker of the mechanisms of power that work in shadowy ways against difference of all kinds: race, class, gender, age, ability, and appearance. At issue are the shapes such animosity takes, the ways in which it is transmitted to and through social environments such as schools or workplaces, and what we wish to do in response to this charged atmosphere of suspicion and fear. In considering how Columbine ever happened, the logic becomes immediately clear to those familiar with the lives of queer youth: difference is not tolerated; it becomes intolerable; and efforts to stamp out difference enter into a recursive relationship with the violence of oppression. The more energy poured into erasing racial, gender, and other social divides, the less awareness and foresight we have to understand our vast cultural variations. Our social heterogeneity requires strategies of teaching that push beyond tolerance of difference. It is not enough to learn how to quietly sidestep things and people discomforting to us. We must learn to welcome and value difference as a means of coping with an ever-changing social landscape.

Our national shock over Columbine—the murder of high school students in a predominantly affluent, quiet suburb of Denver—obscured the reality that at least fifteen youth—predominantly black, male, and living in inner cities—are killed everyday in the United States by handguns. The deaths at Columbine are treated as shocking aberrations rather than the all-too-common reality they reflect. We must ask ourselves why this reality is on the back pages (if in the news at all) while tragedies like Columbine are given so much weight. Ultimately, we must address the disparity in concern for and equality among classes, races, genders, and sexualities if we wish to have any hopes of dismantling the anger that our current social hierarchies generate.

Few of the young people in the narratives excerpted here felt that being queer would hold them back from their career goals, and many elsewhere planned on finding someone special, falling in love, and having children (Gray, 1999). All were committed to making political change for the betterment of the queer community a part of their life's work. They are also undaunted by needing to fight for what they feel they deserve. There are an increasing number of resources available for queer and questioning youth to support them in achieving their goals. Federal grants seeking to address the disproportionately high rates of suicide, substance abuse, and homelessness among queer youth have made their ways to agencies established solely to serve queer and questioning youth (Blumenfeld, 1995; Uribe, 1995).

Sadly, youth are rarely part of the evaluation process of the services established to meet their needs. They are not asked what works or what doesn't and tend to become numbers rather than voices. This is not always the wish of the service provider but the unfortunate by-product of working with limited resources and strict grant deadlines (Irvine, 2001). Taking the time to really assess what youth want or feel they need (let alone create structures that empower the youth to lead themselves) becomes a luxury rather than a priority. With few exceptions, youth are treated as clients of such agencies, presumably seeking shelter from the psychological fallout of living in a homophobic society. Their needs, and by extension, the youth themselves are, as a result, pathologized (Ryan, 2001). They are rarely seen as activists and leaders within the community and are more rarely provided with resources to proactively change their circumstances. They are rarely empowered to shape their own destinies. Although the modern queer movement has come to recognize youth as a part of the community, it is still a battle for young people to represent their needs or put forth their visions of change for the future without being told to stand to the side and wait until they are given their time to speak. The impact is particularly defeating, for without hearing from the young constituents in need of these support services, it is likely their needs will not be met. If these needs are not met, somewhere along the line, their opportunities to reach the futures they imagine rapidly move further from their grasp.

The final questions the young people asked one another in the interview sessions that produced these narratives were, "What do you see for your future?" and "What would you like to say to folks out there—young or old, straight and queer?" Aside from wanting to hear what these young people saw for themselves, what they saw as possible for their community, I wanted to create some way for them to pass on their insights to future educators. They really are the experts in where queer youth support should go and what the next steps should be. The responses certainly reflect the unique experience and needs of each speaker, but there are some notable threads in common. There are sharp criticisms of the adult queer community for the neglect of queer youth. Educators and others in positions of authority receive strong calls to action to intercede and support queer and questioning youth in school environments.

Most poignant to me though, is how many of the speakers call out to other youth like themselves. Several people implore other youth questioning their sexuality or gender to just be proud and love themselves for who they are, wanting them to know they are not alone, that there are others out there just like them. There are valuable messages in these final excerpts, representing a breadth and depth of experiences. Their messages speak to why they all hold such exciting visions for what is possible not only for themselves but for others like them. I believe these parting thoughts from lgbt youth suggest we have good reason to feel optimistic about the possibilities of confronting intolerance towards difference. Their freedom to express their pride serves as a valuable social litmus test of the possibilities of change for the better:

Mary

> I want to tell other youth not to kill themselves, because that's something I came very close to doing. Especially for kids who are somewhat—um, I don't know if eccentric would be quite the word—but kids who don't fit in anyway, what a hard road it is! I mean, if you already don't fit in AND you're a queer, it can be a real uphill battle.

But there is a light at the end of the tunnel, and no, it's not an oncoming train.

It's easier to form an identity of yourself that you determine. Being self-determined is much easier in the gay and lesbian community because there's a lot more acceptance of it. I mean, every lesbian I know is out there trying to find herself. Oh, shit, it's not like there are limited options. So, the queer community can be a lot more accepting of your difference. Ideally, I want more of an cohesive community, so that there could be more of that kind of support for odd girls and everyone.

Anthony

All I've gotta say is: What's the use in hassling kids like me? I mean, is this some kind of way to pick up your own ego or something like that? I have so many questions for people who pick on people like me. Like, okay, you call me this because? Your point by calling me this is? I mean, I think before they clean up anybody else's backyard, they need to clean up their own first.

I think what needs to be done is to have more classes about all this, like in health or Sex Ed. Right now, in Sex Ed, the teachers don't tell you about being gay or anything having to do with gays, you know, only that things have to be straight. I mean, I think they should expand their horizons on that, adding some gay literature for kids to understand. And, I think the parents should do this reading as well. I don't think it's wrong to be gay; I like who I am, you know. I'm a queen, and that is peachy keen with me. I mean, I am a flame, and that is okay! Society needs to stop putting all this emphasis and ridicule on gays. Like, "they're sick, they're unnatural."

I think straight people should accept gay views. No matter if they like it or not, we're still gonna be here. When they die and they're all crippled, we're gonna be here. And they better start accepting us now before it's too late. Teachers have to know how to accept students for being gay or being different, because different is good. I think the parents should go out there and teach their kids that this is okay. You know, just because somebody's different from you doesn't mean you have to back away.

I've been hospitalized for suicide attempts five times last time I counted. One time I tried measuring my life with sleeping pills. Counting, "this one's for living, this one's for dying, this one's for living." I found twenty-nine reasons to die, and I found around eleven reasons to live. I think society should stop saying that gays are so bad and it's not right to be gay and all this stuff. It's not true. I mean, we don't go out there saying that their sexual preference is wrong.

I would also say to the gay kids reading this that everybody has a different time span. If you think you're gay, read books about what that means, go explore what the gay community is like. I'm not saying having sex. I'm saying read books, go places, you know, and just take it one step at a time. When you're ready for one step, go to the next step. Don't try to do it all at once.

Kyallee

I was a lucky one—I had a friend to talk to, and I found a support group. Most gay teens do not have these luxuries. We grow up hating ourselves like society teaches us to. I would not be here today if I had succeeded in my suicide attempt. If someone would've been "out" at my school—if the teachers wouldn't have been afraid to stop the "fag" and "dyke" jokes, if my human sexuality class had even mentioned homosexuality (especially in a positive light), if the school counselors would have been open to discussion of gay and lesbian issues, perhaps I wouldn't have grown up hating what I was and perhaps I wouldn't have attempted suicide.

I tried to die and failed. Many of my peers have succeeded. We have the ability to make this lunacy stop. If you're gay or lesbian or bisexual or transgender, come out and let the youth know that you exist. Be a role model. If you're a teacher, don't tolerate the "fag" and "dyke" jokes—they hurt us and drive us further into the closet. Acknowledge the accomplishments of gays and lesbians in history, too—we have been here all along and surely our contributions count for something . . . and if you're just the average person doing your average thing, don't tolerate the hatred and lies. Put yourself in our shoes—it's a pretty crummy place to be with today's political atmosphere. Don't buy into the stereotypes. Learn the truth about who gays and lesbians are and share this truth with others. Thirty percent of teen suicides are committed by gay teens, and we only number one in ten. It's time to stop the madness.

Lisa

Well, having an out teacher helps a school. At my school, we had Bob Latham, who was out. We had other teachers rumored about, and some people I know for a fact were gay, but no one else was out. I think one other teacher's gonna come out this year. Bob retired, and this teacher's taking over the gay youth group at school. I've known her for quite a while. Having out teachers, having out students, having the administration not let derogatory comments toward gays, or any race really, go unnoticed, that would really help. And just making sure there are punishments for that would help a lot.

I'd say to the straight community that they need to lighten up, they need to really take a look at who we are, get to know somebody who is queer, and then see how normal and sometimes boring our lives can be. For people who are gay, you don't have to flaunt who you are to get accepted. I'm not gonna say don't flaunt who you are, just be yourself. Be happy, be merry, live life to the fullest. Also, just remember, the queer community needs to focus on its youth so that we have more adults in the future who can help us out politically. The more of us there are, the less of them there are out there to work against us.

The community can't be unified if it doesn't know each other. If you have young people who know their elders, then we can kinda see their interests as well as them seeing ours. Different age groups have different interests. There needs to be more of a link between the two groups to see other things, other directions, so that we kind of move in a uniform direction. Because there's a lot of split places in our community. There's the leather community, there's youth, there's the Berkeleyite lesbian separatists, all these diverse people who need to just kinda know each other so that they can see each other's issues. But there need to be more things where people can see each other's issues and kinda figure out where each other are coming from.

Books help that out, and people seeing each other at community centers and stuff, going places with an open mind. You know, we are all supposed to be so open and have such open minds, but a lot of people don't. Even if you're gay, it doesn't mean you have an open mind. You may not be open to this one other person's experience or their lifestyle, but you've got to let them tell you their story, get some knowledge about it before you make a judgment.

Others have just as much of a right to live their life the way they want to as I have the right to live my life the way I want to. My mom raised me with a pretty open mind about other cultures and stuff. I was pretty open minded about a lot of different things, however, I knew there were limits. There were things that you weren't supposed to be; you weren't supposed to be lesbian. Queer was not what you were supposed to be, you know. But, with the way that I was raised, I was open and open to other people's experiences. That's how I get people to accept me.

I won the Bobbie Griffith's Memorial Scholarship Award. What won me that was one sentence, I think. What I put at the end was that I thought that the gay community wasn't gonna get anywhere in Congress the way it was right now, with all the Republicans there. And I said that basically our focus for the time being should be on youth and getting the suicide rate down. You get the suicide rate down, you get more gay adults, okay. You get more gay voters in the future. And then, you'll get what you want.

Paige

I really think awareness needs to be promoted and tied in with education, where we have a little bit of AIDS education, a little bit of sex education, I definitely think there should be some lifestyles education. Maybe even a slight bit of sensitivity training. And I know in Morgan Hill, my home town, the high school has an excellent gay/lesbian/bisexual support group that is sponsored by a teacher at school. I mean, ideally I'd love to see all those things. I don't see why it can't happen, but I know it's not gonna happen any time soon at least in my school. The administration that's there is very old school, and they're not dead yet. And until they die there won't be any fresh people that come through. I mean, Ted—the principal—the guy is, like, 70 years old, he wears two hearing aids in both ears, you have to yell at him to get his attention! We have very few young teachers, and in order to get a more upbeat feeling in the school, we need to have some young teachers and some young blood. And parents: Make it more available for your kids to come to you and say "I'm a lesbian." You know. Just be more open minded, put more things out there for youth.

There is such resiliency in the lives of these young people. They have some good suggestions and directions for us to go. I hope we gain the wisdom to listen to their voices.

AFTERWARD: A LIST OF WHAT EDUCATORS CAN DO TO SUPPORT LGBT YOUTH

1. Make the classroom environment as visibly "gay-friendly" as possible. Youth—whether heterosexual, questioning, or lgbt-identifying—should recognize your classroom or office as a welcoming place respectful of their sexual or gender identity.

2. Don't make heterosexist assumptions about who your students date or what kind of family structure they come from. If you want lgbt youth to feel comfortable at school, make it as easy for them to talk about their same-sex sweethearts or parents as it is for their peers to talk about their boyfriends, girlfriends, and parents of the opposite sex.

3. Display symbols of your support (i.e., rainbow stickers or lgbt-supportive slogans) and keep brochures of lgbt youth resources visibly available.

4. Be involved in an effort to bring more lgbt books and resources to your campus library.

5. Beyond the classroom, students need to see a lgbt-affirming campus that supports its lgbt faculty and staff. If a school community is not a safe place for its lgbt employees or discussion of lgbt topics, imagine the kind of message that sends not only to lgbt youth but their het-

erosexual peers as well. An absence or silencing of lgbt educators, administrators, and staff leaves lgbt youth without role models and implicitly suggests that lgbt people can be—or worse, should be— removed from school environments. Be part of creating a Gay/Straight Alliance or Diversity Task Force that includes lgbt people and concerns. Don't put all the responsibility on lgbt members of the community to lead the effort—they will burn out and their heterosexual peers will feel detached from the issues.

6. Schools must celebrate their lgbt community members as they do all individuals enriching the diversity of the campus environment. Sponsor a "Pride Week" or a day on lgbt issues during "Diversity" or "Tolerance" rallies to get the message across that the campus community cares about these issues and is ready and willing to lead the effort to get discussion going.

7. Lgbt-related issues should be incorporated across the curriculum to illustrate the contributions of lgbt people to all areas of learning and the significance of sexuality and gender to our everyday lives.

8. Administrations should implement policies of zero tolerance for harassment of any kind and put in place an antidiscrimination policy that explicitly protects lgbt students, faculty, and staff. Although it is common to find such policies in place concerning racially motivated hate speech or acts, it is still the norm for antigay slurs, such as "fag" or "dyke," to go unchecked by educators. One of the most common putdowns on school campuses is "that's so gay!" Educators must be willing to challenge their students to think critically about the meaning and impact of their words rather than assume what they say is harmless. The hardest thing for lgbt students to hear is not the slur itself but the silence from their teachers who allow these words to be bandied about without comment. As Fontaine (1997) points out, protecting lgbt students is no longer optional for schools. Legal cases mounted against school districts are being won by former students who suffered daily harassment for being or appearing to be lesbian, bisexual, gay, or transgender without intervention by school administrations.

REFERENCES

Blumenfeld, W. J. (1995). Gay/straight alliances: Transforming pain to pride. In G. Unks (Ed.), *The gay teen: Educational practice and theory for lesbian, gay, and bisexual adolescents* (pp. 211-225). London: Routledge.

Button, J. W., Rienzo, B. A., & Wald, K. D. (2000). The politics of gay rights at the local and state level. In C. A. Rimmerman, K. D. Wald, & C. Wilcox (Eds.), *The politics of gay rights* (pp. 269-289). Chicago: University of Chicago Press.

Conaty, T. (1996). Statement submitted by the National Gay and Lesbian Task Force in support of legislation to permanently authorize the Hate Crime Statistic Act 1. Internet address: *http://www.ngtlf.org*

D'Augelli, A. R. (1992). Lesbian and gay male undergraduates' experiences of harassment and fear on campus. *Journal of Interpersonal Violence, 7*(3), 383-395.

Fontaine, J. H. (1997). The sound of silence: Public school response to the needs of gay and lesbian youth. In M. B. Harris (Ed.), *School experiences of gay and lesbian youth: The invisible minority* (pp. 101-110). Binghamton, NY: Harrington Park Press.

Friend, R. (1993). Undoing homophobia in schools. *The Educational Digest, 58*(6), 62-68.

Gray, M. L. (1999). *In your face: Stories from the lives of queer youth.* Binghamton, NY: Haworth Press.

Gray, M. L. (in progress). *Coming of age in a digital era: Youth queering technologies in the rural United States.* Dissertation work in progress.

Haider-Markel, D. P. (2000). Lesbian and gay politics in the states: Interest groups, electoral politics, and policy. In C. A. Rimmerman, K. D. Wald, & C. Wilcox (Eds.), *The politics of gay rights* (pp. 290-346). Chicago: University of Chicago Press.

Herdt, G. (2001). Social change, sexual diversity, and tolerance for bisexuality in the United States. In A. R. D'Augelli & C. J. Patterson (Eds.), *Lesbian, gay, and bisexual identities and youth: Psychological perspectives* (pp. 267-283). Oxford: Oxford University Press.

Herman, D. (2000). The gay agenda is the devil's agenda: The christian right's vision and the role of the state. In C. A. Rimmerman, K. D. Wald, & C. Wilcox (Eds.), *The politics of gay rights* (pp. 139-160). Chicago: University of Chicago Press.

Herr, K. (1997). Learning lessons from school: Homophobia, heterosexism, and the construction of failure. In M. B. Harris (Ed.), *School experiences of gay and lesbian youth: The invisible minority* (pp. 51-64). Binghamton, NY: Harrington Park Press.

Irvine, J. M. (2001). Educational reform and sexual identity: Conflicts and challenges. In A. R. D'Augelli & C. J. Patterson (Eds.), *Lesbian, gay, and bisexual identities and youth: Psychological perspectives* (pp. 251-266). Oxford: Oxford University Press.

Jordan, K. M., Vaughan, J. S., & Woodworth, K. (1997). I will survive: Lesbian, gay and bisexual youths' experience of high school. In M. B. Harris (Ed.), *School experiences of gay and lesbian youth: The invisible minority* (pp. 17-34). Binghamton, NY: Harrington Park Press.

McLaren, P. (1995). Moral panic, schooling, and gay identity: Critical pedagogy and the politics of resistance. In G. Unks (Ed.), *The gay teen: Educational practice and theory for lesbian, gay, and bisexual adolescents* (pp. 105-124). London: Routledge.

Remafedi, G., Farrow, J. A. et al. (1994). Risk factors for attempted suicide in gay and bisexual youth. In G. Remafedi (Ed.), *Death by denial: Studies of suicide in gay and lesbian teenagers* (pp. 123-138). Binghamton, NY: Harrington Park Press.

Rey, M., & Gibson, P. (1997). Beyond high school: Heterosexuals' self-reported anti-gay/lesbian behaviors and attitudes. In M. B. Harris (Ed.), *School experiences of gay and lesbian youth: The invisible minority* (pp. 65-85). Binghamton, NY: Harrington Park Press.

Rivers, I. & D'Augelli, A. R. (2001). The victimization of lesbian, gay, and bisexual youths. In A. R. D'Augelli & C. J. Patterson (Eds.), *Lesbian, gay, and bisexual identities and youth: Psychological perspectives* (pp. 199-223). Oxford: Oxford University Press.

Rofes, E. (1989). Opening up the classroom closet: Responding to the educational needs of gay and lesbian youth. *Harvard Educational Review, 59*(4), 444-453.

Rofes, E. (1997). Gay issues, schools, and the right-wing backlash. *Rethinking Schools, 11*(3), 1, 4-6.

Rotheram-Borus, M. J., & Langabeer, K. A. (2001). Development trajectories of gay, lesbian, and bisexual youths. In A. R. D'Augelli & C. J. Patterson (Eds.), *Lesbian, gay, and bisexual identities and youth: Psychological perspectives* (pp. 97-128). Oxford: Oxford University Press.

Ryan, C. (2001). Counseling lesbian, gay, and bisexual youths. In A. R. D'Augelli & C. J. Patterson (Eds.), *Lesbian, gay, and bisexual identities and youth: Psychological perspectives* (pp. 224-250). Oxford: Oxford University Press.

Savin-Williams, R. (1998). *"...And then I became gay." Young men's stories.* London: Routledge.

Savin-Williams, R. (2001). *Mom, dad. I'm gay. How families negotiate coming out.* Washington, DC: American Psychological Association.

Sears, J. T. (1991). *Growing up gay in the south: Race, gender, and journeys of the spirit.* Binghamton, NY: Harrington Park Press.

Uribe, V. (1995). A school-based outreach to gay and lesbian youth. In G. Unks (Ed.), *The gay teen: Educational practice and theory for lesbian, gay, and bisexual adolescents* (pp. 203-210). London: Routledge.

CHAPTER FOUR

Unique Problems and Opportunities Within the Southeast Asian Family

Jonas Vangay

Merced College

A Kind of Journey to the U.S.

I still remember well the time when the "Boom! Boom!" of the gunshots invaded a quiet small forest in Laos. Bullets were flying crazily in every direction. A Hmong mother and her children ran as fast as they could down hill. Then, they fell down, apart, one by one. Their screaming cries struck the opening of the ambushed drama set by the communist soldiers, ruled over the ronronnement of the firearms, surpassed the smoky bushes that wrapped them silently to the ground, and finally faded away to the echo of the giant trees that were the only true witnesses that served as an audience. A five minute silence passed by and there was no sign of resistance. Two trembling voices, "Niad, niad, niad, niad, niad, thov zam txim rau wb-os" immerged from the green grass that started to shake as two girls, calling their mother for the last time, agonized slowly one after another. They may have promised their mother not to talk to attract the soldiers. But nothing beyond life was more important than Mother at that particular moment of breath shortage. They were asking for forgiveness from Mother for breaking the rule. Unfortunately, the mother, crawling painfully around a stuffy hedge plant, tried very hard to reach out to her two girls on the other side of the path. Her clothes were covered by blood, her face by sweat, and her long hair by dirt. Then, her body weaker and weaker, the

mother finally put her hands over the baby boy' s head, fighting for
the last seconds of her life to look at the sky as if she wanted to say
to God that there was no justice on Earth.

Randy Mos TxawjThoj

The designation "Southeast Asian" has become well known to many
Americans since the beginning of the Vietnam war. Geographically, Southeast
Asia covers the block of ten countries constituting Vietnam, Laos, Cambodia,
Burma, Thailand, Malaysia, Singapore, Indonesia, The Philippines, and
Brunei. The term "French Indochina," a label coined in the past when France
dominated Vietnam, Laos, and Cambodia, has also been used interchangeably
with "Southeast Asia" in many books. In Laos, the word "Laotian" as both
adjective and noun is supposed to be used respectively as a description of
something from Laos (adjective) and for a person of Laotian nationality
(noun). Sometimes, the appellation "Laotian" is erroneously utilized to
describe the Lao ethnic group in Laos. For the purposes of this essay, the
author will use the term "Southeast Asian" as it usually appears in local newspapers (i.e., the *San Francisco Chronicle* and all the Bee Newspapers in the
Central Valley); it will include all the different groups of Vietnamese people
from Vietnam, all the different groups of Laotian people from Laos, and all the
different groups of Cambodian people from Cambodia. The term "Laotian"
will keep its correct usage as an adjective and noun for everything from Laos.
The term "Lao" will refer to the ethnic Lao and the national language in Laos.

Like other groups of immigrants who carried their diverse historical backgrounds with them to the United States, the Southeast Asian people had their
own histories that propelled them to America. For many of us, the Vietnam
War still chills our hearts because of what we learned, saw, witnessed, fought
for, and remember; yet, many of our children and others in the United States
may know it only as historical events occurring during the presidencies of John
Fitzgerald Kennedy (1961-1963), Lyndon Johnson (1964-1968), Richard
Nixon (1969-1974), Jimmy Carter (1977-1980), and Ronald Reagan (1980-
1988). When the Vietnam War ended in 1975, many Southeast Asians fled
their homelands, to Thailand, the Philippines, Hong Kong, Australia, Canada,
Europe, and the United States (Butterfield & Bowman, 1985). Because of their
close relationship with the U.S. military special forces fighting communism in
that corner of the world, many Vietnamese, Laotians, and Cambodians
obtained entry into the United States over a period of two decades (Office of
Refugee Resettlement, 1995). Many Vietnamese with more Western-oriented
cultural backgrounds found their new homes in urban areas such as Los
Angeles, San Francisco, San Jose, New York, and so forth. Others struggled
painfully to get accustomed to the mainstream of American society. Unlike
their peer compatriots, Laotians and Cambodians tended to converge more
toward small rural regions in the Central Valley of California. The circum-

stances of their immigration and their social movements have created a situation where the acculturation process of these newcomers in the northeastern part of California is far from being finished.

THE ACCULTURATION PROCESS

By definition, the term acculturation refers to the process by which a person from a different culture learns a new culture. Assimilation refers to the process by which a person from a different culture learns a new culture and lives within it (Green & Reder, 1986). The issue of stereotyping the acculturation and assimilation of Southeast Asians becomes sensitive when prejudice or ignorance posits all Southeast Asians as belonging to the same social group, possessing the same business opportunities, having the same educational background, and thus having the same credentials for success in life in the United States. A better overall picture of Asian Americans may be generated through the demographical census conducted by the U.S. Census Bureau. Table 4.1 and Figure 4.1 reflect the states in America where a larger number of Asian families live (U.S. Census Bureau, 1999).

TABLE 4.1

The Ten First Ranked States in the United States	Estimated Asian - Population as of 7/1/99	Population Estimates Base as of 4/1/90	Numeric Change 1990/ 1999	Percent Change 1990/ 1999
CALIFORNIA	4,038,309	2,951,722	1,086,587	36.8
NEW YORK	1,024,625	709,127	315,498	44.5
HAWAII	753,691	695,564	58,127	8.4
TEXAS	577,306	331,428	245,878	74.2
NEW JERSEY	469,435	277,024	192,411	69.5
ILLINOIS	416,006	292,421	123,585	42.3
WASHINGTON	343,690	215,454	128,236	59.5
FLORIDA	281,366	156,444	124,922	79.9
VIRGINIA	258,371	161,195	97,176	60.3
MASSACHUSETTS	233,239	146,030	87,209	59.7

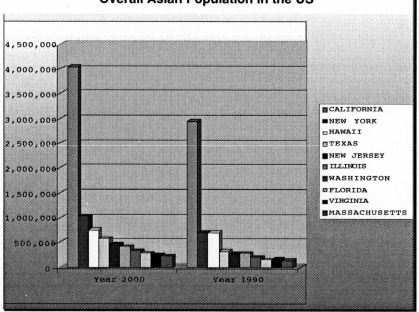

FIGURE 4.1

As recorded in the above table and figure, California has become home to more than four million Asians, far more than in New York and Hawaii combined. Asian language, one of the most important elements of a culture, directly shapes a particular group of people. It defines the ethnicity of that group, their identity, and their social place in the mainstream of society (Taylor & Dube-Simard, 1984). According to the U.S. Census Bureau Report in December 1990 there were about 27,383,547 Californians age 5 or older. Among them, 8,619,334 people (31.4%) spoke a language other than English; 5,478,712 people (20%) were Spanish speakers, and 1,905,985 people (6.9%) spoke an Asian language. A total of 4,422,783 people (16.1%) did not speak English very well; many of them lived in California's Central Valley. The following three tables and figures show the demographic trends in some of the counties in the Central Valley where the concentration of the Southeast Asian population is largest. Per capita, San Joaquin (16%), Merced (10.7%), and Fresno (10.7%) counties host the largest number of Southeast Asians in the Central Valley. According to Mr. Houa Vang (personal communication, June 12, 2001), the executive director of Merced Lao Family Community Incorporated, there are more Cambodians and Lao living in Stockton, Hmong and Mien in Merced, and largely Hmong and Lao in Fresno (see Table 4.2 and Figure 4.2).

TABLE 4.2

County	County Population in 1990	County Population in 2000	Asian Population in 1990	Asian Population in 2000	% Asians Total Population
San Joaquin	480,628	563,183	59,690	90,110	16.0
Merced	178,403	200,746	15,128	21,479	10.7
Fresno	667,490	763,069	57,239	81,648	10.7
Sacramento	1,041,219	2,000,000	96,344	152,811	7.6
Stanislaus	370,522	436,790	19,223	30,575	7.0
Tulare	311,921	358,470	13,319	21,508	6.0

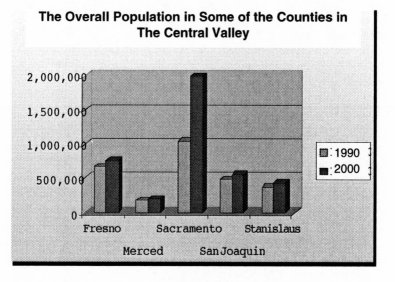

The Overall Population in Some of the Counties in The Central Valley

FIGURE 4.2

A closer look at the Southeast Asians' plight in the Central Valley prompts sociologists and anthropologists to state that geographical, socioeconomic, clan, and family considerations led the majority of the Laotians and Cambodians and some Vietnamese families to locate or relocate to the Central Valley, where farming and the climate are quite similar to what they were used to back in Southeast Asia (Rumbault & Ima, 1987) (see Figure 4.3).

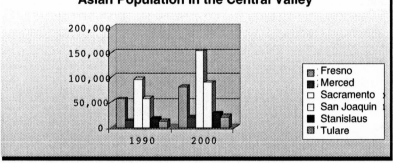

Asian Population in the Central Valley

- Fresno
- Merced
- Sacramento
- San Joaquin
- Stanislaus
- Tulare

FIGURE 4.3

Thus, it is noticeable that the face of the Central Valley is changing in the workplace, schools, and neighborhoods as its population diversifies. A large part of this diversity includes immigrants, particularly the recent influx of Southeast Asian refugees who arrived over a period of 20 years. Legally, most of the Southeast Asians did not enter as immigrants, but as refugees. A refugee is a person who flees her/his native country for safety, especially in time of persecution and war. An immigrant is a person who enters another country for any other reason.

Since the migration of Chinese, Japanese, and Filipinos to the Central Valley, it is possible that other Southeast Asian families may have moved to this agricultural zone before the new influx of the Hmong, Mien, Lao, Lue, and Cambodians in 1980. To draw a parallel to Columbus' discovery, in April 1977, Dan Moua, the first Hmong refugee, moved to Merced with his family in hopes of farming. The San Joaquin Valley holds such a great attraction for refugee farmers that by 1984 more than 10,000 families were concentrated in Merced, Fresno, Sacramento, Stockton, Modesto, and Visalia (Vangay, 1989). The new influx of Southeast Asians to the Central Valley surprised many city, county, and state agencies. This secondary migration occurred regardless of what had been planned by the federal government in accordance with its established refugee and immigration policies.

This sudden arrival has had a dramatic impact on many different public and private social and educational institutions. Beside hospitals, human service agencies, and other social organizations, schools are among the first service providers to undergo emergent responses and solutions to the educational needs of Southeast Asian children. Legal requirements force schools to seek solutions to problems in a timely manner. As an example, in many of the Merced City Elementary Schools, one out of five students is Asian (Parr, personal communication, August 12, 1989). In "Crossing the Schoolhouse Border," Project Director Laurie Olsen and her assistant Marcia T. Chen reported (1984): "We found that the number of immigrant children in the public schools has increased two-and-a-half times in the past decade and is expected to continue to grow at a rate of five to seven percent each year over the next decade" (p. 7).

Anthropologically speaking, as tribal people always move by group, so have the Southeast Asians, especially those with close cultural and familial bonds. The fear of losing their identity, tradition, and culture is their main concern. For the sake of finding prosperous and fertile sites for farming, their migration to the northern part of California has been as natural as the concentration of computer careerists who have followed the development of high technology companies to the Silicon Valley. To their surprise, many of the Southeast Asians came into contact with a totally different farming life style. Pesticides, airplanes, tractors, and bulldozers are American agricultural tools. These new Americans soon found out that the most precious tool they lack is neither the axe nor the shovel, but education centered on academic and professional skills. For many of the Laotians and Cambodians, formal education is relatively new. Time, then, becomes the crucial factor in their new life adjustment patterns.

More than 20 years have passed, and these new arrivals are still finding ways to settle. Despite many barriers that keep them from reaching their goals—goals such as sustaining their families on a small piece of land, acquiring a professional skill, and finding a stable job—these people strongly encourage their children to do well in school; try to enrich their own knowledge, which may range from as little as writing their signature up to college coursework; try to acquire self-sufficiency; and continue the search for new opportunities.

Many questions from Southeast Asian Community leaders continue to remain unanswered: Is education the critical and vital key that will allow the Southeast Asians to leave their traditional doorstep and enter into American civilization, which is well into what social scientists call the "age of information?" Will education help them in making their own life decisions in the United States? What about the Southeast Asian women's educational achievement? How far do they have to go to take their modern places in this society of sexual equality? What happens to Southeast Asians with developmental disabilities? What is their best chance of taking advantage of opportunities offered in the United States? (Vangay, 1989).

THE SOUTHEAST ASIAN DRIVING FORCE IN EDUCATION: IS IT A MYTH, A PURE COINCIDENCE, OR A DRIVING FORCE FOR SOUTHEAST ASIAN STUDENTS' SUCCESS?

Southeast Asian parents may have drawn from a rainbow of cultural values from today's teachers and the many great masters of the ancient times, especially Gautama Buddha, The Old Master Lao Tzu, The Great Master Kong Fu

Tzong (Confucius), and Lord Jesus Christ. For the record, in Southeast Asian tradition, the greatest recognition goes to Master Confucius (or Kong Fu Tzong or Kong), the Great Master. For more than 2,000 years, Confucianism has been inculcated into Southeast Asian family values. Confucianism includes the precepts of (a) family unity or collectivity, (b) humanism, (c) self-discipline, (d) order of hierarchy or filial loyalty, (e) wisdom of the elderly, (f) moderation and harmony, and (g) obligation or filial piety (Smith, 1986). One would suppose that these philosophical teachings are cultural heritages contributing to the Southeast Asian students' success and to the identification of the Asian student body a as "model minority" among other minority groups (Walker-Moffat, 1995). Following are two facets of the Southeast Asian students' education in the Central Valley, both positive and negative.

SOUTHEAST ASIAN STUDENTS IN CALIFORNIA'S CENTRAL VALLEY: SUCCESSFUL OUTCOMES

Regardless of their social and economic situation, family responsibility, cultural mismatch, and lack of adequate academic preparation, the Southeast Asian students in Merced, California have managed to keep their place on the honor roll list. A careful count by Mr. Yia Lor, a Southeast Asian liaison at Merced High School, North Campus, revealed that an average of 28 percent of the honor and high honor graduates from 1990 to 2000 were Asian (about 26% were Southeast Asian) (Lor, personal communication, March 15, 2001). Researchers and scholars would have been quite satisfied with a normal success rate of 10.7 percent as reflected by the racial demographic ratio in Merced County. For this particular standing, the Confucian philosophy of obligation and self-discipline may have been appropriately applied to some extent. Obligation could be interpreted as paying unconditional obedience to teachers, authorities, elderly persons, and superiors. The number one rule in class, "teacher is always right," may have been followed seriously by these successful students. To these students, self-discipline refers to a hard-working attitude, persistence and perseverance, patience and reservation, and boundary markers. The Student Equity Plan at Merced College contends that Asian students performed better than any other ethnic group studied over a four-semester period. Their average score earned in English A (basic English composition and reading), English 1A (English composition and reading 1), English 41 (college-level reading in English), Math A (beginning algebra), Math C (intermediate algebra), and Math 2 (college algebra and trigonometry) was higher than that of other students (Bauer, personal communication, May 20, 2001). These requirements are graduation-applicable courses for an associate degree in arts or an associate degree in science. Again, regardless of the many life difficulties and responsibilities Merced College Southeast Asian students faced at home, the traditional self-discipline and filial loyalty precepts may have been the potential driving force pushing them to stand out academically at Merced College. Many of the Southeast Asian students at Merced College mentioned that their families count on them to excel at school. Their persistence is partially due to the collectivity values that unite the family members together as a societal unit.

THE HIDDEN STORIES OF THE SOUTHEAST ASIAN STUDENTS IN THE CENTRAL VALLEY, CALIFORNIA

In 1989, the author did a research study on Hmong parents' cultural attitudes and the sex ratio imbalance among Hmong high school graduates in Merced. The record showed that out of the total number of Hmong high school graduates every year from 1984 to 1989, the average number of Hmong female graduates represented about 26 percent. In 2000, some ten years later, Mr. Yia Lor's record shows that there has been slight progress toward projected gender equality (Lor, personal communication, March 15, 2001). Lor has been a high school liaison for about fifteen years. From 1990 to 2000, Lor's documentation indicated that every year Hmong female high school graduates numbered about 36 percent of the total number of Hmong high school graduates. This issue of gender imbalance among Hmong high school graduates has its root in Hmong customs and traditions that are critically significant.

To understand the Hmong cultural attitudes leading to the explanation of the educational success and failure of Hmong students, it seems necessary to have some understanding of their cultural knowledge, cultural behavior, and cultural artifacts, distinguished by anthropologists and ethnographers respectively as: what people know, what people do, and the things people make and use. What Hmong people know has been most dramatically affected by their war experiences, which robbed them of a basic educational background. Hmong parents recognize this lack of academic knowledge as a factor contributing to their children's educational difficulties. Formal education in the rural areas of Laos was gaining a small foothold when war swept away what little opportunity the people had for learning. The Hmong, because of communist persecution stemming from their association with the C.I.A., had to live life on the run until they found temporary safety in the camps of Thailand (Chomsky, 1970; Southeast Asian Refugee Studies Project [SARSP], 1987). This temporary arrangement often turned into years of waiting helplessly for sponsorship and clearance to enter a third country, years during which their children ran wild and untutored due to the absence of long-term and/or compulsory schooling, the uncertainty as to which language ought to be learned, and a breakdown in normal cultural and societal controls. As a result, not only Hmong parents but also most Hmong children came to the United States with very little experience of formal education (Lewis, 1992).

Cultural behavior is defined as "what people do." Because of the Hmong clan-based social structure, it is challenging for outsiders to understand or modify Hmong traditional cultural values and behavior. The Hmong clan system remains quite solid but complex. It is what we call a vertically organized, hierarchical, patriarchal, highly disciplined, extended family system. The position of females is that of persons who are indispensable for the supportive functions they carry out, but who are subordinate and interchangeable. As might be predicted, Hmong parents still value their boys more than they do their girls. The boys are desirable in helping to maintain their patrilineal kinship, taking care of the entire family after the father passes away, and furnishing heavy labor.

Hmong cultural artifacts cannot be directly applied toward success in the American technological society. The first problems that Hmong parents have to face in this country is finding a place to live and money to support their families, overcoming the language barrier, and trying to succeed in educating their children and themselves. Upon arriving in the United States, few parents realize that their school age children are learning a culture totally different from theirs. In the United States, new patterns of culture are learned at school whether or not they are overtly taught. Individualism, competition, female equality, and the lack of authoritarianism are aspects of American culture that contrast sharply with the cultures of many Southeast Asian parents. Refugee community members, leaders, and parents wish to preserve their own identity, their own language, their own religion, and their own cultural activities. After one or two years, once they notice some antagonistic behavior from their children who seem to disparage some of the traditional values, the parents' efforts at control become steadily more severe. The children are torn between the two cultures, and the old one is perceived as leading them nowhere, as schools are mainstreaming the students within the dominant culture.

Hmong parents are losing their formerly powerful influence over their children, due to the language barrier, the prevailing influence of the American school system, and the economic displacement of the former heads of households. The ever-changing, technological nature of American society turns the former parent/child relationship into one in which the parent has to depend on the child for knowledge of the outside world. Walker-Moffat (1995) points out that the Hmong elders have lost hope while the children are adapting rapidly. Parents see their children as lost in a world of entertainment. Domestic violence has increased as parents try to assert their traditional authority.

The primary motivation for the Hmong to learn English is the fact that it is necessary for survival and prosperity to speak the dominant language in an industrialized society in which human activity is compartmentalized into highly interdependent areas of specialization and small groups of people are not left alone to fill all of their needs in the ways they see fit. Coming to grips with this fact has caused most Hmong to give up their dreams of recreating life as they knew it in Laos. They now perform an awkward balancing act, knowing that their people must become not only bilingual but also bicultural. It has been a common mistake for people to assume that knowledge of the English language is the only barrier that Southeast Asian refugees have to overcome. Knowledge of Western culture, from its Greek origins to today's technology, is also necessary for success and security.

Immigrating to a new country is difficult, as is continuing one's education in a new language. However, the burden on most of the Hmong is tripled, as they must learn not only a new language but also how to be competitive students, and how to do it in the context of concepts based on a technology few of them encountered until leaving the camps. Hmong students face the task of learning how to operate within the English language—which happens to be a difficult and capricious one—and grasping concepts centuries ahead of those learned in Laos. The enormity of this task causes discouragement among all but the lucky few Hmong students whose families have some educational background and the willingness to sacrifice in order to see their sons succeed. Daughters are rarely accorded this kind of support. Tradition dictates that they marry and work for the benefit of their in-laws; therefore, according to traditional values, sacrifice for a daughter's education would not be a good investment on the part of the family (Vangay, 1996).

Many Hmong parents now see the value of having their daughters at least finish high school. The force of the traditional culture is still in place, however, and the ideas the girls have absorbed throughout their upbringing have more weight than any new requests the parents might make. Many of the early marriages now taking place come about not due to parental force but through the parents' lack of control. Hmong girls and their parents are caught up in a fundamental conflict: the girls, having been taught by precept and by example that a woman's whole future is defined by the man she marries, and caught up in their own adolescent impulses, have always had, in early marriage, a "safe" outlet for their romantic and sexual feelings. Now, in this country, they are being told to save marriage until after graduation while not "bringing shame" on the family through premarital romantic activity.

THE MISSING SUPPORT TO SOUTHEAST ASIAN STUDENTS' ACADEMIC LEARNING— "THE COUNSELING"

After finding homes in the Central Valley for the past 20 years, many Southeast Asian parents continue to raise questions and concerns about the future of their children, who continue to struggle painfully at school. The author had an opportunity to host a TV conference with Mr. Chue Wang Xiong, the media coordinator of Lao Family Community Incorporated in Merced on February 14, 2001. On behalf of the Southeast Asian parents in Merced, Mr. Xiong mentioned that many Southeast Asian children who find life too difficult at school choose any other path to avoid our "compulsory education." The dropout rate is alarming due to many social, familial, and personal factors such as the lack of educational background, early marriage due to cultural pressure from the parents, learning difficulties, lack of support from school and from home, lack of programs, and lack of role models. Through work experience and social activities during the past fifteen years, mainly in the area of leadership in education, the author has noticed that one of the primary problems hindering Southeast Asian students from being successful at school, and thus finishing high school, seems to be the absence of support from families and the schools.

To better encourage and help students to do well at school, parents must realize that their students need to see, know, and understand the contextual environment in which they learn and study. This social adjustment is as critical to school success as academic skill and language acquisition. Southeast Asian students at any level have to adjust to the school world in which they live every-day life in order to compete with their peers. The home culture of many Southeast Asians does not reflect the culture at school. Much of the advice and recommendations by researchers about how to help children at home may not be implemented easily in most Southeast Asian families. Although life situations change gradually over time, extended family structures, living conditions, family distractions, and social gatherings for Southeast Asian students are quite different from what teachers, counselors, and administrators expect them to be. This difference creates a tremendous gap of learning knowledge between Southeast Asian students and other groups. It is difficult for parents to realize that high expectations and valuing their children's education is not sufficient to help children succeed (Janssens, 1987).

Many scholars have repeatedly mentioned that in order for students to suc-ceed academically at school, the culture of the home must be compatible with the culture of the school (Cortes, 1992; Cummins, 1981; Guevara & Kovats, 1989; Krashen & Terrell, 1983). A place to study; books and magazines to read; a typewriter or computer for book reports, essays, and research constitute basic educational elements and tools for every child. Although county and school libraries are helpful, they cannot replace a study center at home. Some parents see practical necessities—a new car and new television—to be more important than improving study conditions at home.

Pushing this cultural philosophy farther, it is indispensable for Southeast Asian parents to start learning their new parenting roles in the United States. A series of parent education trainings for language minority parents is essential in any school district enrolling Southeast Asian students. A parent education pro-gram supervised by a bilingual and bicultural counseling center at school or at any public or private institution will assist the newcomers in acculturating to the mainstream society. The following example illustrates the need for parents' to support their children's education at home and within the community and the need for counseling support for parents in coping with the changing educational society. A group of Southeast Asian leaders in Merced gathered together to discuss what needed to be stressed during the coming years and to find solutions to the abovementioned concerns. After four consecutive meetings with administrators, counselors, teachers, and community leaders from the Southeast Asian community, from the elementary school district, high school district, and the college, the following were recognized as emergency needs:

- Educate Southeast Asian families, leaders, and organizations to support the Police Department.

- Educate parents on alternatives to kicking their children out of the home because of family conflicts about dating practices.

- Begin students' drop out prevention programs at an early age (sixth grade level).

- Invite ex-gang leaders or members to give speeches to Southeast Asian teenagers about their negative past experiences.

- Train parents to understand their children's culture (today's school culture).

- Provide parent in-service training.

CONCLUSION

It is worth reviewing the definition of the term "culture." I have come to appreciate Murdock's definition of culture as adopted by my friend Kirpal Grewal (1989). According to Murdock and Grewal, culture consists of habit forming capacity, social adjustment, academic knowledge, and language for communication. Although the American culture in particular is new to many Southeast Asians in the United States, their Confucian-based cultural heritage has existed for centuries and continues to be a driving force pushing them to overcome their educational difficulties in their new homeland. Oftentimes their habits, social life, survival skills, and language, both oral and written, are incompatible with that of the Americans; yet, they manage to put extra effort in studying not only for themselves, but also for their families.

The key to making it in today's American society is to match the culture at home and the culture at school. Bridging the relationship between the American educational world and the Southeast Asian cultural world lies in improved communication between both parties. A net exchange of information will expand knowledge and understanding. The desired end result will be some needed adjustments on both sides, an increase in Southeast Asian enrollment at school, more parental involvement, a better future for the school's newest ethnic groups, and thus a brighter outlook for the institution itself (Fadiman, 1997).

Academic counseling services at schools fit the needs of the mainstream student population, who are ready for guidance specific to their courses, classes, and majors; the average Southeast Asian counselee has yet to understand the total academic picture. He or she is one step behind most Americans in the type of counseling needed. Southeast Asian students need basic and premajor counseling. Basic information includes individual counseling, family counseling, orientation to the educational system, and an introduction to options available. All counselors having Southeast Asian students should be aware that within the Southeast Asian student population there are three groups with specific needs:

- The newly-arrived K-12 students who are placed in the classroom according to their age, rather than their educational background;

- Young adults who are usually married with children; and

- Older adults who are required by the Department of Human Resources to attend school in order to receive public assistance and justify their continued support.

For the first group, all counseling departments need to give emphasis to mainstreaming junior and senior high school students as soon as possible; counselors should guide them to their majors before they get sidetracked, discouraged, and lost in the shuffle. Remedial courses are necessary to support their English and math skills. Family counseling and group counseling ought to be compulsory to allow all family members to prepare themselves for their new, challenging life. With the help of the counselor, both parents and students will have an opportunity to be exposed to the true ongoing lifestyle of Western people and not to the one shown on television. Optimally, the Southeast Asian family will have the option of seeing and accepting the upcoming changes. A monthly counseling follow-up for at least one year is crucial.

The young adults are a transitional group with their feet in two worlds: they observe the new culture but still live in the old. They have the potential to become self-sufficient but are kept dependent on public assistance by family responsibilities. This group's biggest need is for vocational training specific to local job opportunities. They are the group of students who are squeezed by two cultural worlds and thus may present more absenteeism from school with both reasonable and unreasonable excuses.

Sutara Lor (personal communication, June 2, 2001), a counselor at Merced College, stated that the Southeast Asian elderly students are a lost generation. They have the hardest time learning and see little future in it, just as they see little future for themselves. Many of them suffer from mental, emotional, and physical illnesses. They still dream about going back to their homeland where, according to their dream, land is fertile and life is peaceful.

The relationship between schools and homes could be strengthened by bilingual and bicultural counselors who would work closely with teachers, parents, and community leaders and provide periodic follow-ups with the students.

Such services would give students and parents chances to see the two cultural and educational worlds and make a positive step toward the future. Without such services students may feel frustration, feel their time and money has been wasted, and experience feelings of hopelessness and alienation from institutions.

REFERENCES

Butterfield, F., & Bowman, J. (Eds.). (1985). *The Vietnam war: An almanac* (pp. 348-349). New York: Bison Books.

Chomsky, N. (1970). *Laos: War and revolution.* New York: Harper & Row.

Cortes, C. (1992). The education of language minority students: A contextual interactional model. In Bilingual Education Office (Ed.), *Beyond language: Social and cultural factors in schooling language minority students.* Los Angeles: Evaluation, Dissemination and Assessment Center, California State University.

Cummins, J. (1981). *Schooling and language minority students.* Los Angeles: California State University Center; Evaluation, Dissemination and Assessment.

Fadiman, A. (1997). *The spirit catches you and you fall down.* New York: The Noonday Press.

Green, K., & Reder, S. (1986). Factors in individual acquisition of English: A longitudinal study of Hmong adults. In G. Hendrix, B. Downing, & A. Deinard (Eds.), *The Hmong in transition* (pp. 299-329). Staten Island, NY: Center for Migration Studies.

Grewal, K. (1989). *Southeast Asian cultures.* Unpublished report. Bilingual Teacher Training Program, Merced County School Office, Merced, CA.

Guevara, P., & Kovats. R. (1989). *Bilingual methodology: Handbook for biligual teacher training program.* Riverside, CA: Riverside County Office of Education.

Janssens, L. (1987). *The integration of Hmong adults into American society through the community college: A participatory study of the possibilities of cultural preservation.* Unpublished doctoral dissertation, University of San Francisco, CA.

Krashen, S., & Terrell, T. (1983) *The natural approach: Language acquisition in the classroom,* Hayward, CA: Alemany Press.

Lewis, J. (1992). *Minority cultures of Laos: Khmu, Lua, Lahu, Hmong, and Mien.* Sacramento, CA: SACR.

Office of Refugee Resettlement. (1995). US Department of Health and Human Services: Refugee Resettlement Program, Report to the Congress.

Olsen, L. (1984). *Crossing the schoolhouse border, immigrant students and the California public schools.* A California Tomorrow Policy Research Report.

Rumbault, R., & Ima, K. (1987). *The adaptation of Southeast Asian refugee youth: A comparative study.* San Diego: California State University.

Smith, H. (1986). *The religion of man.* New York: Harper & Row.

Southeast Asian Refugee Studies Project (SARSP). (1987). *A journey from Padong.* Center for Urban and Regional Affairs, University of Minnesota, Minneapolis.

Taylor D., & Dube-Simard, L. (1984). Language planning and intergroup relations: Anglophone and francophone attitudes toward the Charter of the French Language. In R. Bourhis (Ed.), *Conflict and language planning in Quebec* (pp. 148-173). Clevedon, Avon, England: Multilingual Matters.

Vangay, J. (1989). *Hmong parents' cultural attitudes and the sex imbalance of Hmong Merced High school graduates.* Atwater, CA: Mong Pheng Community.

Vangay, J. (1996). *Factors hindering agreement on a common script for the language of academic communication of the Hmong in California.* Unpublished doctoral dissertation, University of California, Davis, and California State University, Fresno.

Walker-Moffat, D. (1995). *The other side of the Asian American success story.* San Francisco: Jossey-Bass.

CHAPTER FIVE

Image Making
and Invisible Minorities

A Case of Arab American Students

Mahmoud Suleiman

California State University, Bakersfield

I AM . . .

I am the daughter of Arab immigrants.
　　they traveled many miles over the sea
　　carrying memories and vested dreams
　　to pass onto my brothers, sister, and me

I am the daughter of Arab parents.
　　they are proud and fluent as expected to be
　　preserving our faith and native tongue
　　many generations have guided me

I am the child of an Arab.
　　childhood memories recalled by fear
　　Life, land, and integrity
　　destroyed by those who hold it dear

A poem composed by Hana' Kheirallah, an Arab American student

I am the faithful American.
> shrouded in mystery and sometimes fear
> of veils and hijab the images tell
> terrorists, religious fanatics is what we hear

I am the colorful American.
> praised for her olive-skin and black eyes
> traditional songs and ancient folklore
> her times have gone with no good-byes

I am the American Alien.
> a familiar stranger amongst my own
> like a puzzle piece that doesn't quite fit
> reality and truth completely unknown

Hana' Kheirallah

Since the terrorist attack upon the United States now known as 9-11 and with the concomitant increase in social instability across the globe, the need to understand the implications of these events and how they affect minority children in the microcosm of today's classrooms is especially significant. In particular, external influences in the universal culture have significantly affected the image making of formerly invisible groups such as Arab Americans and their children. For example, the unstable Middle East has caused many people living in this region of the world to seek refuge and stability elsewhere. Great numbers of immigrants and refugees throughout the Middle East have joined an already large and vibrant Arabic-speaking community in the United States of America.

Although Arab Americans were less visible than other minorities, recent anti-Arab perceptions have made Arab American students more visible in a negative way. Current cultural conditioning does not allow Arabs in America to see themselves positively because of the way Americans see them. Like many other minority populations, Arab American students have long been subject to scapegoating, stereotyping, and prejudice. They have always experienced an "identity crisis" given the negative impact cultural conditioning has on their self-image and intercultural relations.

Social and historical facts about diverse students can be the basis for promoting positive images among ethnic and racial groups. Affirmation of all students in schools should be based on accurate relevant information. Thus, the context of educating Arab American students will be presented in terms of relevant sociohistorical and cultural traits. This should be the basis for integrating culturally responsive instructional treatments in schools.

Based on the Arab American experience, this chapter will examine image making of invisible minorities and highlight relevant cultural and social traits of this unique group and their implications for promoting empathy, understanding, and sensitivity in multicultural settings. It also draws some educational implications for culturally responsive curriculum and instruction in pluralistic schools.

SOCIOHISTORICAL CONTEXT AND BACKGROUND

Arab American students are citizens or residents of the United States, and they are immigrants or descendants of immigrants who came to the United States primarily from the countries that comprise the Middle East. They have not come from one country, but from 22 different states in southwest Asia, North Africa, and the entire Middle East. An Arab American student can be Muslim, Christian, Jewish, or of some other belief. As a result, Arab American learners are very diverse in terms of their country of origin, their religion, historical plight, and the reasons for immigration. Despite their ethnic, religious, linguistic, and racial diversity, Arab American students embody a unique representation of universal values and traits that can enrich the lives of their fellow citizens in American schools.

Many Arab American students trace their family ancestry to the 1890-1940 wave of immigrants from Lebanon and Syria. Although most of the early immigrants were Christians who have assimilated into the American way of life, subsequent waves of Arab American students represent post-World War II immigrants, including Muslims from various Arab states. Other Arab American student populations are descendants of Palestinians who fled after the 1948, 1967, and continuing Arab-Israeli wars. Others do not trace their ancestry to any of these well-known waves of immigration (Banks, 1997).

Arab American learners are represented in almost every American public school district, and they are considered one of the fastest growing groups of immigrants, settling mainly in big cities. Their heavy representation is more visible in such states as Michigan that have the largest single community of Arabs in America. For example, the Detroit-Dearborn area has a population of 250,000 Arabs. New York and California have the largest and most visible Arab American populations in the United States (Banks, 1997; Bennett, 1995).

Historically, Arabs have been able to integrate, rather than reject or destroy, other cultures. This tendency appeared to carry over as they easily entered the mainstream of American culture, placing assimilation above ethnic identification (Banks, 1997). However, in contrast to the Arab Christians, assimilation was much more difficult for the Arab Muslims because of their strong adherence to Islamic faith and law (Banks, 1997).

The Arab community is one of the most heterogeneous in the United States. Yet, it is also one of the most misunderstood. Negative images and stereotypes of Arabs are prevalent (Bennett, 1995). The popular images of Arabs as rich sheiks, religious zealots, or terrorists are gross stereotypes (Nieto, 1996). Because many Arabs are Muslims, their dress and traditions are quite misunderstood. Many Muslim girls wear head covering because of the emphasis on modesty, self-respect, chastity, and honor. Their diet is restricted; it is against Islamic law to eat pork or drink alcohol. Ramadan, in which many Muslim students participate in fasting, is an annual month of reflection upon the Muslim spiritual and cultural upbringing. Also, the Islamic holidays follow the lunar calendar and thus vary from year to year.

Family life is very important for Arabs. Arab Americans are proud of their cultural background. They value the family and take pride in the members of their extended families, communities, and countries. They share certain recognized cultural traits such as generosity, hospitality, courage, and respect for the elderly.

In order to affirm the physical, emotional, and intellectual being of Arab students, it is important to highlight the following cultural traits in the school culture:

- Not everyone living in the Arab world is an Arab; there are other ethnic and racial groups such as Kurds, Druze, Copts, Assyrians, Armenians, blacks, Berbers, Kildanis.

- The Arab world encompasses an array of ethnic, racial, linguistic, and religious groups. The Arab macroculture is pluralistic in nature and is increasingly multicultural.

- The Arab microcultures flourished within a seemingly democratic framework. Historically, the macroculture of the Arab world was marked by a dynamic balance between unity and pluralism during which time the microcultures flourished in an atmosphere of harmony and coexistence.

- The Arab value system centers around the family. Arabs are family oriented; children are highly valued, with a great sense of pride in individuals, families, communities, and society at large.

- Religion and language are among the most important identifying traits of individuals and communities among Arabs. Islam, intricately related to Judaism and Christianity, is seen as a way of life, a means of cultural and social growth, and a political and economic paradigm of behavior at individual and group levels.

- The Arabic language, once a lingua franca, has a religious prestige because it is the language in which God chose to reveal the Quran (Kura'an) to Muhammad, the Prophet of Islam. Quranic (Classical, or High) Arabic is the language of the mosque, media, and education. It is the language that is supposed to be used by the elite educated Arabs.

- Arabic speaking peoples are dilingual due to the diglossic situation in Arabic; two functional forms of the language are equally important in meeting the communicative needs of their speakers.

- Quranic literacy is widely common among hundreds of millions non-Arab Muslims across the globe. About one billion Muslims know Arabic.

- Arab Muslim civilizations flourished throughout history; their empire spread from Spain and Europe to China. Arabs have contributed to world civilizations in nearly all aspects.

- Foreign/second language learning is highly valued by Arabs and Muslims. Multilingualism is viewed as a social and religious asset, not a liability.

- Arab and Muslim Americans are among the largest ethnic groups in the United States.

The Arab diversity stems from geographic, ethnic, religious, political, and socioeconomic factors found throughout the Arab world. It is diverse in nature despite the common cultural and linguistic traits found in various Arab societies. Arab student populations represent diverse backgrounds. In fact, Arabic-speaking students in American public schools represent a variety of sociocultural and linguistic backgrounds, and their educational expectations and attitudes reflect these numerous differences.

Whereas some Arab communities have assimilated to the American way of life, others have tried to maintain a meaningful level of multiculturalism (Grant, 1995). Still others have developed a feeling of resentment towards the sociocultural adjustment process because of the alienation and sense of nonbelonging they experienced within American society (Bennett, 1995; Grant, 1995). In other words, most Arab Americans feel that they are deprived of their full participation in the democratic process (Nieto, 1996). Although there are many factors that shape the Arab American experience and influence the educational needs of their children, many Arab American students have been met with unfair and prejudiced treatment.

IMAGE MAKING AND UNFAIR TREATMENT

For years, Americans have largely ignored Arabs and their contributions to American civilization. Misinformation and lack of information about Arab culture plays a significant role in American misperception and misunderstanding of Arab American students. Arab American student populations have been a constant target of discrimination, prejudice, and stereotyping.

The underlying premise of the paradoxes in American democracy (Chomsky, 1999) has been demonstrated in the American treatment of Arabs. For example, when Arab states cut oil production in the 1970s and raised oil prices, Arabs received more attention (Banks, 1997). The Gulf War made Arabs more visible, but in a negative way (Al-Khatab, 1998). In the midst of all that, Arab American students and their families have become, according to Nicholas

Von Huffman (as cited in Orfalea, 1998), "the last ethnic group safe to hate in America" (p. 5). This unpleasant status has reinforced Arab American silence (Orfalea, 1988), especially in social and educational institutions. The 1990s brought little change in the way Arabs are perceived or depicted. Paul Findley (as cited in Bennett, 1995) discussed the weak and almost nonexistent political stand of Arab Americans when he stated, "Even if a congressman had wanted to hear the Arab viewpoint, he would have difficulty finding an Arab spokesman to explain it" (p. 142).

These sociopolitical conditions have affected the interaction patterns with Arab student populations in many ways. Cultural conditioning has become the driving force that filters the image of these students, thus affecting their self-image and role in American society. Sharpe (1992) discusses the impact of cultural conditioning on human and public relations in American democracy. He maintains that several American institutions such as mass media have for a long time promoted an individualistic culture. In order to overcome the negative impact of cultural conditioning, Sharpe (1992) suggests that the "best advancement is to learn all we can about other cultures and impart it to our students and fellow practitioners. It allows us to more clearly see ourselves as others see us" (p. 107). Hence, we need to make accurate educated assessments about the behavior of individuals, groups, and institutions to "facilitate change that truly contributes to the social harmonizing process for the benefit of the global society" (Sharpe, 1992, p. 107).

As a case in point, consider what happened to so many students across the United States on April 19, 1995 when the Alfred Murrow building in Oklahoma City was bombed, killing 168 people and injuring hundreds more. As a result of careless accusations and innuendo, many innocent Arab American students suffered from physical and emotional harassment. What makes this tragedy even more disturbing was the spontaneous and erroneous assumption of Middle Eastern cuplability during the first two days after the bombing, even though there was no evidence to support such accusations. The media, especially the mainstream newspapers and television news stations, played a huge part in concentrating exclusively on Arab terrorists and perpetuating stereotypes about Arabs as terrorists. By pointing unrelentingly and with bias at Arabs as the perpetrators of the terrorist act, the media catalyzed and reinforced stereotypes against Arab Americans. As a result, many students were beaten and threatened by their peers in schools. Unfortunately, these negative stereotypes were only reinforced by the later destruction of the World Trade Towers.

This automatic reaction to blame Arabs and Muslims is a result of many years of stereotyping and racialization in many forms of literature and visual media. For instance, many of the villains in contemporary films are usually foreigners and most often Arab or Muslim. In a recent Hollywood movie The Siege the villains are Arabs who quote the Koran and perform ablution before heading off to blow up innocent civilians. The movie depicts Muslims at prayer juxtaposed with acts of violence. The Siege follows a succession of more than a dozen films and made-for-television movies produced in the 1980s and 1990s featuring murderous Muslim fanatics, among them Executive Decision, True Lies, Voyage of Terror, and Terrorist on Trial. Terrorist has become synonymous with Arab or Muslim especially in the realm of visual media, including news broadcasts. One of the first programs reporting the bombing was initially entitled Terror in the Heartland. When it was later learned that the criminals were white male Americans, the title was changed to Tragedy in Oklahoma. In contrast, a religious fanatic who shoots an abortion doctor is referred to as a gunman not a terrorist; but an Arab or Muslim who commits a crime is always a terrorist.

It has been assumed that language speaks us as much as we speak it. In the attack upon the Trade Center, the language used to describe the assumed perpetrators was replete with negative connotations in reference to Arabs and Muslims. Language seems to have disclosed a lot of racial stereotypes in the mainstream mind as Arabs and Muslims were negatively portrayed.

In the case of the Oklahoma bombing, after the initial shock of the blast subsided, anger became the driving force in pursuing justice. Americans could not imagine anyone besides foreigners who could commit such an act. This was the heartland of America. The predominately white Christian community could not identify the terrorist as one of their own. It seemed much easier to identify foreigners as terrorists and eventually scapegoats. This seemed to be the product of the countless news reports, movies, television shows, and other media tools that enhanced such negative images.

Many people assumed that this bombing was committed by Arabs and Muslims. Frequently people erroneously conceive these two terms as synonymous. In order to dispel the stereotype, one must differentiate between two terms: Arab and Muslim. An Arab is a person whose native language is Arabic and who lives by Arab cultural traditions and values. He or she is not tied to any particular religion. Religious diversity is characteristic of both the Arab world and the Arab American population. In the United States, where the majority of Arab Americans are Christians, there are still several thousands who belong to the Jewish faith.

Undoubtedly, negative perceptions and attitudes are the outcome of personal experiences of individuals, parental influences, social ingredients, and mass media, all of which help to shape attitudes of individuals and groups. In particular, the media plays a significant role in enhancing stereotypes especially about Arabs. According to Anderson (1991), "In the United States, anti-Arab propaganda is a hot commercial item . . . and the media have done their part to encourage Arab bashing" (p. 29). This over the years has made Arabs more visible in a reprehensible manner. Negative images about Arabs have been incubated in the minds of the public and carried into today's classrooms. So whenever external incidents take place, Arabs seem to be most vulnerable to blame. Abourezk (1993) demonstrated how Arab Americans and their children lose their civil rights due to the social climate in American society; according to him, "Arabs are America's new scapegoats, and anti-Arab hysteria has been building in this country for many years" (p. 26). Abourezk cited several incidents that reflect the behavior of agents of American governmental and social institutions in their intimidation of Americans of Arab descent.

For a long time Arabs have been plunged into the realm of stereotyping and victimization (Adeeb & Smith, 1995; Al-Ani, 1995; Nieto, 1996; Santos & Suleiman, 1991; Suleiman, 1993; Zogby, 1981). This has resulted in misinformation about the merits of Arabic culture and its contributions to humanity instead of acknowledging it as a vital part of American pluralism. Thus, cultural conditioning marked with a great deal of error about Arab societies has negatively affected the images of Arabic speaking children as seen by their peers and the images of themselves. Consequently, the Arab American child, according to Nieto (1996), is "one of the most misunderstood, shrouded in mystery and consequently stereotypes" (p. 137). Part of the problem is the scarcity of accurate information and unbiased resources about Arabs. Another reason lies in the lack of a true representation in the media that gives fair credit to Arabs and their cultures.

Despite the interaction Arabs have with Americans, it has been found that indirect contact with Americans has little impact on promoting stereotypes (Kamal & Maruyama, 1990). At the same time, more direct contacts between Americans and Arabs will likely lead to developing mutual positive attitudes (Suleiman, 1993). In fact, the most frequent contact Americans have with Arabs and their countries is through media channels. This clearly reflects the role of the media in the cultural and social conditioning process.

Arabic speaking students have had their share of discrimination due to cultural conditioning. Numerous reports document cases of Arab American students at different levels being harassed by their peers in times of political fluctuations. Although the American public has become conditioned to accept negative stereotypes, educators can play a significant role in the social harmonization process in the school culture and in society at large. In particular, bilingual/multicultural teachers have the power to prevent cultural conditioning from taking its toll. After all, students are the ultimate consumers of teachers' input and overall educational services provided by the school system. Cultivating a more positive cultural conditioning is a key ingredient for providing the best education for all and for empowering individuals and groups regardless of their backgrounds.

EDUCATIONAL IMPLICATIONS

Fortunately, education is a major investment in Arab cultures. It is a source of pride in Arab American families for their children to achieve success within American schools. Nonetheless, many schools have not yet acknowledged Arab culture and history or even tried to dispel negative stereotyping among non-

Arab students. As the number of Arab American students in public schools has increased, so has the need for affirming their cultural being in curriculum and instruction. Very little has been done to promote culturally responsive practices relevant to the experiences, histories, and diversities of Arab American student populations.

Apart from the fact that Arab Americans are generally racially invisible, their immigration patterns have been uneventful. Their transition has also been relatively smooth. Most importantly, Arab students have not suffered any significant failures in schools as have some other ethnic groups.

According to the 1980 U.S. census, Arab Americans have a higher educational achievement level and significantly higher number of high school and college graduates than the U.S. population as a whole (Banks, 1997). A powerful motivational force for Arab students is religion, because it stresses seeking knowledge and education as the duty of every individual.

Placed in mainstream classrooms, Arab American students are often confronted by preconceived prejudices and biases. Influenced by a prejudiced, uninstructed film industry and print and television media, American perception of Arabs ranges from the overly romanticized to the harmfully negative (Grant, 1995). According to Banks (1994), one of the most fundamental dimensions of multicultural education is the knowledge construction process. It relates to "the extent to which teachers help students to understand, investigate and determine how the implicit cultural assumptions, frames of references, perspectives, and biases within a discipline influence the ways in which knowledge is constructed within it" (p. 5). This dimension is also important because it intricately relates to other dimensions such as reducing prejudice, empowering the school culture and social structure, equity pedagogy, and content integration. A dynamic balance between these dimensions is necessary to empower all students from diverse, racial, ethnic, linguistic, religious, and cultural backgrounds. Furthermore, understanding students' characteristics, feelings, attitudes, and experiences can help teachers and educators develop more democratic values and attitudes and become more active participants in the pluralistic society (Banks, 1995; Bennett, 1995; Grant, 1995; Nieto, 2000).

Sadly, learners whose cultures are not acknowledged in schools feel alienated, and the American educational system has been ineffective in reducing stereotypical images about Arabs. Furthermore, students feel that whatever the school does not teach is not worth learning. Because the Arab culture in American public schools is "referred to in only negative ways" (Nieto 1996, p. 137), "all students are mis-educated to the extent that they receive only a partial and biased education. The primary victims of biased education are those who are invisible in the curriculum" (p. 213). Thus, if contributions of a given group are not highlighted in the school curriculum, students will receive conflicting messages about who they are and what their roles should be. And if a group of learners are portrayed negatively in the school's culture, then an "identity crisis" will be inevitable. These meanings have been echoed in the experiences of many Arabic speaking students going to American educational institutions, including at the university level (Suleiman, 1993).

Therefore, foundation and methodology in a multiculturally infused program should address "information on the contributions of diverse people to the various disciplines" (Chisholm, 1994, pp. 57-58). Unfortunately, the Arab civilization, which has greatly contributed to humanity in almost every aspect of world civilization (Al-Qazzaz, Afifi, & Shabbas, 1978), has largely been ignored by American educational institutions and their educational programs. In an account of the lack of serious efforts to acknowledge and "celebrate" the Arabic language and culture in U.S. public schools, colleges, and universities, Starr (1990) demonstrates how the United States has failed to be sensitive to the Arab language and culture in these educational institutions; he also reveals the United States' "provincial" trend in dealing with other cultures and languages. Although, "Arabic is the language of one of the world's great civilizations, and one to which the West has been profoundly indebted for over a millennium in fields as diverse as mathematics, chemistry, geography, and philosophy" (Starr, 1990, p. B2), no profound commitment to its inclusion in the curriculum has been made.

Schools can make sure that Arabs are accurately and fairly represented in the curriculum and school activities. For instance, there are many inaccurate texts covering Middle Eastern geographical, social, and cultural facts. Schools can take action against discrimination and incidences of racism. They can also provide professional training for their staff and teachers and provide them with accurate textbooks. Schools can avoid discriminating against all Arabs, especially those who are Muslims, by being aware of food taboos, dress codes, and restrictions on male and female interaction.

Knowledge of Arab Americans and their culture should help educators to construct a more realistic picture of their students. Teachers should be sensitive to their students' feelings and behavior. Because harassment of Arab American students increases when negative news reports about political events that involve Arabs, or even seem to involve them, are aired teachers need to be prepared to respond. It is very important for teachers to recognize the diversity within Arab culture and the differences and similarities between previous and new immigrant groups (Grant, 1995). One of the most important determiners of effective teaching of Arab American students is maintaining a positive attitude about Arabs and their culture. In addition to understanding how Arab Americans are viewed, it is important to understand Arabs' perceptions of Americans.

Affective characteristics of minority learners, such as attitudes toward the dominant group, have a marked effect on learning/teaching and interactional processes in diverse settings (Lustig & Koester, 1996; Seelye, 1993). For instance, affective predispositions (i.e., the learner's beliefs, feelings, and intentions) towards the target language community are likely to explain a proportion of language achievement (Olshtain, Shohamy, Kemp, & Chatow, 1990). These affective variables deal with social/political contexts from which attitudes and motivation are derived.

Attitude formation, according to Brown (1987), develops in the early stages of one's life and is the result of parents' and peers' attitudes. It is also the result of "contact with people who are 'different' in any number of ways, and interacting affective factors in the human experience" (p. 126). For instance, students whose experiences with English or its speakers are unpleasant tend to have unfavorable attitudes towards the host country and its language (DuBois, 1956). This is true of Arab minority students who develop certain types of attitudes, negative or positive, towards English and Americans, given several intervening factors.

Although these issues have been largely overlooked by researchers who have worked with Arab American students, it has been found that Arab attitudes toward Americans and the United States are shaped in terms of various determiners (Suleiman, 1993). There are several factors that shape cross-cultural attitudes: (a) the individual's previous and current perceptions about the target group; (b) individual's experiences with the group in the host country; and (c) the media and its roles in enhancing positive and negative stereotypes. In a large-scale study conducted on Arab university students, Suleiman (1993) concludes that Arab attitudes vary in terms of these determiners. For instance, the erroneous portrayal of Arabs in the American media negatively affects attitudes of Arabs towards Americans. Likewise, Arabs who have several unpleasant experiences with Americans tend to have unfavorable attitudes toward Americans.

In order to ease the adjustment of Arabic speaking students and cultivate more positive attitudes in American schools, several guidelines must be kept in mind. These guidelines should be implemented whether in the delivery of input or in the interactional process in various social and educational settings. Teachers and school administrators should be held accountable for creating conditions that are conducive to the expectations of Arabic speaking children and their parents. These desired goals can be achieved through:

1. Awareness combined with mutual understanding and appreciation of cultural differences;
2. Frequent direct contact with the target group, which would lead to greater understanding and comfort, not to mention the improvement of the students' command of the language;
3. Teaching/learning approaches that should *not* be disconnected from teaching cultural aspects of that language;
4. Educational programs that should enhance the notion of intercultural communication as a requisite for development;
5. Multicultural programs that are based on the needs assessment of students;
6. Teachers and educators who deal with Arab students with sensitivity to their needs and characteristics.

Given the alarming cultural conditioning that fosters negative stereotypes about Arab cultures and peoples, teachers in multicultural settings should maintain a positive outlook and a meaningful interaction with Arab American students in U.S. public schools. By understanding the microcultures of these particular groups, educators will promote a greater understanding of the dynamics of effective interaction in diverse classrooms. This will enhance their ability to deal with real-life issues and maintain peace in pluralistic schools.

Finally, educators dealing with Arabic speaking students need to be sensitive to their unique needs. Through communication with students and their families and by suspending prejudicial assumptions about Arab American's linguistic, racial, and ethnic backgrounds, educators can develop better bonds with this important group. By giving credence to Arab cultures in the school's curriculum and culture, educators can enhance students' pride and ensure their success.

REFERENCES

Abourezk, J. G. (1993). The Arab scare: When the heat is on, Arab Americans lose their rights. *The Progressive, 57*(5), 26-29.

Adeeb, P., & Smith, P. (1995). The Arab Americans. In C. Grant (Ed.), *Educating for diversity: An anthology of voices*. Boston: Allyn & Bacon.

Al-Ani, S. (1995). Muslims in America and Arab Americans. In C. Bennett (Ed.), *Comprehensive multicultural education: Theory and practice* (3rd ed.). Boston: Allyn & Bacon.

Al-Khatab, A. (1998). In search of equity for Arab-American students in public schools of the United States. *Education, 120*(2), 254-261.

Al-Qazzaz, A., Afifi, R., & Shabbas, A. (1978). *The Arab world: A handbook for teachers*. Berkeley: NAJDA. (Available from Women Concerned about the Middle East, Box 7152, Berkeley, CA 94707.)

Anderson, J. (1991). Blame the Arabs: Tensions in the Gulf bring bigotry at home. *The Progressive, 55*(2), 28-29.

Banks, J. (1994). *Multiethnic education: Theory and practice*. Boston: Allyn & Bacon.

Banks, J. (1995). Multicultural education: Historical development, dimensions, and practice. In J. Banks & C. Banks (Eds.), *Handbook of research on multicultural education*. New York: Macmillan.

Banks, J. (1997). *Teaching strategies for ethnic studies* (6th ed.). Needham Heights, MA: Allyn & Bacon.

Bennett, C. (1995). *Comprehensive multicultural education: Theory and practice* (3rd ed.). Boston: Allyn & Bacon.

Brown, H. D. (1987). *Principles of language learning and teaching* (2nd ed.). Englewood Cliffs, NJ: Prentice-Hall.

Chisholm, I. M. (1994). Preparing teachers for multicultural classrooms. *The Journal of Educational Issues of Language Minority Students, 14*, 43-67.

Chomsky, N. (1999). *Profit over people.* New York: Seven Stories Press.

DuBois, C. A. (1956). *Foreign students and higher education in the United States.* Washington, DC: American Council on Education.

Grant, C. (Ed.). (1995). *Educating for diversity: An anthology of voices.* Boston: Allyn & Bacon.

Kamal, A., & Maruyama, G. (1990). Cross-cultural contact and attitudes of Qatari students in the United States. *International Journal of Intercultural Relations, 14,* 123-134.

Lustig, M., & Koester, J. (1996). *Intercultural competence: Interpersonal communication across cultures.* New York: Harper Collins College Publishers.

Nieto, S. (2000). *Affirming diversity: The sociopolitical context of multicultural education* (3rd ed.). New York: Longman.

Olshtain, E., Shohamy, E., Kemp, J., & Chatow, R. (1990). Factors predicting success in EFL among culturally different learners. *Language Learning, 40,* 23-44.

Orfalea, G. (1988). *Before the flames.* Austin: University of Texas Press.

Santos, S., & Suleiman, M. (1991). Teaching English to Arabic-speaking students: Cultural and linguistic considerations. *NABE, '90-'91,* 175-180.

Seelye, H. N. (1993). *Teaching culture: Strategies for intercultural communication.* Chicago: NTC Publishing Group.

Sharpe, M. L. (1992). The impact of social and cultural conditioning on global public relations. *Public Relations Review, 18*(2), 103-107.

Starr, S. F. (1990, April 10). Colleges can help America overcome its ignorance of Arab language and culture [Opinion]. *The Chronicle of Higher Education,* p. B2.

Suleiman, M. F. (1993). *A study of Arab students' motivations and attitudes for learning English as a foreign language.* Doctoral dissertation, Arizona State University, Tempe, AZ.

Zogby, J. J. (October, 1982). When stereotypes threaten pride. *NEA Today,* p. 12.

CHAPTER SIX

Organizational Behavior and the Consequences for the Culturally Different

Gregory Lomack

California State University, Fresno

I, Too

I, too, sing America.

I am the darker brother.
They send me to eat in the kitchen
When company comes,
But I laugh,
And eat well,
And grow strong.

Tomorrow,
I'll be at the table
When company comes,
Nobody'll dare

Say to me,
"Eat in the kitchen,"
Then.

Besides,
They'll see how beautiful I am
And be ashamed—

I, too, am America.

Langston Hughes

THE SOCIOACADEMIC CANON OF THE CULTURALLY DIFFERENT: NATIONAL LEVEL

Longstanding social, economic, political, and educational disparities continue to predominate among U.S. racial, ethnic, and language minority groups, particularly when comparing success rates of African American, Hispanic American, Native American, and Pacific Island American groups to their European American counterparts. These disparities are at times masked and at others glaring. These differences are based upon many factors, including the particular group, context, period, and variables under examination.

In the United States schools are often characterized by policies that are antithetical to meeting our nation's purported goal of delivering a comparable education to its culturally and racially diverse populace. For example, norm-referenced testing that attaches monetary reward to academic achievement and sanctions to academic underachievement tends to do a disservice to schools that service predominately low-income and ethnically different student populations. These schools may spend large amounts of time on test-prep to improve test scores and ranking while sacrificing quality instruction. The negative effects of these policies and practices on the elementary and secondary schooling outcomes and identities of African American, Hispanic American, and other designated minority-group students are clear, widespread, and growing in scope and complexity.

For all of our history the issue of how to successfully include cultural minority students in public education has been hotly debated (DeVillar, Faltis, & Cummins, 1994). The willingness of educators to discuss the identity and psychosocial adjustment needs of all of the members of the human family is insufficient if minority students still are treated as subhuman and slaves. In order to construct an understanding of the present, we must look back through a chronology of federal and state laws. The decisions pertaining to the education of cultural minority students in public schools illuminate the depth at which exclusion is entrenched.

Slavery was a state and national practice that permeated our society from approximately 1619 to 1870, despite the slave trade (as opposed to slavery) being officially banned by Congress in 1810. Africans in America were involuntary immigrants bereft of rights, including those we consider primordial: life, liberty, and the pursuit of happiness. Schooling African Americans in bondage, expressly teaching them how to read and write, which have led to a sense of achievement and participation in their destiny, was virtually forbidden throughout the southern states (Myrdal, 1944). Ironically, what appeared on the surface to be in the best educational and psychosocial interest of the marginalized group was socially beneficial for all involved. Schooling in the North evinced a reciprocal desire by African Americans and European Americans for segregated schooling, albeit for different but related reasons.

Schools, for example, were physically integrated as early as the 1640s in parts of Massachusetts. The early educational leaders thought school integration would be a method through which all could adjust to the changing social and educational environment. As a result of the historical relationships between African Americans and European Americans, early attempts to provide schooling to both groups in the same location were less than amicable. They were characterized by social hostility in the form of mistreatment and racial insults toward African Americans by their European American teachers and student counterparts, practices that led organized groups of troubled African Americans to clamor for segregated schooling after the Revolutionary War. These environments would be less hostile but also less good (Brooks, 1990).

Concerned parties understood early that for African Americans to make a healthy adjustment from identity confusion to identity salience, equal access to social and physical accommodations, including quality schooling, was tantamount. Being in close proximity to people who despised you was not the central issue. Having equal access to knowledge and the hope of a better life was.

PLESSY VS. FERGUSON

Undoubtedly, the most serious blow to the educational efforts of African Americans was the momentous decision rendered in the *Plessy v. Ferguson* Supreme Court case of 1896. This case involved a challenge from Homer Plessy, a black man, to a Louisiana state law requiring that blacks and whites use separate train car facilities. The Supreme Court concluded that racial segregation did not constitute discrimination under the Fourteenth Amendment so long as the separate facilities were equal. The doctrine of "separate but equal" meant that the federal government sanctioned segregation. Subsequently, laws requiring racial segregation in education and other social and political domains were enacted throughout the South (Orfield & Eaton, 1996).

Plessy vs. Ferguson resulted in a dual system that was indeed separate but manifestly unequal. As time passed inequalities continued to occur. For example, in the 1940s new school facilities were constructed for white students, whereas black students inherited the deteriorating schools vacated by whites or remained in dilapidated, often overcrowded, and sometimes widely dispersed schools. Black students often had to walk fifteen to twenty miles to schools while buses transporting white pupils to school passed them en route. Inequities also occurred in the availability of educational resources such as textbooks, libraries, musical instruments, laboratories, and physical education facilities. A separate curriculum for blacks and whites constructed to maintain a system of segregation and patterned superordinate-subordinate relations between the races also resulted from this dual system (Blackwell, 1985).

BROWN VS. BOARD OF EDUCATION

Opening the door for educational leaders to assist minority students in making the required psychosocial adjustment in schools and fostering a healthy identity development during postwar America, there came a series of federal and state court decisions. Prying the door of opportunity open were Brown I and II; these decisions implied that access to quality education for minorities could only be achieved by bringing them to academic environments with the majority. In the 1954 case of *Brown v. Board of Education Topeka*, 347 U.S. 483 (1954) (Brown I) the constitutionality of segregation was tested. The National Association for the Advancement of Colored People (NAACP) selected cases that were representative of the persistent problems stemming from the separate-but-equal decision. A cadre of black lawyers, including Thurgood Marshall, argued five cases: *Brown v. Board of Education Topeka* (Kansas); *Briggs v. Elliot* (South Carolina); *Davis v. County School Board of Prince Edward County* (Virginia); *Gebhart v. Belton* (Delaware); and *Bolling v. Sharpe* (District of Columbia). Armed with voluminous and convincing evidence from social research, they persuaded the Supreme Court to respond favorably (Blackwell, 1985).

In the lead case of *Brown v. Board of Education Topeka*, Kansas, the Supreme Court unanimously concluded that state-imposed segregated schools were "inherently unequal" and must be abolished. This decision, regarded by many as the landmark Supreme Court decision of the century, struck down the "separate but equal" doctrine (Orfield & Eaton, 1996).

These decisions caused the modern high school, in particular, to become the central laboratory in which diverse groups came together and interacted. For example, in the 1930s about 50 percent of working-class students attended high school, whereas by the 1960s this figure exceeded 90 percent. Additionally, between the early 1940s and the late 1950s the percentage of black students who finished high school doubled. But if the high school was becoming more heterogeneous, it was more along class than racial lines, even though the Supreme Court had unanimously ruled in Brown I that the Fourteenth Amendment required equal admission of all students to public schools (Franklin, 1997).

Because school districts throughout the country were slow to implement policies to desegregate and quick to evade tenets set forth in the 1954 decision, in 1955 the Supreme Court decided on Brown II, 349 U.S. 294. This was the Supreme Court's first attempt to define how and when school desegregation would be achieved. In Brown II, the Court hedged on Brown I's powerful anti-segregation stand, setting no standard or deadline for desegregation to occur. Desegregation, the court said, should occur with "all deliberate speed" in plans developed in federal district courts. In *Green v. County School Board of New Kent County*, 391 U.S. 430 (1968), the Supreme Court ruled that schools must dismantle segregated/dual systems "root and branch" and that desegregation must be achieved with respect to facilities, staff, faculty, extracurricular activities, and transportation.

HISPANIC-AMERICANS

By the late 1970s patterns of race and ethnicity were undergoing a transformation. The roots of this transformation can be traced to the Immigration Reform Act of 1965, which abolished national origin quotas and promoted unforeseen changes in the composition of the immigrant population and the competition for fewer jobs with lower wages (Franklin, 1997). These population changes added to the necessity of social institutions, especially schools, to provide environments that promoted healthy psychosocial adjustment. The success of the new immigrant children and their ability to become productive citizens was assured by this adjustment. The Hispanic population was not only overwhelmingly urban, it was also relatively young. Its median age was 22 years, compared with 30 years for non-Hispanic Americans.

Compared to other immigrant groups, Hispanics were also a relatively poor population with low levels of educational attainment. The low level of educational attainment provided an obstacle to Mexican Americans in establishing a positive identity. This also added to the erroneous generalization that members of this group were inferior (Franklin, 1997). The practice of segregation historically rested upon irrational notions of "racial" inferiority and the general unsuitableness of Mexican Americans, and other Hispanic Americans, for integration into American institutions. The general response to a survey conducted in the Imperial Valley of California, for example, reasoned that segregation was justified due to "a consciousness of racial difference" (Wollenberg, 1978, p. 111).

This purposeful racial-ethnic ambiguity has been used as a segregation device throughout Hispanic American students' educational experiences and has been consistently challenged by Hispanic Americans. In California, *Roberto Alvarez v. the Board of Trustees of the Lemon Grove School District* (1931) successfully challenged the notion that Mexican American students could be legally segregated from their Anglo American peers. In the same year, the Bliss Bill, which attempted to have Mexican Americans designated as Indians and thereby subject to legal school segregation, was defeated (Trueba, 1988). In 1947, yet another court case in California, *Mendez v. Westminister*, ended the State's de jure segregation of Mexican Americans, with Texas and Arizona following suit in 1948 and 1950 (Wollenberg, 1978).

The obvious intention of defeating de jure segregation of Mexican Americans was to provide access to quality education. The less obvious intent may have been to demonstrate that, given an opportunity, it would be seen that Hispanics were just as capable as their white peers who had the same racial classification.

The customary classification status of Americans of Mexican descent as Caucasians has also been used by school districts, although unsuccessfully, as a device to legally provide the means to exclude European American students from having to attend schools with African Americans. In 1970, almost two decades after the Supreme Court's decision in Brown I and II, schools in Texas were still placing Mexican American students in segregated schools with African American students on grounds that, as Mexican American students were Caucasian, this practice met the Court's desegregation decree. This objectionable practice was successfully challenged in *Cisneros v. Corpus Christi Independent School District* (Salinas, 1973).

Another court case, recognizing the rights of Latinos to desegregation as well as that of African American students, was *Keyes v. Denver School District No. 1, 413 U.S. 189* (1973). Under Keyes, school districts were responsible for policies that resulted in racial segregation in the school system, including constructing new schools in racially isolated neighborhoods and gerrymandering attendance zones. Once intentional segregation was found on the part of the school board in a portion of the district, the whole district was presumed to be illegally segregated. The entire district was held accountable for the actions of some (Orfield & Eaton, 1996).

SOUTHEAST ASIANS

In addition to Hispanic immigration into the United States, the 1970s saw another major pattern of race and ethnicity transformation: the immigration of Southeast Asians. The recent immigration of Southeast Asians can be viewed in "waves." The first wave of Southeast Asian immigrants came from Vietnam.

These were most often the educated professional class who left their war-torn homeland with the evacuation of the American military. The second wave of immigrants, who did not come from a tradition of schooling, consisted of Cambodians, highland Hmong, lowland Lao, and Tai Dam (Westlander & Stephany, 1983). Within these very divergent groups, there are different social cultural factors that affect school age children. In addition to the usual linguistic and acculturation difficulties that exist for refugees, consideration must be given to the time of arrival, social class background, and the amount of trauma the children may have experienced (Ima & Rumbaut, 1989).

One Southeast Asian population that has recently been examined by researchers is the Hmong. The majority of these refugees entering the United States did not have any formal education. Among the Southeast Asian refugees, the Hmong has the largest percentage of individuals without formal education. The Hmong did not have a formal written language until the mid-1950s (Rumbaut & Morrow, 1989). Within Hmong and other Southeast Asian populations, cultural values that are transmitted through the family and education have a strong foundation in Confucian and Buddhist traditions. These traditions add to the Southeast Asian work ethic and concept of achievement. Belief in one's own ability to effect change or attain goals was a critical component of achievement and motivation (Caplan, Choy, & Whitmore, 1992). Caplan, Choy and Whitmore (1992) convincingly argued that these refugees' sense of control over their lives could be traced to family identity. The sense of familial efficacy proved critical, as opposed to the more Western concept of personal efficacy.

African Americans, Hispanics, and Southeast Asians, through legal, emotional, physical, and intellectual persistence were desirous of full participation in American life. Full inclusion within American society is linked to a quality education. With hard fought battles against legal segregation, it appeared that the United States was ready to move forward in its efforts to provide all children with equal access to quality education. Unfortunately, the social malady of racism was only submerged. In the early 1990s courts made decisions that would effectively reverse years of progress toward academic inclusion and the educational leader's ability to help students negotiate their identities (Orfield & Eaton, 1996).

BACK TO THE FUTURE: THE RE-EMERGENCE OF SEGREGATION

Nearly a half century after the Supreme Court's unanimous 1954 school desegregation decision, *Brown v. Board of Education*, the Supreme Court reversed itself in the 1990s. After decades of bitter political, legal, and community struggles over civil rights, there was surprisingly little attention to the new school resegregation policies spelled out in key 1990s decisions in *Board of Education of Oklahoma City v. Dowell*, 498 U.S. 237 (1991); *Freeman v. Pitts*, 112 S. Ct. 1430 (1992); and *Missouri v. Jenkins*, 115 S. Ct. 2038 (1995). These decisions outlined procedures for court approval of the dismantling of school desegregation plans. These plans, despite the well-publicized problems in some cities, have been one of the few legally enforced routes of access and opportunity for millions of African American and Latino schoolchildren in an increasingly polarized society (Orfield & Eaton, 1996).

Dowell and Pitts embrace new conceptions of racial integration and school desegregation. These decisions view racial integration not as a goal that segregated districts should strive to attain, but merely as a temporary punishment for historic violations and an imposition to be lifted after a few years. After the sentence of desegregation has been served, the normal, "natural" pattern of segregated schools can be restored. As mentioned earlier, Green ordered "root and branch" eradication of segregated schooling and specified several areas of a school system such as students, teachers, transportation, and facilities. Under Dowell, a district briefly taking the steps in Green can be termed "unitary" and is thus freed from its legal obligation to purge itself of segregation. Unitary might best be understood as the opposite of a "dual" system, in which a school district, in essence, operates two separate systems, one black and one white. A unitary district is assumed to be one that has repaired the damage caused by generations of segregation and overt discrimination (Orfield & Eaton, 1996).

In 1992, a year after Dowell, the *Freeman v. Pitts* decision went even further, holding that various requirements laid out in Green need not be present at the same time. This meant, for example, that a once-segregated system could dismantle its student desegregation plan without ever having desegregated its faculty or providing equal access to educational programs (Orfield & Eaton, 1996).

In 1995, the *Missouri v. Jenkins* decision found the Court's majority determined to narrow the reach of the "separate but equal" remedies. This decision prohibited efforts to attract white suburban and private school students voluntarily by providing excellent programs (i.e., "magnet schools"). The goal was to create desegregation by making inner city schools so attractive that private school and suburban students would choose to transfer to them. Because possible desegregation was limited within the city system by a lack of white students, the emphasis was put on upgrading the schools. When the district court said it would examine test scores to help ensure that the remedy actually helped the black children who had been harmed by segregation, the Supreme Court said no. This ruling emphasized the limited role of the courts and the need to restore state and local authority quickly, regardless of remaining inequalities. Ironically, the politically conservative movement that claimed it would be more productive to emphasize choice and "educational empowerment" over desegregation, won a constitutional decision in Jenkins that pushed desegregation in big cities toward simple, short-term racial balancing within a city, even though the

African American and Latino majority is so large that little contact with whites is possible. In just five years, Dowell, Pitts, and Jenkins had reduced the long crusade for integrated education to a formalistic requirement that certain rough indicators of desegregation be present in school districts and individual schools (Orfield & Eaton, 1996). The rough indicators lacked the impetus to create equal and quality education.

In his 1954 opinion in *Brown v. Board of Education*, Chief Justice Earl Warren wrote that "education represented a central experience in life" (Franklin, 1997, p. 130), because it alerted children to cultural values. In Warren's view, the ideas that children learned in school remained with them for the rest of their lives. The ideas learned in school and the sociocultural experience of educational exclusion provided the background central to the identity development of cultural minority children. This is a history that educational leaders, especially classroom teachers, must understand in order to have positive expectations and create learning environments that help culturally different students attain success.

WITHIN PYGMALION: ORGANIZATIONAL BEHAVIOR AND STUDENT OUTCOMES

The educational success of culturally different populations, to a large degree, depends upon our response to history. The history works to shape our expectations of culturally different populations and also our expectations of what we have to offer as educators. What we expect of students is important, however, what we expect of ourselves and how we communicate our expectations in relation to the students we serve is critical to their educational success.

An excellent illustration of expectations is found in George Bernard Shaw's play *Pygmalion* (1916). In *Pygmalion*, Professor Henry Higgins insists that he can take a Cockney flower girl and, with some vigorous training, pass her off as a duchess. He succeeds. But a key point lies in a comment by the trainee, Eliza Doolittle, to Higgins' friend Pickering: "You see, really and truly, apart from the things anyone can pick up [the dress and the proper way of speaking and so on], the difference between a lady and a flower girl is not how she behaves, but how she's treated. I shall always be a flower girl to professor Higgins, because he always treats me as a flower girl, and always will; but I know I can be a lady to you because you always treat me as a lady, and always will" (SIRS, p. 1). Just as the character, Eliza Doolittle, suggests that a person's place in society is largely a matter of how he or she is treated by others, a study by Rosenthal and Jacobson (1968) concluded that students' intellectual development is largely a response to what teachers expect and how those expectations are communicated. As an example, the original Pygmalion study involved giving teachers false information about the learning potential of certain students in grades one through six in a San Francisco elementary school. Teachers were told that these students had been tested and found to be on the brink of a period of rapid intellectual growth. In reality, the students had been selected at random (SIRS, p. 1). At the end of the experimental period, some of the targeted students, and particularly those in grades one and two, exhibited performance on IQ tests that was superior to the scores of other students of similar ability and superior to what would have been expected of the target students with no intervention. These results led the researchers to claim that the inflated expectations teachers held for the target students (and, presumably, the teacher behaviors that accompanied those high expectations) actually caused the students to experience accelerated intellectual growth (SIRS, p. 2). Consciously or not, we communicate our expectations. We exhibit thousands of cues, which can be as subtle as the tilting of heads, the raising of eyebrows, or the dilation of nostrils. Most are more obvious, and people pick up on those messages.

The Self-fulfilling Prophecy was conceptualized by Robert Merton, a professor of sociology at Columbia University. In a 1957 work called *The Self-fulfilling Prophecy*, Merton, said the phenomena occurs when "a false definition of the situation evokes a new behavior which makes the original false conception come true" (p. 198). In other words, once an expectation is set, even if it is not accurate, we tend to act in ways that are consistent with the expectation. Surprisingly often, the result is that the expectation, as by magic, comes true.

Expectancy theory focuses on people's need for achievement and success; it suggests that people's expectations of success and the value they place on them direct their behavior. A key element of expectancy theory is that a person's thoughts guide behavior. The social motives and needs that a person develops are not physiological in origin; they are not initiated because of some physiological imbalance. People learn through their interactions in the environment to have needs for mastery, affiliation, or competition. These needs lead to expectations about the future and about how differing efforts will lead to various outcomes (Lefton, 1999).

The expression "self-fulfilling prophecy" suggests that those who expect to succeed, will; those who don't, won't. Expectations for success and failure can influence the outcome of an effort if those expectations help shape the person's behavior. Thus, a teacher who expects a student to fail may often treat the student in ways that increase the likelihood of failure. Things tend to turn out just the way the teacher expected (or prophesied) they would. Expectancy thus becomes a key component of the whys of behavior (Lefton, 1999). The Pygmalion study is seen as a self-fulfilling prophecy effect, because the imminent intellectual blooming of target students was "false information" given to teachers. The information presumably led teachers to act in such a way as to make the false conception a reality. Sustaining expectation effects are said to occur when teachers respond on the basis of their existing expectations for students rather than to changes in student performance caused by sources other than the teacher (Cooper & Good, 1983). Good and Brophy (1984) expressed that self-fulfilling prophecies are the most dramatic form of teacher expectation effects, because they involve changes in student behavior. Sustaining expectations refer to situations in which teachers fail to see student potential and hence do not respond in a way to encourage some students to fulfill their potential.

Delpit (1995) admitted that we say we believe that all children can learn, but few of us really believe it. Teacher education usually focuses on research that links failure and socioeconomic status, failure and cultural difference, and failure and single-parent households. It is hard to believe that these children can possibly be successful after their teachers have been so thoroughly exposed to a canon containing much negative indoctrination. When teachers receive that kind of education, there is a tendency to assume deficits in students rather than to locate and teach to strengths. When entire school districts internalize this attitude the focus is shifted from authentic teaching and learning to test-driven curricula, the result being the expectation and deliverance of a mandated noncurricula. An illustration of this expectation is the manner in which culturally different students are treated when it comes to testing. In schools where the focus is on improving test scores as opposed to improving academic performance there is a tendency to focus significant amounts of instructional time on test-taking strategies.

PRINT WARS AND UNINTENDED CONSEQUENCES

In classrooms, schools, and school districts that educate large numbers of culturally different students, there is often a focus on passing a standardized assessment as opposed to quality teaching aligned with standards. Haycock (2001) suggests that standards won't make a difference if they are not accompanied by a rigorous curriculum. Yet in too many schools, some students are taught a high-level curriculum, whereas other students continue to be taught a low-level curriculum that is often not aligned with standardized tests. It is here where the effects on low-performing students, particularly minority students, begin to skew the possibilities for their access to a richer education. A balance between test-taking strategies and a major emphasis on the core subject areas must be established and maintained to improve the environmental print of culturally different students. If this balance is not achieved our students will continue to be set up for academic and social impoverishment.

Environmental print is what the environment's critical areas (home, school, community, and society at large) write on your experiences. As a result of the writing, you experience the environment differently than someone with a different environmental print. Students who do well on a standardized assessment have an environmental print similar to the reference group whose knowledge formed the basis for the standardized assessment. These students have had similar experiences in their environment's critical areas. In addition, each of these critical areas works to reinforce the other. What happens in the home and community is reinforced in the school, and what happens in the school is reinforced in the home and community. This is true in affluent attendance areas where the majority of staff lives in the community. The reinforcement works to create a common knowledge (canon) that students with a similar environmental print are consistently immersed in. In many cases, not only do the culturally different students have a dissimilar environmental print, but are also having different informational experiences reinforced in their environment's critical areas. This creates a knowledge immersion common only to the culturally different student.

Test-taking strategies separate from core subject content and negligent of environmental print promote unintended consequences for the culturally different. Students who become test-savvy but lack adequate skills in the core subject content areas are ill-prepared to compete with their peers who have been immersed in the core subject areas. The assessment results misrepresent what the test-savvy students have mastered, promoting a false sense of achievement for the students, school, and district. It may also reinforce the false need to continue the practice. Teachers are reporting that the kind of test prep frequently done to raise test scores may actually hamper students' ability to learn to read for meaning. Elementary teachers note that so many months of "reading" the practice samples and answering multiple-choice questions on them undermines their students' ability to read sustained passages of several pages. The reading samples are material the students are meant to forget the minute they mark their answers. At all grade levels this read-and-forget activity is using up the school year with a noncurriculum. That this is happening chiefly in African American and Latino schools means that the gap between what these children learn and what the children in nontest-prep–usually middle-class and white–schools learn is widening even more dramatically. The gap continues in high school. Almost three-quarters of high school graduates go on to higher education, but only about half of them complete even a midlevel college-preparatory curriculum (four years of English and three years each of math, science, and social studies). If we also include two years of foreign language and a semester of computer science, the numbers drop to about 12 percent. The numbers are worse for African Americans, Latinos, and low-income students (Haycock, 2001).

THE PSYCHOLOGICAL CONTRACT

The goals of the school district, school, and classroom determine the relationship between academic and social inputs and student outcomes. Culturally different students come to our schools with a historical canon. This canon helps shape the manner in which they are perceived by everyone in the school organization, including themselves. Subsequently, this perception determines the attitudes, actions, and programs that are implemented. If the school organization perceives that culturally different students are economically, socially, and academically deprived, a "savior" posture may be taken. This posture suggests that what culturally different students bring to school in the way of skills and behaviors are inadequate and contradict what is required for academic and social success. The "savior" posture tends to promote dependent attitudes and behaviors for the culturally different student. They begin to believe that what their immediate environments (home and community) have taught is not as valuable as what the school is teaching. The students also become less reliant on what their immediate environment encourages (respect for traditions and customs and an awareness of cultural sensitivities), and increasingly dependent upon a knowledge base void of familiar contextual clues. The "savior" posture may provide temporary assistance to individual students. However, if this posture prevails, the school organization may undermine the culturally different students' ability to bridge their immediate and school environments. If the school organization perceives that culturally different students are vocation-bound and lack the requisite parental and social support for professional pursuits, a "custodial-maintenance" posture may be taken. This posture suggests that culturally different students' interests lie primarily in what their immediate environment offers. Interests that lie outside of the immediate environment are considered beyond their potential and are discouraged. The "custodial-maintenance" posture works to build and maintain artificial limits on the potential of culturally different students. This is much like the baby elephant that is kept in a location chosen for it using a rope and stake that, when the elephant becomes adult and is easily able to remove the stake, remains in the chosen location because of what it has been taught. The culturally different students are taught not to develop interests outside of their immediate environment. Thoughts and interests to the contrary are only briefly entertained and never acted upon. All culturally different students are not going to attend college or pursue professional careers. The "custodial-maintenance" posture may provide an excuse for those who seek to insulate students from a cold, callous, and competitive world. However, if this attitude prevails, the school organization may provide a narrow and distorted vision of future possibilities. If the school organization perceives that culturally different students have the same access to academic, social, and economic resources as their peers, an "idealist" posture may be taken. This posture suggests that culturally different students have the same opportunities as their peers. They are free to pursue and take advantage of intellectual and career pursuits unhampered by ethnic and class status discrimination. Interests within and outside of immediate environments are encouraged. Culturally different students, like their peers, will find intellectual and social meaning in school activities. What is taught in school is reinforced in the home, and what is instilled in the home is mirrored in the school.

The "idealist" posture, as the name suggests, is based on our ideals. This posture works to encourage and build a bright and productive future for all of our children. The "idealist" posture is based on a "leveled playing field" model, where all have equal and equitable access to societies' resources and rewards. Culturally different students and their peers are viewed as a monolithic group, in school to seek challenge and learn to take full advantage of their potential. Go to school, work hard, get good grades, and you will have a good job, is the mantra. The "idealist" posture may serve as a motivating force that encourages culturally different students to compete and seek challenge and pursue interests within and outside of their immediate environments. However, if this posture prevails without consideration for and sensitivity to real or perceived barriers (i.e., nonleveled playing field, ethnic and class-status discrimination, and an unequal and inequitable access to resources and rewards), culturally different students will be positioned for a culture shock as they begin to negotiate an environment less inviting but more real than school.

The "realist" posture, as the name suggests, takes into consideration that the primary goal of the school organization is to build bridges to help culturally different students go from where they are to where they need to go. The school organization ought to anchor students to constructive inputs of their immediate environment. The respect for home and community, value of unique cultural contributions, necessity of self-reliance and improvement, and recognition of interdependence with all of humanity will serve as the foundation upon which competencies can be built, reinforced, and extended.

School organizations do a remarkable job with children who come from homes and communities with similar references for success. Culturally different students need to be instructed (structure put on the inside) to take custody of, develop, maintain, and improve their competencies. The school organization will facilitate this process through the acknowledgement, appreciation, and acceptance of what culturally different students bring to school from their immediate experience. The school must help the students in their present condition first. When the student is able to use what the school offers to negotiate the immediate environment, success may be transferred to the school as a whole. This will enable the school organization to do its duty to assure that culturally different students are afforded equal and equitable access to all the resources within the school's purview.

All history is brought forward. All of us have had assistance in our ability to walk, talk, eat, and comprehend. These basic competencies are a part of the foundation that enables successful negotiation of the current environment. School organizations can insure that culturally different students develop the necessary competencies for current and future success by facilitating the process of building bridges of learning and hope from the past to the future.

REFERENCES

Blackwell, J. E. (1985). *The black community: Diversity and unity* (2nd ed.). New York: Harper & Row.

Brooks, R. L. (1990). *Rethinking the American race problem.* Berkeley: University of California Press.

Caplan, N., Choy, M., & Whitmore. J. (1992, February). Indochinese refugee families and academic achievement. *Scientific American*, pp. 36-42.

Cooper, H. M., & Good, T. L. (1983). *Pygmalion grows up: Studies in the expectation communication process.* New York: Longman Press.

Delpit, L. (1995). *Other people's children: Cultural conflict in the classroom.* New York: The New Press.

DeVillar, R., Faltis, C., & Cummins, P. (1994). *Cultural diversity in schools: From rhetoric to practice.* Albany: State University of New York Press.

Franklin, D. L. (1997). *Ensuring inequality.* New York: Oxford University Press.

Good, T.L., & Brophy, J.E. (1984). Teacher expectations. In *Looking in classrooms* (Chapter 4). New York: Harper & Row.

Haycock, K. (2001, March). Closing the achievement gap. *ASCD Educational Leadership, 58*(6).

Ima, K., & Rumbaut, R.G. (1989, June). Southeast Asian refugees in American schools: A comparison of fluent-English-proficient and limited-English-proficient students. *Topics in Language Disorder*, 54-75.

Lefton, G. (1999). *How are expectations bringing out the best in others.* School Improvement Series (SIRS). Northwest Regional Educational Laboratory.

Merton, R.K. (1957). *Social theory and social structure.* Glencoe, IL: Free Press.

Myrdal, G. (1944). *An American dilemma: The negro problem and modern democracy.* New York: Harper & Brothers.

Orfield, G., & Eaton S. (1996). *Dismantling desegregation: The quiet reversal of Brown v. Board of Education.* New York: The New Press.

Rosenthal, R., & Jacobsen, L. (1968). *Pygmalion in the classroom.* New York: Henry Holt.

Rumbaut, R., & Morrow, S. (1989). *Research concerns associated with the study of Southeast Asian Refugees.* Washington DC: National Institute of Mental Health.

Salinas, G. (1973). *Voices from el grito.* Berkeley, CA: Quinto Sol.

Shaw, G. B. (1915). *Pygmalion.* New York: Brentano.

SIRS (1989, November). School Improvement Research Series: School Improvement Program. Kathleen Cotton & Karen Reed Wikelund, *Expectations and Student Outcomes.* North West Regional Educational Laboratory.

Trueba, H. (1988). Comments on L. M. Dunn's bilingual Hispanic children on the U.S. mainland: A review of research on their cognitive, linguistic, and scholastic development. *Hispanic Journal of Behavioral Sciences, 10*(3), 253-262.

Westlander, D., & Stephany, G.V. (1983). Evaluation of English as a second language program for Southeast Asian students. *TESOL Quarterley, 17*, 473-480.

Wollenberg, C. M. (1978). *All deliberate speed: Segregation and exclusion in California schools, 1855-1975.* Berkeley: University of California Press.

CHAPTER SEVEN

Ethnic Validity
for Educators

Karen T. Carey

California State University, Fresno

FOR THE CHILDREN

The rising hills, the slopes
Of statistics
Lie before us.
The Steep climb

Of everything, going up.
Up, as we all
Go down.

In the next century,
Or the one beyond that
They say,

By Gary Snyder, from Turtle Island, Copyright ©1974 by Gary Snyder. Reprinted by permission of New Directions Publishing Corp.

Are valleys, pastures,
We can meet there in peace
If we make it.

To climb these coming crests
One word to you, to
You and your children:

Stay together
Learn the flowers

Gary Snyder

How do we insure that every student is given the opportunities needed for him/her to succeed? How do we make certain that we are doing everything we possibility can to help a student succeed academically, socially, and personally, rather than merely focusing on whether the student meets arbitrary academic standards? These are difficult issues for educators facing rooms of male and female students from varying cultural and social backgrounds. One way for us to address a student's diversity within the school setting is through the use of validity.

Validity is a concept that confuses many preservice and inservice educators. However, the importance of validity is paramount, particularly when working with students from populations of different ethnic and cultural backgrounds. In this chapter, a discussion of validity, particularly ethnic validity, and its importance will be presented.

Validity is defined as the degree to which a construct measures what it claims to measure. In other words, does a particular instrument, test, concept, or other definable thing measure what we think it does? For example, in a math class on fractions the teacher would not test the students on geography. There are essentially three basic types of validity: content, criterion, and construct. Briefly, content validity is based on whether the content of a particular instrument, test, or concept is fair and representative of the domain in question. Content validity is based upon common sense and logic. For example, the content validity of a student's behavior such as noncompliance would include an examination of specific behaviors (crying, screaming, ignoring adults), the settings where the behavior occurs (school, home, community), whether the commands or requests by the adult are understood by the student (appropriate for age, ability, gender, ethnicity), and whether there are other factors contributing to the student's behavior (adult anger, depression, physical problems, language difficulties).

Criterion-related validity refers to the relationship between a particular instrument or test and a specific criterion of performance. Criterion-related validity can be separated into concurrent (current) validity and predictive (future) validity. For concurrent validity the scores from a particular instrument or test are associated with some already established measure, or the relation-ships between some behavior the student exhibits and other measures of the problem (e.g., observations and doctors' reports). As an example, a student's ability to make friends can be related to the student's aggression or social with-drawal. For predictive validity the scores from a particular instrument or test are used to predict future performance or the effectiveness of some program on a student's anticipated behavior problem over a long period of time. The most common example is that of the Scholastic Aptitude Test used to predict how well a student will do in college. Another example, using social skills as above, would involve evaluating a student with some test such as the Social Skills Rating System (Gresham & Elliot, 1993) and making predictions about the stu-dent's behavior at some future time.

Validity is also important when we think about targeting different areas of a student's life for change. Do we really need to involve ourselves in a student's life and be making changes in the student's life? And more importantly, should we be, particularly when our involvement may be in direct opposition to the values, beliefs, and needs of the student's family. Many constructs currently used to diagnose students, such as attention deficit disorder and learning disabil-ity, are used by educators and parents alike, but as educators we need to be sure that the label truly does describe the individual student and that our involvement can produce the positive changes we wish to accomplish; if not, we are doing a grave disservice to the student. For example, a student labeled as having atten-tion deficit disorder may in fact, simply be bored with a minimally stimulating classroom environment. Many educators who attend conferences or presenta-tions become bored and talk, laugh, and carry on while someone is speaking. Our own students are no different. Thus, construct validity is important when we identify a student's challenging behaviors, and we must select appropriate measures to help define and describe such problems (Hayes & Nelson, 1986).

Furthermore, when a student exhibits a problem, we must pay close atten-tion to our own personal constructs and those used by the student's parents. Personal constructs (Kelly, 1955) are those that we use to "perceive, think, interpret, and experience the world" (Mischel, 1981, p. 486). Thus, we must make certain that any "diagnosis" or plan we intend to implement in the class-room fits parents' and other educators' beliefs about such problem behaviors, interventions, presumed causes of behaviors, and the possibility for change. The racial, ethnic, and cultural aspects of one's personal constructs are obvious, but we must also carefully examine the personal constructs of parents from varying socioeconomic backgrounds as well as mothers and fathers. Mothers and fathers will often have different views of why their children are engaging in specific behaviors and what should be done about it.

Identifying students with either overt or hidden problems and then devel-oping interventions is difficult for every educator. Doing so for students of dif-fering ethnic, racial, cultural, and/or economic backgrounds, however, is espe-cially arduous. It involves making allowances for many individual and cross-cultural variables that can influence our own and others' decision making including language differences, limited opportunities or experiences, varying ways of adapting and coping with life, and always the possibility of mistrust and prejudice between individuals. We can never know with any certainty how directly a student's problems are linked to the complex interactions between social, economic, political, situational, and individual factors. When a student's problems stem from profound economic or familial dysfunction, we may not be able to do much for that student (Barnett & Carey, 1992). But by no means should we give up. We must remember that every student has the potential for success, and our continued encouragement and expression of belief in the student may influence the student in the long term to overcome his/her life adversities. We have a responsibility to address the individual needs of every student in appropriate and positive ways regardless of the student's cultural, socioeconomic, or ethnic background. By incorporating the theoretical construct of ethnic validity into practice, we will be able to increase our success in working with all students.

ETHNIC VALIDITY

The concept of ethnic validity was first proposed by Savage and Adair (1980) in order to insure the fairness of assessment procedures for African American students in response to concerns about test bias for this population. They suggested that five components of behavior be sampled, including affective, behavioral, cognitive, cultural, and social. They recommended that the evaluator become immersed in the African American culture for long periods of time in order to insure an overall understanding of the student's experiences. However, Savage and Adair noted several potential problems with their model. Most people could simply not commit to spending the extended period of time required for a thorough assessment or spend the needed time immersing themselves in the culture. Further, they felt that some individuals might experience difficulties when attempting immersion in the African American culture.

Another model of ethnic validity was proposed in 1991 by Tyler, Brome, and Williams. This model was specific to psychotherapy. They suggested that the psychotherapy (Freudian) model was ethnocentric and based on white American male values. However, to meet the needs of all people, including those of different ethnic groups, Tyler et al. proposed a model based on three assumptions. The first assumption stated that there are many ways of living, and different lifestyles have both positive and negative aspects. The second assumption was that people are influenced by the characteristics and social contexts of the individuals with whom they interact as well as their ethnic/cultural backgrounds. The final assumption was that a person's identity is established at both individual and group levels. The overarching idea of this model was that the therapist needed to recognize, accept, and respect the similarities and differences in every individual's development and experiences. Thus, although the therapist might have different opinions, perceptions, ideas, and attitudes about the world, he/she would have to develop the ability to empathize and understand the views of the client. Thus, the emphasis is placed on what is acceptable and meaningful to the individual client within the client's cultural group.

The model proposed for educators was developed by Barnett and associates (1995). They expanded on the two models described above and incorporated the concept of social validity into their model. Social validity refers to the judgments, beliefs, and values made by others about the acceptability of goals for a specific treatment or intervention, the procedures used in the treatment or intervention, and the potential outcomes of such a treatment or intervention. For example, does the student who is experiencing problems in school believe that additional tutoring will make a difference in her grades? Do the parents? Does the family of a student who has difficulty paying attention in class believe that the only way to assist the student is through medication? Social validity emphasizes the importance of taking into consideration the feelings and beliefs of the individual identified, the family, the culture, and the larger society.

Expanding on social validity, Barnett et al. (1995) defined ethnic validity as "the degree to which problem identification and problem solving are acceptable to the client in respect to the client's belief and value systems, as these are associated with the client's ethnic/cultural group" (Barnett et al., 1995, p. 221). Thus, ethnic validity stresses values associated with one's particular cultural or ethnic group and focuses on the student experiencing difficulties as a member of a group with shared values and perspectives.

To insure ethnic validity when working with students and families of differing ethnic backgrounds a collaborative process using team members of the same gender, culture, social status, race, and/or ethnic background as the student and family can be used to establish and "anchor" the cultural appropriateness of meeting with parents, identifying problems, and developing solutions. The principles of ethnic validity are based on eco-behavioral analysis, collaborative problem solving, and decision making.

Eco-behavioral analysis refers to a complete evaluation of the student's natural environment in relation to his/her behavior. Using Bandura's (1986) reciprocal determinism, we analyze each situation in terms of the relationships between the environment, behavior, and people present. For example, does the student's behavior improve in different situations and with different individuals? An eco-behavioral approach provides us with alternatives for resolving problem situations: (a) by allowing us to modify the problem behavior(s); (b) by altering or clarifying our expectations and the expectations of others encountering the problem behavior(s); or (c) by changing the student's situation or environment. By using an eco-behavioral approach we can pinpoint the specifics of situations that then allow us to make improvements in the student's life.

Sometimes changing the student's classroom, getting ourselves and others to be able to see the student's strengths rather than weaknesses, or by some form of direct intervention we can make important changes in the student's life that can lead to productivity and success.

PROBLEM SOLVING

In addition to eco-behavioral analysis, other methods for establishing ethnic validity are problem solving, acceptability, and teaming strategies. To address the individual needs of racial, ethnic, and culturally different students and families we can take several important steps. First, we can establish ourselves as advocates for the student and his/her family. Families who view us as being on their side will not take us to fair hearings or create problems for us in other ways. Second we need to understand and accept the racial, ethnic, and cultural differences of the family and the community in which they live. We must remember, however, that even within groups there are differences between individuals. We must also pay careful attention to our own prejudices and biases and make certain that we do not simply stereotype people based on how they look or where they live. Third, we should make every attempt to involve professionals and other community members of the same background as the parents and student in any meetings concerning the student. People from the family's own community will help the family feel at ease and make the transition from the community to the school. Finally, we should use a collaborative consultative approach when working with students and their families when any decisions are going to be made. The stages of collaborative problem solving are: (a) problem identification, (b) problem analysis, (c) plan development, (d) plan implementation, and (e) evaluation (Curtis & Meyers, 1988). This problem-solving model is based on team members who have a mutual respect for one another and interact with openness and trust. Each stage of the process requires that the team evaluate the gender, socioeconomic, and cultural context and the influence of each on the specific problem under discussion.

In the problem identification stage, for example, we must first determine if a student's behavior is viewed as a problem in all of the situations and environments, which involves interaction on the part of the student. If the behavior is only a problem in certain circumstances, under certain conditions, or with certain individuals, the "problem" may not be a problem at all. The purpose of the problem identification stage then is to define the problem as specifically and as comprehensively as possible.

The second stage, the problem analysis stage, continues the exploration of the student's problem and tries to identify the antecedents and consequences of the problem. Plan development requires that all persons involved in the student's life come together to develop a plan of action to solve the problem. Everyone must "buy in" to the plan and agree to carry it out as proposed by the team. Plan implementation involves the actual use of the plan in the setting where the problem is seen. Finally, the evaluation stage requires a careful analysis of the effectiveness of the plan.

By using this process and including individuals with knowledge about the student's background and culture, many school- and home-related problems can be understood and solved. This process can also be adapted to different classrooms, programs, practices, and philosophies to achieve the goals we are looking for with our students.

ACCEPTABILILITY

Acceptability refers to the judgments students, families, educators, administrators, and the larger society make about the plans to change a student's behavior in regard to the appropriateness, fairness, reasonableness, intrusiveness, and normalcy of the plan (Kazdin, 1980). In other words, do parents, teachers, and others with whom the student interacts believe that the plan will be helpful in correcting the problem. Our plans must be compatible with the needs, values, and customs of the student, the student's family, and the community. The analysis of potentially effective plans is based on their viability for a specific group in relation to the student's race, ethnicity, or culture. Only by asking members of the student's group if the plan is viable will the team know if the plan developed will be viewed as a positive by members of that group. Thus, the cultural context and differences among participants could become factors in determining the appropriateness of any plan for any student. And, importantly, plans viewed as unacceptable by the racial, ethnic, or cultural group will result in failure for the student, and the problem will not be resolved. Thus, we must do all we can to determine if the plan is acceptable to the significant others in a student's life and if they believe it has the potential to change the student's behavior.

TEAMING

The use of teams within school settings is vital to insuring that every student is provided the best possible services, and almost every decision made within a school setting requires a team decision. Most educators are familiar with multi-disciplinary teams including student study or child study teams, and most often such teams are used for making decisions related to a student's need for special education. Student study teams are composed of individuals with specific professional titles and generally include a site administrator, such as a principal; a regular education teacher; a special education teacher; people who have evaluated the student including a school psychologist, a speech therapist or pathologist, a school nurse, and others; and the student's parents. However, regardless of the type of team working to assist a student, team membership and participation should vary depending on the specific student situation being addressed. The important features of a team approach that address ethnic validity include an interactive and collaborative problem solving approach as described above; racial, ethnic, and/or cultural group representation and participation that deal with language or other potential barriers, and distributed decision making power. Team decisions should be just that—team decisions. No one individual should press his or her agenda, but those persons most familiar with an individual student's life experiences should be listened to and their beliefs and values carefully considered.

The inclusion of racial, ethnic, and/or cultural representatives on the team allows the team to evaluate goals, procedures, and outcomes with regard to the student, family's, and community's values, perspectives, and daily practices. Inclusion insures that the team will not overstep its bounds and make cultural mistakes that would be virtually impossible to repair. And, it shows that the team truly does respect and value the individual student and his/her family and clearly wants the best for the student.

GUIDELINES FOR ETHNIC VALIDITY

Barnett et al. (1995) developed six questions for teams to ask when working with racially, ethnically, or culturally diverse students. First, the team should determine whether the student's cultural community has preferences for solving problems and if so, those preferences should be adhered to and respected by all members of the team. Second, the team members must have taken the time to understand their own values, beliefs, and other attitudes that may influence their ability to understand others. If individual team members do not have an understanding of their own beliefs and values, they will have great difficulty working with members of other racial, ethnic, and cultural groups. Third, each team member and the team as a whole needs to determine what can be accepted in terms of attitudes and beliefs that conflict with their own. For example if prayer is the intervention of choice for a family, how does the team respond in terms of what is acceptable in a school situation? Fourth, the interactions between the team members, including the family representative(s) (whether from the student's racial, ethnic or cultural group), the student, and the student's family must be determined with respect to defining and acknowledging ethnic validity. In other words, are the team members "in line" with the family in terms of what is acceptable for the family and the student? If there are significant differences between the representative, the student, or family members, and individual team members, team membership may need to be reconfigured in order to best meet the needs of the family. Fifth, the team needs to identify effective ways to resolve differences in views between team members, including family representatives and the family members. In some situations, a student may have parents and relatives of differing ethnic backgrounds resulting in familial conflict over potential problem solutions and plans. Such conflicts must be resolved and all team members must be in agreement about any potential plans to be implemented, or the plan will certainly fail. Sixth, the team members must determine the best way to measure ethnic validity for an individual student. Ethnic validity may be expressed as positive relationships between the team and family or representative, or positive feelings regarding the values, beliefs, and attitudes of the family, representative, and individual team members.

CONCLUSION

Taking the needed time to identify all aspects of an individual student's race, ethnicity, and culture while taking into consideration the student's gender and social class can lead to positive long-term outcomes for the student and his/her family when dealing with difficult school-related problems, whether they be behavioral or academic. Ignoring this information will result in less than satisfied team members, and most importantly, possible educational failure for the student. At this time the concept of ethnic validity is simply theoretical. Research is needed to verify the applicability of the concept. However, the model as described above may help educators understand different problem situations and the ethnic and cultural aspects of such problems. Understanding the multicultural components of problem situations and potential remedies may result in practices that enable the student's true identity to be taken into account. The model can provide educators with a greater understanding of the world around them and a new appreciation of the students they serve.

REFERENCES

Bandura, A. (1986). *The social foundations of thought and action: A social cognitive theory*. Englewood Cliffs, NJ: Prentice-Hall.

Barnett, D. W., Collins, R., Coulter, C., Curtis, M. J., Ehrhardt, K., Glaser, A., Reyes, C., Stollar, S., & Winston, M. (1995). Ethnic validity and school psychology: Concepts and practices associated with cross-cultural professional competence. *Journal of School Psychology*, *33*(3), 219-234.

Curtis, M. J., & Meyers, J. (1988). Consultation: A foundation for alternative service delivery in the schools. In J. L. Graden, J. E. Zins, & M. J. Curtis (Eds.), *Alternative educational delivery systems: Enhancing instructional options for all students* (pp. 35-48). Washington, DC: NASP.

Gresham, F., & Elliott, S. N. (1993). *Social skills rating system.* Circle Pines, MN: American Guidance Service.

Hayes, S. C., & Nelson, R. O. (1986). Assessing the effects of therapeutic interventions. In R. O. Nelson & S. C. Hayes (Eds.), *Conceptual foundations of behavioral assessment* (pp. 461-503). New York: Guilford.

Kazdin, A. E. (1980). Acceptability of alternative treatments for deviant student behavior. *Journal of Applied Behavior Analysis, 13,* 259-273.

Kelly, G. A. (1955). *The psychology of personal constructs* (Vols. I & II). New York: Plenum.

Mischel, W. (1981). A cognitive-social learning approach to assessment. In T. V. Merluzzi, C. R. Glass, & M. Genest (Eds.), *Cognitive assessment* (pp. 479-502). New York: Guilford.

Savage, J. E., & Adair, A. V. (1980). Testing minorities: Developing more culturally relevant assessment systems. In R. L. Jones (Ed.), *Black psychology* (2nd ed.). New York: HarperCollins.

Tyler, F. B., Brome, D. R., & Williams, J. E. (1991). *Ethnic validity, ecology, and psychotherapy: A psychosocial competence model.* New York: Plenum.

CHAPTER EIGHT

Who's At Risk?
The Chaotic World of
Diverse Populations

Greg S. Goodman

Victor Olivares

California State University, Fresno

"The deepest impulse was to make learning part
of the process of social change itself."

Chantal Mouffe (1988, p. 42)

WEREWOLF FRIENDS

I was a werewolf, age 17,
Gnawing a leftover pork chop on the back porch,
My chin lost in teenage fuzz, eyebrows dark,
I looked in a hand mirror–yes, my face was bristly.

My friend Stevie rode up on his bike,
He too a werewolf, tongue red as a petal
In the cheese-chunk of his ugly face. He kicked
The kickstand down,
And we sat on the porch,
Each of us sneaking quick glances into the mirror.

"Werewolf Friends" from A Natural Man by Gary Soto ©1999. Published by Chronicle Books, LLC. Used with permission.

We did our werewolf thing—beat each other on the lawn,
Then scratched because the grass was itchy.
We drank water from the garden hose, peed
On a rose bush, and wrestled over a half-chewed Snickers,
Bellies sloshing like fish bowls. By then,
My stepfather was home, a werewolf himself,
Hairy from the tug of decades of moonlight and such.
He drank his werewolf grog at the kitchen table
And beat his fists on the table top—
Something about Republicans,
Hairless, balless,
But what fat wallets!

Stevie and I left on his bike,
Me bouncing on the handlebars.
Dusk. Hot enchilada dinners sifted through the sycamores,
Scenting our dirty little town with meat.
We biked to the levee–other teenage werewolves
Jumping up and down, lashing more pee into the current,
Hurling ourselves against each other.

We threw the bike down.
This is A-OK, Stevie crowed
And piled onto the others, the sweat
Of teenage years flowing among these friends.
A sensitive werewolf, I leaned a shoulder into a young tree,
And spun my shoes. Something had to come down,
Tree or this suffering. I looked skyward—
Moonlight! I stepped around the wrestling werewolves
And dragged my teenage soul through the dust,
Luring leaves and cockles, burrs, and foxtails.

I howled at the godless sky.
I ran toward the moonlight on the canal,
Wild hair up my ass, some unraveling from my armpits
And groin, curly bushels on my palms,
Hair like static frying over my body,
Arms stretched out, fingers wiggling,
I ran and, like everything
I desired—girls with their peachy fuzz, dammit!—
The moon's cleanly shaved face was just out of reach.

Gary Soto

As we begin the 21st century, today's educators are confronting difficult problems in nearly every area of education: assessment, special education, provision of free and appropriate public education, recruitment of staff representative of diversity, technology, the incursion of corporate America in the school, multicultural education, and myriad other issues. As educators, our challenge is to speak from our souls and to articulate that which is best for all students/learners, not just the top of the class (Goodman, 2001). In the process of creating schools that result in success for all students, 21st century educators must seek democratic and inclusive school organization and praxis based upon a philosophy well versed in critical theory (Giroux, 1997; McLaren, 1999).

The students at the top have had many opportunities to experience the rewards competitive culture affords them, and they will continue to receive them. Often coming from affluence and possessing the cultural capital (Bourdieu, 1993) that perpetuates success, the students at the top of academic success live a world apart from the majority of their fellow students. Esteemed by the possession of expensive cars, the wearing of designer clothing, and surrounded by other accouterments that brandish the advantage of class or money, students with cultural capital experience the world in fundamentally different ways than their less advantaged peers. Praised at graduation or baccalaureat, the best of the class are featured.

In competitive systems, being at the top is the reward for good work. Peter McLaren (1999) calls this process, "a ritual of self-perpetuation" (p. 289). The problem created by this identification of individual icons of system success, for example valedictorians, is the cost of virtually ignoring the 25 to 50 percent of the class that dropped out. This group of alienated students should also include those who remain in school and cling on to hope that they can survive school despite the fact that they are disenfranchised in many ways. While in school, this group of alienated or disaffected students frequently requires the majority of disciplinary or other administrative attention. The anger in these students is often the precursor to fights, classroom disruption, and destruction of school or individual property.

More important, the cost of school failure can be societal exclusion such as relegation to low-paying/status careers, incarceration, and/or other forms of alienation. A report on educational attainment and work force characteristics concluded, "Persons with lower levels of educational attainment were more likely to be unemployed than those who had high levels of educational attainment" (*Digest of Educational Attainment*, 1998, p. 2). For example, "The 1997 unemployment rate for adults (25 years and older) who had not completed high school was 8.1 percent compared with 4.3 percent for those with 4 years of high school and 2.0 for those with a bachelor's degree or higher" (*Digest of Educational Attainment*, 1998, p. 2). Furthermore, although not always the case, the correlation between school failure and incarceration is too great to ignore. Ninety-eight percent of all American youth entering the prison system lacked a high school diploma or a General Education Diploma (GED) (Ingersoll &

LeBoeuf, 1997). Sonia Nieto (1996) speaks to this well when she states, "That many students are alienated, uninvolved, and discouraged by school is abundantly clear. This fact is most striking, of course, in dropout rates. A national study found that one of the main characteristics of dropouts is alienation from school life. Students who drop out are usually uninvolved and passive participants in the school experience" (p. 101). The effect of this disconnection with success is devastating for the students' families and the communities that inherit the school's failures.

Racism continues within institutions in the implementation of rules and regulations known as zero tolerance. Zero tolerance policies were enacted by schools in the 1990s to "send a message" to communities that violence on school campuses would be dealt with severely, for example, by expulsion. Everyone agrees that schools must be safe places. However, rules that work to exclude students rather than rehabilitate are often more exclusive of certain groups over others. When disproportionate numbers of African American, Hispanic, and Hmong students are recommended for expulsion in comparison to white, majority students, the question "Is this institutionalized racism?" begs for response. At issue is equity and justice for the students considered others or outsiders (werewolves?). According to W.G. Secada [as cited in Herb Kohl's *I Won't Learn From You* (1994)], "The heart of equity lies in our ability to acknowledge that, even though our actions might be in accord with a set of rules, their results may be unjust. Equity goes beyond following rules, even if we have agreed that they are intended to achieve justice. . . . Educational equity, therefore, should be construed as a check on the justice of specific actions that are carried out within the educational arena and the arrangements that result from those actions."

We write to address this group that never makes it to the event of graduation. They may be working in a fast food restaurant that night or live their lives ensconced behind bars. The groups for whom we write beg for an answer to the question of why they did not make it. Why did they fail? Our passion is to debunk the myths of the failure of the underrepresented. Most commonly, school failure is accompanied by blame. The students frequently blame the school at the onset of their departure, expulsion, or removal. Later, the students turn the blame inward and fault their poor behavior and lack of respect. This confusion of who is to blame may be called the failed student's dilemma (Goodman, 1999). The students are in a quandary as to whom to blame, and they have good reason to be confused. The majority of American society is perplexed by misinformation and in spurious debate about whom to blame, too (Hinds, 2000).

Moreover, the problem of failure is not going to be resolved successfully through finding an inadequacy or a deficiency upon which to place blame. School failure is not attributable to conservative political arguments of poor attempts or bad work on the part of either students, teachers, administrators, or parents. The wholesale failure of up to one half of our students (*Digest of*

Educational Attainment, 1998) is the result of the mismatch of a traditional, hegemonic pedagogy and the educational leadership's inability to develop alternative educational methods sufficient to rectify or ameliorate the immense and diverse problems disaffected students possess. It is frustrating that our systems are so slow to adopt change (Vygotsky, 1978). However, for several reasons, we remain mired in the same cycle of failure and expulsion of our school failures. Making changes in this loop of disaster means first accepting that we are reinforcing this pattern with our curriculum, policies, and procedures (Senge, 1990). An even deeper level of questioning is posed by John Willinsky (1998), in his award-winning work on imperialism's lingering effects upon our schools and their role in maintaining and replicating hegemony, *Learning to Divide the World*. Willinsky states, "We need to consider what we have learned about a world that was, in no small measure, divided and instructed under the sponsorship of imperialism. We have to ask what the young learn of the question, 'Where is here?' and the part that schooling has long played in defining who belongs where" (p. 244). The problem of the underrepresented is very complex, and reversal of school failure is not simply rectified (Sarason, 1990).

That we have not been able to develop a solution to the problems posed by at-risk students is clear, but why the disaffected receive so little positive attention is our question. Is it that the disaffected have been too easy to dismiss; each leaving school as an individual and, therefore, not having to be considered as a large group? Could it be that these students come from families that do not have strong advocacy skills? Are these departures, removals, or dropouts a function of institutionalized racism? Are our educational leaders so enmeshed in a white-thinking, monocultural perspective that they are unaware of the racist implication of disproportionate numbers of nonwhite dropouts and school failures? Is the leadership uninformed or unaware that large numbers of expulsions and dropouts among students of color perpetuates hegemonic relationships and continues to alienate subordinated groups? Although questions of race will vary depending upon the demographics of each school community, within urban schools the issues of race and class are irrefutably enmeshed in the political economy and educational practices of the schools.

Throughout the United States the phenomenon of poor academic performance by up to one half of all students is as old as the institution of education itself. The debate among educators about the causes and cures of poor academic performance has been discussed in public forums, journals, books, and at conferences. Increasingly, the debate has moved from research institutions to the media (Suoranta, 1999). Subsequently, the public has seen reports on education slowly evolve into a pattern that is disconcerting to many citizens of this country—high drop-out rates, school violence, and low academic achievement scores. As a result, the public sentiment is that education should be the priority. According to one recent mid-term election poll, education was viewed as the biggest problem facing California (Howard, 1998). Likewise, Californians voted accordingly at the polls. The gubernatorial candidate that espoused education as his top issue was elected over the primary challenger who chose to make crime the centerpiece of his campaign. To further support education, Californians signaled to the public policy makers of the state that they were ready to reinvest in education by approving a $9.2 billion school bond measure to provide monies for improving the facilities of public schools and publicly owned colleges and universities. Thus, the voters of California—one of the most ethnically diverse in the nation—seem to have come together to acknowledge that education is a common value among people.

One potential reason for explaining the public's sentiment for education is that most observers view education as the road to a good life. Studies have linked education with character formation and increased income potential (Etzioni, 1983). Conversely, there is much to be lost from an uneducated citizenry: higher unemployment rates or marginal incomes, and therefore, a lower tax base to draw from to meet the fiscal needs of the nation. And therein lies the commonality of our individual endeavors and patriotism: the high value placed on education is not only one that serves personal interest, but also one that serves the entire community.

The impact of this juxtaposition of individual and ethnic group failures and national needs has kept researchers laboring on studies aimed at understanding poor academic performance. Unfortunately, the answer to the question of why some students fail in our institutions of learning continues to elude us. From the broad literature on students experiencing academic difficulties, it appears that the paradigms for researching this phenomenon have been unsuccessful for accounting for such widespread school failure. Frequently, the public is confused and swayed by politically motivated arguments exclusively supporting economic interest.

Money alone is not the answer to preventing the alienation of certain groups of students from the educational system. To illustrate this point, $150 billion dollars were spent on K-higher education in 1960. Thirty-eight years later, in 1998, education expenditures rose to an estimated high of $584 billion dollars. "Elementary and secondary schools spent 60% of this total, and colleges and universities accounted for the remaining 40%" (*Digest of Educational Statistics*, 1998, p. 2). Despite these huge expenditures, the average achievement of high school students on most standardized tests is unchanged, or in some cases, lower than in past decades (Catterall, 1998; McChesney, 1997; National Commission on Excellence in Education, 1983; Newman & Boyer, 1985). Recent studies indicate that there are deficits in the average proficiency scores of all students in the core courses of reading, writing, mathematics, and sciences. One study found that nationwide, high school students graduate with reading scores that are slightly below the eighth-grade level. There are even wider gaps in the proficiency scores between white students and Hispanics, blacks, and American Indians/Alaskan Natives. And in California, African-Americans and Latinos continue to have the lowest eligibility rates for college (California Postsecondary Education Commission, 1998).

Educational attainment is dependent on a broad, complex spectrum of resources and experiences (Posner, 1995). For example, academic and social integration, teacher perception, and discourse are interrelated factors that affect student attrition rates (Steinberg & Kincheloe, 1997). In addition, researchers have posited the elements of extrafamilial resources such as financial capital, human capital, and social capital to be key elements in student success/failure within white or hegemonic systems (Hao & Bonstead-Bruns, 1998; Hoggerth, Boisjoly, & Duncan, 1998; Zhou & Bankston, 1994). The important extrafamilial elements are linked to success for underrepresented students, and the concept of extrafamilial resources is relevant to the studies that link education with increased character formation and future success (Etzioni, 1983; President's Commission for a National Agenda for the Eighties, 1980). The level of schooling is likely to influence the probability of educational attainment for the future children of these families (Haveman & Wolfe, 1994; Rumberger, 1995, both cited in Hoggerth et al., 1998). For example, the Public Policy Institute of California report (Bretts, Rueben, & Danenberg, 2000) concluded that, "Student SES and school resources, especially teacher characteristics and AP course offerings, are strongly related. Notably, educators' level of preparation can explain a significant portion of the variation in course offerings in high schools. Not surprisingly, smaller schools offer fewer advanced placement courses than other schools" (p. xxii). In a similar report on teacher qualifications, by the Center for the Future of Teaching and Learning (Clemings, 2000), a collaborative report authored by the University of California and the California State University System, found that: "California children with the lowest test scores-those who most need great teachers—are five times less likely to have qualified instructors that students in high achieving schools" (p. A1).

The report further stated that today there are 28,500 underqualified (i.e., noncredentialed, on emergency permits) educators staffing our schools, compared to 15,400 in 1995-96, before the state began reducing class size. Also, one-fifth of the schools have more than 20 percent underqualified teachers. Those schools are likely to be low-performing schools with high percentages of poor, minority, and limited-English-speaking students. A closer look at the third grade reading scores from a statewide test suggests a correlation between low performing schools and underqualified teachers. The authors of the report found that "nearly 1,000 schools with the lowest scores have on the average 22% under-qualified teachers. The 900 with the highest scores have on the average 4% under-qualified teachers" (p. 19).

It is important to note that no specific information was provided in these reports that clarified the correlation was a result of a school's capacity to offer the advanced college preparation courses or variations in the demand for college preparation courses. Nonetheless, schools with few resources have less qualified teachers and this may be the cause for low-performing schools. Put in another way, lower income students are, in many cases, being denied their fundamental right to equal access to equal schools. It is clear that fueling schools with more

money, and outdated ideologies about curriculum and school environments—
English only curriculum, stiffer standards, safe schools, zero tolerance, and the
assurances of teacher accountability rallied in clichés such as "English for our
kids' sake"—serve to only create a mismatch of the school systems purpose and
needs of disadvantaged students. The get-tough-on-academic-standards
approach shuns education's historical role in determining "How can we most
effectively bring about student learning?" (Gronland, 1998). In other words, if
educators fail to ask and confront these types of questions, "Why should we
expect what we will now recommend will be anymore effective than our past
efforts?" (Sarason, 1990, p. 5). If the real purpose of school is to bring about
learning for all students, then we must step into the world of the disadvantaged
student to understand why these students have the greatest distance to travel to
reach success in school; then, we can see the mismatch between the school's
purpose and the needs of disadvantaged students. This is the critical first step in
moving toward aligning the needs of the disadvantaged student and the school
systems' purpose.

Attributing poor academic performance solely to dismal economic conditions and low parental educational level does more to limit our understanding of
academic attrition than to provide answers. How this mismatch of the school's
purpose and the needs of disadvantaged students is perpetuated can be seen
through the lens of cultural reproduction theory (Bourdieu, 1993). Cultural
reproduction theory states that groups or social classes tend to develop systems
that reinforce the power and position that those groups hold. In the case of
schools, success is marked by grades and advanced placement. These successes
are the product of having the cultural capital (Bourdieu, 1993) to succeed within
that system. Examples of cultural capital are homework, vocabulary, and personal experience. Students from economically and educationally disadvantaged
backgrounds are more likely to struggle in school or leave school because of a
lack of social or cultural capital (Bourdieu, 1993). According to McLaren
(1994), "Schools systematically devalue the cultural capital of students who
occupy subordinate class positions" (p. 198). We would suggest that a pervasive
lack of hope of future success is also a part of the equation. A student without
the tools for success—for example, a strong and supportive family or habitus—
is at a disadvantage. In cultural reproduction theory, they are already marked to
repeat the failure from which they came. Again, according to McLaren (1994),
"The end result is that the school's academic credentials remain indissolubly
linked to an unjust system of trading in cultural capital which is eventually
transformed into economic capital, as working-class students become less likely
to get high-paying jobs" (p. 198).

Recent studies on the successes of students at risk suggest that social capital, an element of extrafamilial resource, can offset the negative impacts of
poverty and a lack of parental education (Catterall, 1998; Hao & Bonstead-
Bruns, 1998; Hoggerth et al., 1998; Zhou & Bankston, 1994). Social capital is
defined as the relationships between parents and children and the relationships

between parents and other individuals and institutions that affect children's development. Relationships between parents and children center on the types of relationship that parents establish with their children through nurturing, mentoring, and caring for them. The relationship between the parents and other individuals and social institutions addresses the ties with networks outside the family, such as community affiliations—civic or school based (Coleman, cited in Hoggerth et al., 1988). In the context of education, social capital or family networks serve as teams of informal resources that can help the student excel in education. The family network may provide access to educational materials, exposure to role models, or something as basic as having access to someone who has a formal education to serve as an education resource and role model. Shared expectations about education by family and the community can promote academic achievement (Hao & Bonstead-Bruns, 1998; Zhou & Bankston, 1998).

Proponents of social capital provide a credible argument for educators to explore how to integrate ethnic social capital ideologies into mainstream offerings by the school for parent involvement (Parent Teacher Associations and the like). And in recent years some schools have begun to develop school, home, and community-based models; however, this has mostly occurred at the public school level, and not the institutions of higher learning. According to Coleman (cited in Hoggerth et al., 1988), "the basis for academic achievement is an underlying social bond between students and their schools" (p. 211). Parents play an important role in facilitating this bond. It is a bond that results from positive social interactions between the parents and school staff. This bond promotes the psychological development of the student. Thus, a student who feels connected to the institution of learning will experience greater levels of academic and social integration into the campus community. Conversely, parents who do not interact with school staff will have little understanding of the complex environment within which their sons and daughters participate. Even worse, these parents are unable to identify resources to direct their children to when they encounter difficulties on the campus, or relate to the plight of their children. These students who have a strong adherence to traditional family values and a strong commitment to the ethnic community feel alienated from white culture and the inextricable links to (white) privilege (Ignatiev & Garvey, 1994).

Monica provides a good example of a failed relationship between student, family, and school. One of fifteen students interviewed in an ethnographic study of at-risk college students (Olivares, 1999), Monica's experience exemplifies what can happen when parents not only never make contact with a teacher, but they fundamentally do not comprehend the school experience. Most of the students in the study were first-gener ation students; that is, they were the first of their families to attend college. These students commonly reported that they did not have computers at home, and for many, transportation was a problem. In the case of these students, the elements of extrafamilial resources were limited.

Monica is 19 years old and of Mexican descent. She is dressed casually.

(I = Investigator; S = Student)

I: Can you tell me what you do when you are studying late at night and have a question about homework?

S: I really can't study at home. I live with 12 people in my house. I live in the living room. When I get home, I have to do a lot of chores. I have to cook and clean.

I: Is they're anyone in the home you can ask for help when you have a question about homework?

S: I am the only one going to college. I can't ask my dad and mom. They didn't go to school. In fact, I can't even go the library on the weekends. I have to lie to my dad about what time I get out of school just so I can go the library.

I: Can you explain this a little more to me?

S: I think my dad thinks that I would be hanging around the college just to meet guys. They are not very supportive of my education.

This may not be a case of the parent's failure to support their student's education as much as it may be an example of the disconnection of two different worlds. In this situation, traditional education reflects a white, postcolonial, and monocultural perspective, not a multicultural view representative of the diverse students of today. The effect of this dominant ideology in America is that barriers to success are experienced as personally inhibiting of success and maintaining of a white social domination (MacLeod, 1995). In attempts to mitigate these obstacles to diverse students' success, counseling programs have been initiated that include improving communication with parents. However, a far better solution would be for the institution of learning to foster interaction with the various sociocultural communities, creating a pipeline for information sharing about academia that fosters multiculturalism.

In order to reach and teach underrepresented students, the teacher needs to recognize and remember that the influences that lead to the patterns of failure are deeply imbedded in the habitus of that student (MacLeod, 1995). Jay MacLeod eloquently describes the role of habitus and social reproduction theory in his ethnography of disaffected youth in a Massachusetts housing project. MacLeod (1995) states, "Put simply, the habitus is composed of the attitudes, beliefs, and experiences of those inhabiting one's social world. This conglomeration of deeply internalized values defines an individual's attitudes toward, for example, schooling" (p. 15). From this habitus, there tends to be a reproduction of values over time. Although not all poor and delinquent students perpetuate habitus characteristics among themselves, the large majority continue the "traditions" set by older siblings, parents, and close friends. Breaking away from those values is the exception to the rules of social reproduction. In order to break the chains of habitus and to develop routines that foster success in school, a major paradigm shift needs to occur within the student. For educators to gain the trust of at risk students, they must first abandon their old connections and belief systems (habitus) before they can learn new ones.

Our responsibility as citizens governing the educational system is to reconsider our position vis-à-vis the outsiders. The cost of continuing to be in denial of the deleterious effect of school failure are staggering. According to Noam Chomsky (1999), "Democracy functions insofar as individuals can participate meaningfully in the public arena, meanwhile running their own affairs. . . . Functioning democracy presupposes relative equality in access to resources . . ." (p. 131). Certainly access to a free and appropriate public education (FAPE) should be the cornerstone of the entire process of democratic citizenship.

At-risk or disaffected students come in all sizes, shapes, sexual orientations, and colors; lack of entitlement knows no boundary. Moreover, it may be safe to say that all students are at risk to a large degree in adolescence and young adulthood (Cairns & Cairns, 1994). As educators, we must learn to identify those most at risk for school failure, and we need to find a way to develop a relationship with those students or to see to it that someone in our school is representing the interests of those students. Only through a connection with the teacher will at-risk students be able to forge a relationship to the work that a teacher presents (Pianta & Walsh, 1996).

Herb Kohl (1994) describes relationships as the cornerstone of student success. In his book *I Won't Learn From You*, Kohl posits that many students choose to not learn from particular educators. Kohl states:

> Not learning tends to take place when someone has to deal with unavoidable challenges to her or his personal and family loyalties, integrity, and identity. In such situations, there are forced choices and no apparent middle ground. To agree to learn from a stranger who does not respect your integrity causes a major loss of self. The only alternative is to not-learn and reject the stranger's world. (p. 6)

Frank Smith (1986) furthers Kohl's argument by noting, "None of us can learn something that we don't understand, that we are not interested in, or we don't see as the kind of thing people like ourselves learn" (p. 53). This statement reflects what some educators feel about the teaching pedagogy of the American education system—that it has failed to connect the curriculum with the needs of the students (Beane, 1997). In relation to K-12 as well as higher education and student academic performance, this is an essential and critical issue that cannot be ignored in light of student disengagement and the increase in the diversity of the student population.

At the heart of change, educational leaders must redefine the purpose of schools in the new millennium. One scholar, Boyer (1995), asks, "That is, what is an educated person? What should schools be teaching to students" (p. 16). As we become increasingly aware of the historical contributions of diverse ethnic groups to American society, we are now confronted with the question of which dream of the nation is to be transmitted to future generations. For example, many of the inventions created by people of color over the years are not showcased in our history books, nor are the nonmainstream perspectives of an event or concept. This raises issues of our moral and ethical responsibility to create curriculum that presents a more balanced perspective of history. History gives us our sense of identity. A multicultural perspective of history stands a better chance to bridge our identities for the common good. It is time to retell the traditional, white monocultural story of America to include all of our experiences and to reverse the negative consequences of imperialistic pedagogy (Willinsky, 1998).

The inclusion of multicultural content in education should not be limited to what is taught, but should be expanded to include how information is taught. Too little priority has been given to the culturally conditioned learning styles, verbal and nonverbal learning patterns, and the behavioral and response mechanisms of diverse groups (Baker, 1983, cited in Ford, 1992; Bennett, 1988; cited in Ford, 1992). Triesman's (1992) study reviewed the need for expanding teaching methodologies to better represent the women, Asian, African Americans and Latino/a college students whom they serve. This researcher demonstrated that successful teaching pedagogy mixes cultural identities to solve problems by creating a sense of equal value among group members, building a sense of community across ethnic and gender identities and exposing students to different problem solving techniques that are rooted in culturally influenced learning styles.

Very often the disconnections between student and teacher can be linked to a cultural component. Although an overt act of racism within the classroom walls is rare, institutionalized racism and covert racism continue to work to effectively sever connections between many minority students and their schools. All participants in the school community need to work actively to construct truly multicultural and equitable pathways to learning. You, as the teacher, are the key in the process. In the classroom, students directly confront the reality of their success and failure. With each teacher there exists the possibility for the construction of present-time and/or future hope or despair. Students that fail in our school system are labeled as "at risk." Although the term is applied in general ways rather than with clear meaning (Catterall, 1998), it still prompts many to believe that something must be done immediately. Risk factors for student failure have historically been attributed to poor socioeconomic conditions, behavioral deficits, learning disabilities, and limited exposure to social skills development opportunities. Traditional remediation strategies for addressing such deficits have focused more on academic interventions rather than including strategies that enhance critical thinking and problem solving skills.

In particular, we need to address the effects of racism and persecution on our at-risk and diverse student population. More than any other issue of imperialism, the continuation of hegemonic relationships within our schools needs to be confronted (Freire, 1970). Racism and its negative effect upon us all is a demon that feeds itself. The means by which racism continues to avoid extinction is eloquently explained by Cornel West (1999):

> What is distinctive about this precious experiment in democracy called America is that it has always been inextricably interwoven with white supremacy and its legacy. Although some scholars call it irony, I call it hypocrisy. John J. Chapman described it accurately when he concluded that white supremacy was like a serpent wrapped around the legs of the table upon which the Declaration of Independence was signed by the founding fathers. It haunted America then and nearly 200 years later it still does. The challenge for America is whether it will continue to deny, evade, and avoid various forms of evil in its midst. (p. 7)

Furthermore, the implications for a successful transition into academe is complicated as the number of ethnic minority students, reentry students, and female students continue to increase (National Center for Educational Statistics, 1995; Newman & Boyer, 1985; Upcraft & Schuh, 1996). For example, studies (National Center for Educational Statistics, cited in McLeary, 1995) indicate that of the students enrolled in a baccalaureate degree program, whites and Asian/Pacific Islanders are more likely to graduate than members of other ethnic groups. Of those students that enroll in college, a disproportionate number of certain groups—ethnic minorities—come ill prepared to start college and may never catch up, and many do not graduate (California Post Secondary Education Commission, 1988; National Center for Educational Statistics, cited in McLeary, 1995).

For our schools to be collectively successful, we need to teach each individual how to participate in the totality of constructive activity within our communities. As the educational leaders of democratic communities, we need to express our deepest concerns for the success of all. This is accomplished by instituting the best educational practices and considering the needs of the whole community in the implementation of school programs and alternatives. School boards and superintendents need to work closely together to plan for the successful schooling of all the community's constituents (Goodman, Fulbright, & Zimmerman, 1997). This chapter's purpose is to represent the voices that often are left out of the board's meetings. Through our listening to our students' stories, we may help to promote a greater understanding of the unique educational requirements possessed by so many of our students and of what can be effective in providing them with school success.

How this can be accomplished will depend greatly upon your ability to help all of your students to forge a connection between themselves and the tasks that you present for them. The more relevant and engaging the assignment, the greater will be the outcome in student achievement. We have great problems to solve in the next 100 years. We face tremendous challenges within our communities to develop citizens who feel valued and esteemed as opposed to marginalized and alienated. Educators must be ever cognizant of the need to include everyone in the prosperity and opportunity our communities can provide. Success for all is not an unrealistic goal; it is the goal (Slavin, 1996).

None of this can occur without the leadership of a teacher and an administration supportive of high levels of quality instruction for all the school's students. According to Slavin (1996), "The only way to substantially increase the effectiveness of educational practice, to ensure that the tireless efforts of dedicated teachers actually pay off in greater student learning, is to put into teachers' hands methods and materials capable of ensuring success for every student" (p. 2). Whatever program or methodology you employ as a teacher, the key element is that you strive to make every student a success. The ultimate test for each of us as responsible citizens living within an active democracy is to work for the attainment of civil, political, and social rights fundamental to democracy's perpetuation (Mendieta, 1999). If we all work together, we can create communities that are safe, sacred, and esteemed by their inhabitants. If we fail, we will leave a shameful legacy. As educators, our calling is to work toward the successful resolution of these fundamental social problems. This is the praxis and the pedagogy of love.

This chapter is written to appeal to you, the beginning educator, to look for the werewolves in your class and to not be afraid of their scratch or bite. These outsiders are waiting for an invitation to be included, and you have to be the one that extends yourself to them to accept your invitation. This is our chance to learn ways in which we can improve the pedagogy and praxis that we, as the educators and stewards of our communities, are called upon to perform. Working in the field of education today is the most difficult and challenging work that anyone can do. However, teaching every student means not giving up or letting a student convince you that they are unworthy of your love. This is not a romantic love. Teaching is the manifestation of a love of humanity (Freire, 1970), and it requires a sense that no matter how the student wishes to present, you still see the potential for his or her success in your classroom. Cornel West (1999) states, "Democracy always raises the fundamental question: What is the role of the most disadvantaged in relation to the public interest" (p, 9). Our most disadvantaged and challenged students are telling us, "It is time for a change!"

REFERENCES

Beane, J. A. (1997). *Curriculum integration: Designing the core of democratic education.* New York: Teachers College Press.

Bourdieu, P. (1993). *The field of cultural reproduction.* New York: Columbia University Press.

Boyer, E. L. (1995) The educated person. In J. A. Beane (Ed.), *Toward a coherent curriculum: The 1995 ASCD Yearbook.* Alexandria, VA: Association for the Supervision and Curriculum Development

Bretts, J., Rueben, K., & Danenberg, A. (2000). *Equal access, equal resources? The distribution of school resources and student achievement in California.* The Public Policy Institute. [Online]. Available: http:/www.ppic.org/publications/PPIC128/index.html

Cairns, R., & Cairns, B. (1994). *Lifelines and risks: Pathways of youth in our time.* Cambridge, England: Cambridge University Press.

California Post Secondary Education Committee. (1998). As cited in the California State University web site. *What are the eligibility rates of 1996 public High School Graduates for the California State University?* [On-line]. Available: www.cpu.edu/postedu.htm

Catterall, J. (1998). Risk and resilience in student transitions to high school. *American Journal of Education, 106*(2), 302-333.

Chomsky, N. (1999). *Profit over people.* New York: Seven Stories Press.

Clemings, R. (2000). School scores, credentials linked. *The Fresno Bee, 7,* p. B1.

Digest of Educational Attainment (1998). All levels of education. [Online]. Available: http://nces.ed.gov/pubs99/digest98/

Digest of Educational Statistics (1998). Outcomes of education. [Online]. Available: http://nces.ed.gov/pubs99/digest98/

Etzioni, A. (1983). *An immodest agenda.* New York: McGraw-Hill.

Ford, B. A. (1992). Multicultural education training for special educators working with African-American youth. *Exceptional Children, 59(2),* 107-115.

Freire, Paulo. (1970). *Pedagogy of the oppressed.* New York: Continuum.

Giroux, H. (1997). *Pedagogy and the politics of hope: Theory, culture, and schooling.* Boulder, CO: Westview.

Goodman, G. S. (1999). *Alternatives in education: Critical pedagogy for disaffected youth.* New York: Peter Lang.

Goodman, G. S. (2001). *Reducing hate crimes and violence among American youth: Creating transformational agency through critical praxis.* New York: Peter Lang.

Goodman, R., Fulbright, L., and Zimmerman, W. (1997). *Getting there from here: School board-superintendent collaboration: Creating a school governance team capable of raising student achievement.* Arlington, VA: Educational Research Service.

Gronlund, N. (1998). *Assessment of student achievement.* Boston: Allyn & Bacon.

Hao, L., & Bronstead-Bruns, M. (1998, July). Parent child differences in educational expectations and the academic achievement of immigrant and native students. *Sociology of Education, 71,* 175-198.

Hinds, M. deC. (2000). *Violent kids: Can we change the trend?* Dubuque, IA: Edward J. Arnone.

Hoggerth, S. L., Biosjoly, J., & Duncan, G. (1998, July). Parent's extrafamial resources and children's school attainment. *Sociology of Education, 71,* 246-268.

Howard, P. W. (1998, November 4). Lundgren's losing campaign infected republican morale. *The Fresno Bee*, pp. A1, A14.

Ignatiev, N., & Garvey, J. (1994). *Race traitor*. New York: Routledge.

Ingersoll, S., & LeBoeuf, D. (1997, February). Reaching out to youth out of the educational mainstream. *Juvenile Justice Bulletin*, pp. 1-11.

Kohl, H. (1994). *I won't learn from you: And other thoughts on creative maladjustment*. New York: The New Press.

MacLeod, J. (1995). *Ain't no makin' it*. Boulder, CO: Westview Press.

McChesney, J. (1997). *What works in schools: Forum and reform for the 21st century*. [On-line]. Available: ericae.net/edo/htm

McLaren, P. (1994). *Life in schools: An introduction to critical pedagogy in the foundations of education*. New York: Longman.

McLaren, P. (1999). *Schooling as a ritual performance: Toward a political economy of educational symbols and gestures*. New York: Rowman & Littlefield.

McLeary, B. (1997). Survey of remedial education in higher education more relevant to politics than to teaching and curriculum. *Composition Chronicle, 10(4)*, 1-22.

Mendieta, E. (1999). Becoming citizens, becoming Hispanics. In D. Batstone & E. Mendieta (Eds.), *The good citizen*. New York: Routledge.

Mouffe, C. (1988). Radical democracy: Modern or postmodern? In A. Ross (Ed.), *Universal abandon? The politics of postmodernism* (pp. 31-45). Minneapolis: The University of Minnesota Press.

National Commission on Excellence in Education. (1983). *A nation at risk: The imperative for educational reform*. Washington, DC: U.S. Government Printing Office.

Newman, F., & Boyer, E. L. (1985). *Higher education and American resurgence*. Princeton, NJ: The Carnegie Foundation.

Nieto, S. (1996). *Affirming diversity: The sociopolitical context of multicultural education*. White Plains, NY: Longman.

Olivares, V. (1999). Making sense of the chaos in the classroom. Unpublished ethnography, Fresno, CA.

Pianta, R., & Walsh, D. (1996). *High risk children in schools: Constructing sustaining relationships*. New York: Routledge.

Posner, G. J. (1995). *Analyzing the curriculum*. New York:McGraw-Hill.

President's Commission for a National Agenda for the Eighties (1980). *The quality of American life in the eighties*. Princeton, NJ: A Report to the Panel on the Quality of Life.

Sarason, S. B. (1990). *The predictable failure of educational reform*. San Francisco: Jossey-Bass.

Senge, P. M. (1990). *The fifth discipline: The art and practice of the learning organization*. New York: Doubleday.

Slavin, R. E. (1996). *Education for all*. Lisse: Swets & Zeitlinger

Smith, F. (1986). Why learning fails: Wastelands of school instruction. In *Insult to intelligence: The bureaucratic invasion of our classrooms*. New York: Arbor House.

Soto, G. (1998). Werewolf friends. In J. Ragan & L. Rodriguez (Eds.), *Rattle: Poetry for the 21st century*. Los Angeles: Bomb Shelter Press.

Steinberg, S. R., & Kincheloe, J. (1997). *Changing multiculturalism*. Buckingham, England: Open University Press.

Suoranta, J. (1999). Memory and the construction of identities: The integrated media machine as a tool for cultural learning. In M. Yla-Kotola, J. Suoranta, & S. Inkinen (Eds.), *The integrated media machine: A theoretical framework*. Helsinki, Finland: University of Lapland.

Triesman, U. (1992). Studying students studying calculus: A look at the lives of minority mathmatics students in college. *The College Mathematics Journal, 23(5),* 362-372.

Upcraft, M., & Schuh, L. (1996). *Assessments in student affairs*. San Francisco: Jossey-Bass.

Vygotsky, L. S. (1978). *Mind in society: The development of higher thinking processes*. (M. Cole, V. John-Steiner, S. Scribner, & E. Souberman, Eds. & Trans.). Cambridge, MA: Harvard University Press.

West, C. (1999). The moral obligations of living in a democratic society. In D. Batstone & E. Mendieta (Eds.), *The good citizen*. New York: Routledge.

Willinsky, J. (1998). *Learning to divide the world*. Minneapolis: University of Minnesota Press.

Zhou, M., & Bankston, C. (1994). Social capital and the adaption of the second generation: Case of Vietnamese youth in New Orleans. *International Migration Review, 28*(4), 821-942.

CHAPTER NINE

The Art(s) of Multicultural Education

Susan Schlievert

California State University, Fresno

"Not everything that we want to say can be said in language."

Elliot Eisner (1998)

Pablo Picasso, Guernica, 1937.
©2003 Estate of Pablo Picasso/Artists Rights Society (ARS), New York

The arts are the most basic element of the school curriculum. The arts are the language of civilization, the fundamental medium of communication, and the framework for culture. They provide a means to understand different groups by exploring both diversity and the common elements and functions of arts across cultures.

Ask students about their favorite subject or activities at school, and the majority will include the arts. Not math facts, not reading and answering questions from the end of a chapter, not a written book report. Rather, they will most often cite art activities as their most memorable experiences. Why? Because it was fun? Because it was a respite from other subjects? Or was it because it involved all students, regardless of background, ethnicity, disability, or preferences?

In our society and in our schools, we place great emphasis on linguistic and mathematical intelligences (Gardner, 1993). We test students in reading, language, and math. If students do poorly, society labels them and increases the same regimen. But research shows that the arts actually increase performance in all curricular areas (Catterall, Chapleau, & Iwanaga, 2000). Yet many people continue to downplay these results and decrease or eliminate arts instruction. Teachers must understand that the arts cannot be relegated to the category of "extra," or "reward," or "free time."

A few years ago I received a letter from a former student. He had been asked to write about his favorite year in school and his favorite teacher. I was honored, of course, that he had chosen me, but I was even more interested in the reasons why he chose me. "We built an Egyptian tomb," he said. He had made tomb paintings, pounded papyrus, swathed a mummy, and painted a sarcophagus. What he didn't add was that he had learned history, geography, math, science, and, yes, art skills through the project. He read and wrote about Egypt. He compared civilizations and analyzed societal practices. But this was fun! The arts enabled the student to effectively learn about ancient Egypt, a subject required by state frameworks and district standards.

So why should the arts be included in the curriculum? For cultural awareness and appreciation? To integrate with other disciplines? To motivate? To promote cognition? In actuality, the arts encompass all of these reasons, while presenting a comprehensive view of the contributions of all groups.

While acknowledging the contributions of different cultures and groups, the arts encourage students to understand art from other cultures and therefore to understand other cultures in general. They have the power to transcend language barriers and bring diverse groups together. An arts curriculum integrates universal, cultural, and individual features, so that nothing need be foreign in a multicultural society (Katter, 1991).

"First in the heart is the dream. Then the mind starts seeking a way."

Langston Hughes (1995)

Students need to be understood and they need to express themselves, but language is not the only way to express ideas or emotions. An arts curriculum is the vehicle that allows students to communicate with others, regardless of language.

We comprehend the world in many ways. To a journalist, a devastating storm may be described in terms of human suffering and of the property destruction caused by it. A meteorologist might view the same storm as isobars and subsequent forecasts. An artist may depict the storm in bold strokes of color and huge waves or threatening winds. A composer may utilize the unique sounds of the instruments to convey the force of the storm. None of these things produces a total understanding of the nature of a storm, but taken together they provide a more complete representation than any one of them individually. The combination happens because of the way the brain processes information—in both a linear fact-based manner and in a holistic, emotion-based manner. Students need to engage in both.

The arts afford students the opportunity to express themselves in different ways. The arts embrace the concept of novelty, valuing new perspectives and different methods. They form cultural connections, both to the native culture and as a window to different ones, and show how cultures are interconnected and interrelated. The arts open a genuine dialogue between student artist and the audience.

Tan was a student who came to California from Vietnam. He was very quiet and shy, having little interaction with his classmates. One day, before winter break, he pulled out some colored paper and started folding. He soon had made complex forms (animals, lanterns, flowers) out of folded paper. The other students were fascinated and asked him to show them how he did this. His artistic endeavors opened up a dialogue with others, and he eventually explained the cultural significance of his work. Subsequently, his schoolwork improved.

Dave's family escaped from the fighting in Eastern Europe. He, too, was a quiet student who underestimated his abilities. One day, instead of writing a report for class, he asked if he could do a project. He made a collage out of his grandfather's collected scraps: a piece of his entry documentation to the United States, pictures of the bombed neighborhood where his family had lived, drawings of lost objects, photographs of missing relatives, bits of fabric and ribbon. He told the story of their escape and relocation without writing a paragraph. Both students and teachers were impressed with his project and asked him about his experiences. He was asked to present his work to a large organization.

Eddie came from the poorest section of town. He had difficulty processing language, both in English and in the Spanish spoken at home. He was overweight and spoke with a lisp. In short, Eddie was either ridiculed or ignored. Then Eddie enrolled in drama. His director cast him in a major role that required Eddie to memorize lines and speak clearly. The director worked with Eddie to learn material in different ways. Eddie succeeded, and other students noticed him. After high school, Eddie was offered a job in New York as a production assistant to a major Broadway producer.

Mira felt that she was different because of her Persian background and Muslim beliefs. She rarely volunteered or contributed in her middle school classes; she kept to herself. One day Mira's history teacher introduced Islam with a tessellation mosaic project. Mira volunteered to explain the practice of nonrepresentational art in Muslim culture. Her art project was an example for the other students, and they learned more about her.

Danny was very small, resembling a seven-year-old when he was in reality fourteen. He had been teased and taunted for years. Then he was cast in a touring production that addressed smoking, substance abuse, and healthy living. He was an instant hit! The young audience related to him, his cast members valued him, and other students looked at him differently. He was included in social events, and he gained confidence. In addition, students learned about the medications he took daily that contributed to his small stature.

Sherri was obese. The 200 pound high school student liked to read and study complex issues. She sang in the choir, but few students realized how talented she was. Then Sherri was cast as the lead in the school play. She was required to sing, dance, and be a leader. The response was overwhelming. The newspaper wrote about her, she was voted into student government, and she won an award. Other students looked at her accomplishments instead of her weight.

Jamahl was a middle school student who wanted to be "tough and cool." A guest artist came to his U.S. history class and taught the students how to make cornhusk dolls. She explained the legend and background of the dolls, and then she showed the students how to make them. Jamahl was hesitant at first; this was not an activity that fit his image of "tough and cool." After some coaxing, he started to make the doll. He became engrossed in the project and had a wonderful experience. The next day, he told his classmates that the guest teacher was "mega-cool!"

Alicia was the daughter of a football player and a cheerleader, but Alicia did not fit their mold. She resembled her father in stature and style. She was creative, introspective, and uninterested in the family tradition of sports and sororities. She was losing interest in school until she auditioned and was cast as the lead in the school play. When her family came opening night to see her, they were amazed! They had no idea that she could act or perform. Their expectations and pressures changed, and they found value in her activities and preferences. They sent her to the university of her choice, not the college of her relatives. She was finally valued for herself, not as a reflection of her parents.

Jerry was not a good student. His parents had doctoral degrees, but Jerry did not excel in school. His teacher caught him drawing during a lecture; the teacher recognized his talent. He asked Jerry to draw birds for a classroom project. When Jerry's parents came to school for a conference, the teacher pointed out the drawings to them without identifying the artist. One parent said, "Audubon?" The teacher replied, "No, your son!" The parents were shocked. They did not know that Jerry could draw. He had never shown them his drawings because he felt that they would not be valued. The parents realized that they had neglected to recognize their son's talent. In an emotional exchange, they praised their son.

All of these students were from some minority or repressed group. They all benefited from artistic experiences, as did their fellow classmates. Their teachers all embraced diversity and variety, though their roles varied from didactic to enabling, from guiding to tutoring. The arts were the "hook" that drew the students in and kept them by encouraging, or rather demanding, active participation.

"Education is experience."

John Dewey (1938)

Recently, I talked to a woman who had returned from a vacation in Mexico. While there she had visited Chichen Itza. She was astounded by the pyramids, not just because of the architecture and design, but because she had no idea that pyramids even existed outside of Egypt. She had learned about pyramids in school, but only about a few in Egypt. She added that she had learned about several artists in school, but that all were European males. Art contributions from other groups had not been presented, and she was surprised to learn about female composers and artists. As teachers, we must insure that arts are defined so that they encompass other cultures and diversities; they are not just pretty pictures or nice music.

Although the arts are action-based and open-ended, that does not mean that they are not "disciplined." The arts are not a "free-for-all" activity. Just as an architect creates an innovative design based on solid mechanical knowledge, so should students' work be based on an arts foundation. Teachers set standards, establish rubrics, and provide examples. To acquire such skills requires hard work, rigor, and discipline. They are assessed on a common set of standards (Getty Center, 1990). Trying to create without a study of what has gone before puts one in the unfair role of "first artist."

The arts remove student resistance to engagement and attract students' attention. They support collaboration, often a characteristic of cultures. They are "more of a dialogue than a monologue, more of a conversation than a lecture" (Eisner, 1994). They allow the students to apply, extend, synthesize, and relate knowledge. Arts generate intrinsic motivation and assessment. They encourage reflection, including "What more do I need to know?"

Lessons involving the arts spark interest in a topic; they relate content with importance, relevance, and connection. They help to develop the reasoning and problem-solving skills necessary for a productive work force and to the learning of other subjects. They can be viewed through different lenses: structural, historical, cultural, aesthetic. They should be highly valued, not deemed nonacademic, elective, cocurricular, or extracurricular.

*"There is unity among art's functions across cultures
and a diversity in its form."*

F. Graeme Chalmers (1996)

State Departments of Education, too, have called for the arts to be taught. For example, California's Visual and Performing Arts Framework represents a "strong commitment to include dance, drama/theatre, music, and the visual arts in the educational life of all students as they progress from kindergarten through high school" (1996). The Frameworks promote "using the arts to motivate, enhance, and enlighten learning" (p. 125). In addition, some school districts have developed a comprehensive matrix to address multicultural artist and activities (Schlievert & Johnson, 1998). Teachers can use these resources to begin introducing the arts to students.

> *"A painter takes the sun and makes it into a yellow spot.*
> *An artist takes a yellow spot and makes it into a sun."*

Pablo Picasso in Siler (1996)

How does the classroom teacher incorporate the arts into the curriculum?

The first step is an awareness—of the importance of the arts in appreciating diversity, of their benefit to cognitive development, of the relationship between arts and other academic achievement, and of the ability of the arts to transcend language. The teacher must examine his/her own beliefs and knowledge about the arts in order to present lessons that utilize the many contributions of different groups.

The next step is to add lessons that include ethnic/diverse content. For example, quilts can be incorporated as a part of history lessons, including Amish quilts, Rinngold's African-American representations, and Hmong story quilts.

Students can compare and contrast styles. Culture is the entire pool of artifacts accumulated by a group during its history (Cole, 1996). Students need to realize that artifacts were also produced by cultures other than the dominant one. They need to learn to evaluate, appreciate, and value different media and techniques.

Finally the students can use art to confront social issues (Banks & Banks, 1993). The arts perpetuate, change, and enhance culture (Gerbrands, 1957). For example, the topics of slavery and intolerance manifest themselves in artwork and cross many cultural boundaries. Music, too, has served to expose and reflect on social issues, from Negro spirituals to jazz, from troubadours to English ditties.

In a similar manner, Zimmerman (1990) suggested five approaches to art education. The first approach was to add lessons with multicultural content. The second approach used cross-cultural celebrations, such as holidays. The third approach examined the arts of particular groups. The fourth approach reflected diversity in a multiethnic and multicultural arts curriculum. The fifth approach, decision making and social action, required students to question and challenge the arts.

Although art lessons stand by themselves, they can easily be incorporated into other curricular lessons: singing to augment reading and spelling (think

"Conjunction Junction" on cartons), using rhythms and chants during math, enhancing science lessons though drawings, dancing for P.E. and social skills, recreating history through the arts, putting on a play to dramatize a piece of literature, and studying artwork to develop higher-level thinking and vocabulary development. Arts activities train students to use their entire intellectual capacity.

An effective way to include the arts of different groups is to teach through themes. Animals, portraits, people at play, people at work, the sea, landscapes, fantasy, realism, flowers, abstract, masks, sculpture, ritual, architecture, power, leadership, and textiles are just a few of the possibilities. For example, masks are prevalent in most cultures, but students in the United States associate them with Halloween. This provides an easy introduction to the masks of Africa, to Oceanic masks, to Venice Carnival masks, to Mardi Gras masks, to German Fasching masks, to Native American masks, and to makeup. Portraiture can be examined through eighteenth-century painters, Sepik River masks, Moche portrait vessels, and gold Benin sculptures. Sculpture can be studied through Michelangelo, Henry Moore, African akua'ba, and South American Olmec heads. Animals can include Colima dogs, Oaxaca painted animals, British paintings, Garcia's Blue Dog series, and many others.

Music is another area where students can find crossovers from many cultures. Much "pop" music reflects the styles of other cultures, from Latin to African, from Asian to Haitian. Current dance is an amalgam of many cultures and styles.

"If I could tell you what I want, I wouldn't need to dance."

Isadora Duncan (1927)

What better way is there to address multicultural education, to include all cultures, than through the arts? Primary grade students are aware of social attitudes (Chalmers, 1996). This is where the arts of diversity need to begin. They sustain interest, address all modalities, incorporate different styles and processes, and express different viewpoints. Students can discern similarities in objects and uses. These students should view artwork and be involved with a variety of materials. Upper elementary school students can recognize the purposes for art. They can discover similar reasons for art production by different groups. Middle school students look for meaning. They can identify styles and work more independently at art production. High school students can be urged to consider aesthetics and connections. They can relate the arts to their own experiences.

At an educational forum, an award-winning poet was asked if "rap" was poetry. He replied that it was, but that a lot of it was not very good poetry. His comments spoke to the alienation some students feel about the arts. If "rap" is legitimized by a renowned poet, perhaps student rappers could be encouraged to listen to other poetry. After all, it is just another style, and not all "serious" poetry is good.

With high-stakes testing, one hears concern about having enough time to teach everything. Arts education can actually increase instructional time and efficiency. Imagine driving down the street and coming to a corner. A sign tells you to decrease your speed by removing your foot from the accelerator, apply pressure to the brakes, and to not enter the intersection. Or, you could see a stop sign. Some things are easier to understand and quicker to teach, explain, or learn through nonverbal means. In this case, a red hexagonal stop sign delivers the message.

It is almost impossible to teach the arts in isolation. The arts include specific, inherent outcomes, such as learning to paint a flower. There are ancillary outcomes, as well: science (pistil, stamen, stem, petals, leaves, pollen, moisture), math (number of petals, symmetry, pattern) or language (describe the painting to others, increasing vocabulary). But for students, it's just fun to paint a picture of a flower. Thus, the arts are the tool to integrate curriculum.

> *"There are four main things people do with art. They make it.*
> *They look at it. They understand its place in culture over time.*
> *They make judgments about its quality."*

> Elliot Eisner (1996)

We read about youth spray painting, flashing signs, yelling and stomping. Through the arts, we could read about those same students painting a mural, flashing signs in a drama production about life on the streets, or making sounds through the use of a synthesizer or drums. After all, Keith Haring based his art on graffiti. Teachers can show students a way to express themselves and social concerns in an acceptable way; art on paper, rather than sprayed on public buildings.

At a time when concern has increased about morals, school violence, and values, the arts are in a unique position to address these issues, as well. Educational research about learning through the arts suggests that they contribute to academic success and the development of positive habits and behaviors (Heath, Soep, & Roach, 1998). If, as a society, we value respect, responsibility, fairness, caring, trustworthiness, and citizenship, then we can illustrate and promote these values through the arts.

One way to use the arts to promote character includes reviewing shared values, showing the work(s) of art (prints/reproductions, overheads, internet, PowerPoint) that illustrate the values, eliciting student reaction (Examples: Describe the work? What value does this illustrate? How did the artist express this? How does this relate to you?), and asking students to produce their own artwork, based on a virtue (Examples: posters for environmental issues, "monuments" for special people, t-shirt designs). This encourages classroom discussion by utilizing concrete examples for abstract concepts. The images stimulate discussion about values and ethics. Table 9.1 shows an example of virtues and related artworks.

TABLE 9.1 Values and Examples of Artwork

Value	Artwork
Respect, tolerance, and acceptance	Bartholdi: Statue of Liberty Curtis: Chief Joseph Lin: Viet Nam Wall
Responsibility, duty	Rembrandt: *Night Watch* Audubon: Collection Warhol: *Endangered Species* Hmong story quilts
Fairness, justice	Ringgold: Martin Luther King, Jr., Quilt Lawrence: *Harriet and the Promised Land* Mayer: *Blind Justice*
Caring, concern	Kollwitz: *The Tower of Mothers* Rivera: *The Flower Carrier* Curtis: *Mother and Child* Ghirlandaio: *An Old Man and His Grandson* Tanner: *The Banjo Lesson* Cassatt: *The Bath* AIDS Quilt
Trustworthiness, integrity	Hicks: *Peaceable Kingdom* Homer: *Snap the Whip*
Citizenship	Leutze: *Washington Crossing the Delaware* Trumball: *Signing of the Declaration of Independence* Rosenthal: *Iwo Jima Flag Raising* Rockwell: *Freedom of Speech* Wood: The *Midnight Ride of Paul Revere* Hassam: *Allies Day*

Sometimes an excuse for the exclusion of the arts is monetary; some say that they cannot afford materials. Find them! Ask printing companies for the extra unused paper they ordered for special jobs. Save fabric scraps, egg cartons, old magazines. Reuse aluminum foil to make sculptures. Include dance and drama; they require little or no materials. Make musical instruments out of almost anything. Waste no paper; use half sheets if possible. Approach a parent club or community organization to sponsor art materials. Access the myriad images from the Internet (ex. www.artsednet.getty.edu). Write a grant. Visit an online museum. Ask! Look for alternate means and aim for less ethnocentrism.

"Differences are easy to find. It's the similarities you really have to dig for."
Pasco said, "Sometimes the differences overwhelm the similarities."
"But only if you let them," Lorraine replied.

Neil Bissondath (1993)

The arts are the language of civilizations. The visual and performing arts are a basic medium of communication that motivates and integrates. They promote cultural awareness. Therefore, students need a comprehensive, written, sequential arts program at all grade levels, from kindergarten to twelfth grade. In addition, the arts should be included just for arts' sake.

With a global economy, and the subsequent interest in competitors' student performance, some tend to believe that the United States can compete with Germany, Japan, or others simply by adding more time to the day or by adding more math and language courses to the curriculum. But other countries aren't teaching less art than we do; in many cases they are teaching more. Japan, for instance, requires two class periods per week in music and two in art in the elementary school grades. Two more classes in each subject per week are required in grades seven and eight and one course each per week in grade nine. In secondary school there are additional requirements in music and calligraphy. Hungary, a leader worldwide in achievement by eighth and ninth graders in science, requires both voice and instrument training twice a week throughout the first eight years of schooling (Schlievert, 1997).

The Secretary's Commission on Achieving Necessary Skills (SCANS, 1992) emphasized a need for creative, skillful workers and innovative leaders. These skills are intrinsic in the arts. Arts courses train students to use their entire intellectual capacity, and they encourage independent thought.

The arts span cultures and time; they cross disciplines. Who doesn't like some kind of music? Who leaves an office, room, or cubicle blank, not decorated with something? Who has never tapped out the beat to music, or clapped to a song? Artistically literate children need the "basic" that is the arts.

The United States is a nation of immigrants; it has a common culture that is multicultural. As educators, we must insure that all students have access to an arts curriculum—a curriculum that embraces all groups and emphasizes the unity of our world.

Teaching the arts to students gives them the power to express meaning in ways that nothing else can match. The arts are active, creative, self-expressive, and entertaining. The arts endure.

One ought, every day at least, to hear a little song, read a good poem,
see a fine picture and, if it were possible, speak a few reasonable words.

Johann Wolfgang von Goethe, 1749-1832

REFERENCES

Banks, J., & Banks, C. (1993). *Multicultural education.* Boston: Allyn & Bacon.

Bissondath, N. (1993). *The innocence of age.* Toronto: Penguin.

California Visual and Performing Arts Framework for California Public Schools. (1996).

Catterall, J., Iwanaga, J., & Chapleau, R. (1999). Involvement in the arts and human development. In E. B. Fiske (Ed.), *Champions of change: The impact of the arts on learning.* The Arts Education Partnership; The President's Committee on the Arts and Humanities; The John D. and Catherine T. MacArthur Foundation; and the GE Fund.

Chalmers, F. (1996). *Celebrating pluralism: Art, education, and cultural diversity.* Los Angeles: Getty Education Institute for the Arts.

Cole, M. (1996). *Cultural psychology.* Cambridge: Harvard University Press.

Dewey, J. (1938). *Experience & education.* New York: Collier Books.

Duncan, I. (1927). *My life.* New York/London: Liveright.

Eisner, E. (1992). *The role of disciplined-based art education in America's schools.* Los Angeles: Getty Center for Education in the Arts.

Eisner, E. (1994). *The educational imagination.* New York: Macmillan College Publishing.

Gardner. H. (1993). *Frames of mind: The theory of multiple intelligences.* New York: Basic Books.

Gerbrands, A. (1957). *Art as an element of culture.* Leiden, Netherlands: E. J. Brill.

Getty Center for Education in the Arts (1990-1998). *Proceedings.* Harvard University: Project Zero (REAP: Reviewing Education and the Arts Project).

Heath, S.B., Soep, E., & Roach, A. (1998, November). Living the arts through language and learning: A report on community-based youth organizations. In *Americans for the Arts Monographs*, *2*(7), 1-20. Washington, DC: Americans For The Arts.

Hughes, L. (1995). Freedom's plow. In A. Rampersad (Ed.), *The collected poems of Langston Hughes.* New York: Vintage Classics.

Katter, E. (1991). Meeting the challenge of cultural diversity. *Visual Arts Research, 17*(2), 28-32.

Schlievert, J., & Johnson, P. (1998). *Visual and performing arts standards.* Clovis, CA: Clovis Unified.

Schlievert, S. (1997). *The economy and education.* Doctoral dissertation. University of California, and California State University Joint Doctoral Program.

Secretary's Commission on Achieving Necessary Skills, U.S. Department of Labor. (1992). *Learning a living: A SCANS report for America 2000.* Washington, DC: Government Printing Office.

Siler, T. (1996). *Think like a genius.* New York: Bantam Books.

Zimmerman, E. (1990). Questions about multiculture and art education. *Art Education, 43*(6).

CHAPTER TEN

What Our Second–Language Students Can Teach Us About Learning

Case Studies of Two Hmong High School Boys

Pauline Sahakian

University of California, Merced

HOW I LEARNED ENGLISH

It was in an empty lot
Ringed by elms and fir and honeysuckle.
Bill Corson was pitching in his buckskin jacket,
Chuck Keller, fat even as a boy, was on first,
His t-shirt riding up over his gut,
Ron O'Neill, Jim, Dennis, were talking it up
In the field, a blue sky above them
Tipped with cirrus.

And there I was,
Just off the plane and plopped in the middle
Of Williamsport, Pa., and a neighborhood game,
Unnatural and without any moves,
My notions of baseball and America
Growing fuzzier each time I whiffed.

So it was not impossible that I,
Banished to the outfield and daydreaming
Of water, or a hotel in the mountains,
Would suddenly find myself in the path
Of a ball stung by Joe Barone.
I watched it closing in
Clean and untouched, transfixed
By its easy arc before it hit
My forehead with a thud.

I fell back,
Dazed, clutching my brow,
Groaning, "Oh, my shin, oh my shin,"
And everybody peeled away from me
And dropped from laughter, and there we were,
All of us writhing on the ground for one reason
Or another.

Someone said "shin" again,
There was a wild stamping of hands on the ground,
A kicking of feet, and the fit
Of laughter overtook me too,
And that was important, as important
As Joe Barone asking me how I was
Through his tears, picking me up
And dusting me off with hands like swatters,
And though my head felt heavy,
I played on till dusk
Missing flies and pop-ups and grounders
And calling out in desperation things like
"Yours" and "take it," but doing all right,
Tugging at my cap in just the right way,
Crouching low, my feet set,
"Hum baby" sweetly on my lips.

Gregory Djanikian

WHO ARE THE HMONG?

The Hmong are the newest immigrants to come to America. They came from the plateaus of northern Laos. They are known to have been one of the most ancient peoples of Asia. During prehistoric times their ancestors resided in central China until they came under attack by the Han Chinese. Faced with humiliation, imprisonment, and death, they migrated southward to the mountains of southern China. But some continued on, crossing the border into northern Vietnam or journeying westward to the hills of Laos. Out of necessity, they turned from lowland farming to adopt a slash-and-burn method and organized their villages to be almost completely self-sufficient. In Laos, as the population grew, the Hmong began moving into central Laos. By 1947 they were recognized as official members of the Laotian community (Bliatout, Downing, Lewis, & Yang, 1988; Long, 1992).

Now citizens of Laos, the Hmong defended their new country, helping the American military against the North Vietnamese (1961-1973). Thousands of Hmong were killed, their fields and villages burned. They became "displaced persons" surviving on rations provided by the military and the U.S.-supported government. In 1975, the communist military again retaliated against the Hmong, who sought refuge by swimming and rafting across the Mekong River to escape into Thailand. Those who had close ties with the United States were granted asylum in America (Bliatout et al., 1988). Brought by the CIA at the end of the Vietnam War, the Hmong were settled into agriculturally rich regions such as California's Central Valley to integrate into a strong agricultural economy.

The Hmong are a new culture to the American scene. This chapter will reveal the struggles and expectations of the children and grandchildren of Hmong immigrants who are attending our schools and attempting to succeed in their new homeland. As you read about the progress of two Hmong high school boys—Kaying and Mua—you will learn how their writing in English developed. You will also come to understand how their learning was influenced by their attitudes and actions, their classroom instruction and socialization experiences, and their acculturation to life in America.

THE EDUCATIONAL DISADVANTAGES OF HMONG CHILDREN

Many Hmong students enrolled in California high schools are the children and grandchildren of Laotian villagers who were barred from education by not only a lack of money but also the long distance between the village and school. Some who stayed in the Thai refugee camps did attend the Thai government school and learned to read and write in Thai. However, most possess no writing literacy in either Hmong or the Laotian language and have no written language base from which they can transfer the skills required in written discourse (Cummins, 1981, 1983; Krashen, 1981, 1982). Consequently, Hmong children are at an educational disadvantage in our schools.

Historically, the records indicate that we have not been very successful with most second-language learners (De La Luz Reyes, 1992; Delgado-Gaitan, 1987). Moreover, learning to speak English is only the beginning of their struggles. The difficult transition from conversational to academic English—the reading and writing proficiency demanded of our students to succeed in American society—delays academic progress for most second-language students at the high school level (Collier, 1990; Ramirez, 1992).

To address the problems of second-language learners, a large body of research has focused on models of second-language acquisition (Dulay, Burt, & Krashen, 1982; Ellis, 1994). Other researchers have examined how first-language learning relates to second language learning (Cummins, 1981, 1983; De La Luz Reyes, 1992; Long & Richard, 1990), and how individual factors such as age and motivation influence learning (Gardner, 1985; Schumann, 1978). Still other researchers have focused on the writing of second-language learners (Canale, Frenette, & Bélanger, 1988; Kroll, 1990). Researchers of second-language writers have relied on the studies of writing development and writing processes of native English speakers such as Britton (1970), Elbow (1973), Flower and Hayes (1977), Graves (1983), Moffett (1968), and Murray (1968).

The findings from these researchers have guided second-language writing research, and the results establish the similarities between native and nonnative speakers' writing development (Kroll, 1990). More specifically, research shows the composing processes of skilled writers are similar, whether they write in their primary or second language. Similarities in composing processes also exist between unskilled writers in either language. Furthermore, unskilled writers, native and nonnative speakers alike, seem to lack composing competence more than linguistic competence (Krapels, 1990). Having established the similarities, current researchers are beginning to ask about differences in composing between native and nonnative speakers—an area that undeniably needs more study (Kroll, 1990). This chapter will present case-study research that contributes to our understanding of the differences by examining the elements that influence the progress of second-language writers and by identifying patterns of writing development.

The literature suggests that although second language students may rapidly achieve competency in spoken, conversational English, the development of competent reading and writing skills in English takes much longer (Cummins, 1981; Krashen, 1982). Writing competence in particular is critical to secondary academic achievement as well as to college and university success. If we believe that education transforms individuals, liberates them to make informed choices about their lives, then those who "have not" become the powerless in a society (Freire, 1985). Therefore, Hmong students whose families have little or no experience with written language are particularly at risk (Schieffelin & Cochran-Smith, 1984). Inadequate, uninformed writing instruction further limits their opportunities in a democratic society (De La Luz Reyes, 1992).

THE COMPLEX NATURE OF WRITING

There is no question that writing is a difficult, complex activity. Research on writing processes has demonstrated the complexity of producing written text even for the skilled writer (Flower & Hayes, 1981). Some argue that writing involves cognitive processes that are qualitatively different from the processes involved in reading comprehension, listening comprehension, and oral expression (Britton, Burgess, Martin, McLeod, & Rosen, 1975; Moffett, 1968; Smith, 1973). They assert that oral language must be reconstructed to function independently when conveyed in written composition. Moreover, writing is more difficult because it requires creating text—assembling and organizing relevant meanings in harmony to the purpose of the writing, tailoring meanings to the experience and expectation of the reader, and encoding meanings in language that clearly, grammatically, cohesively, and gracefully conveys one's message (Canale, Frenette, & Bélanger, 1988). Finally, the thinking process required for writing development in a first or second language is more difficult to examine than oral communication and reading comprehension. Levels of language acquisition, rate, and means of development, as well as questions about what constitutes proficiency, compound the problem of investigating the writing development of nonnative speakers.

By shedding light on the struggles of Kaying and Mua, and by identifying patterns of change or lack of change in their writing based on Odell's linguistic cues (1977), this chapter will inform teachers of all disciplines as to how they might contribute to their students' improved writing performance and literacy achievement. As you read each case study, try to answer the following questions: What particular factors in the learner's attitude and actions, as well as factors in the school and home environments, inhibit or frustrate this second-language writer? How can your knowledge of these factors inform your teaching? What are the indicators of growth beyond grammatical proficiency that reflect the second-language learner's writing development? Answers to these questions helped to identify the literacy problems and progress of Kaying and Mua, two Hmong high school students. However, the results are applicable to all second-language learners (Sahakian, 1997).

GETTING TO KNOW THE BOYS

Kaying and Mua are cousins who have similar backgrounds: their Hmong cultural heritage, their parents' immigration from refugee camps in Thailand, their entrance into American school after having attended Thai school, their culture shock as non-English speakers, their multiple moves and resettlements, and their experiences attending and graduating from the same high school. Growing up, their culture dominated their lives. Their friends in school and out of school were Hmong. They spoke in Hmong with brothers and sisters at home. They could only relate to their parents in Hmong. They lived in a Hmong world, out of which they stepped for a few hours a day. Only then were they required to think and communicate in English. Each story is similar, yet different in subtle ways, the greatest difference being in the boys' ability to move beyond their fears and feelings of isolation to take charge of their learning.

KAYING'S STORY

Kaying was born in a Lao village in 1976, and three months later, because of the war, the family moved from village to village until they were able to get passage on a boat and crossed the Mekong River to the safety of Ban Vinai refugee camp in Thailand. His mother told him stories of about how she carried him on her back, walking almost on tiptoes, trying hard to be quiet and to keep him quiet, knowing they could have been shot and killed at any moment.

In the camp the families lived together, shifting from one bamboo hut to another. Home meant being under any number of roofs where aunts and uncles lived. Kaying remembered little about his schooling in the Thai camp although he went to school for six years. He said that these early years were very blurry to him, "like something in my eye and can't see clear." What he did remember most was playing with his cousin Mua. They would play war games, mostly using sticks for guns. He also remembered a time he and Mua sneaked out of the camp and then sneaked back in under the wire fence without being caught. Kaying later wrote a story about this adventure. He recalled the guards being "very mean and scary." In 1989 when Kaying was thirteen years old, he and his family moved to California and settled in the Central Valley with an uncle who had sponsored them. No one in the family spoke or understood any English, although they had been through relocation training before coming to America.

KAYING'S ATTITUDE TOWARD LEARNING

Kaying began to learn English in a bilingual class in sixth grade. He described his pace as rather slow and a continual source of frustration for him. In school he felt very lonely most of the time and sometimes scared. His cousin Mua had been placed in another classroom. Kaying said he hated being separated from Mua and felt that he had lost his childhood too soon, forced to learn to survive in a strange land with a difficult language—a task he felt ill prepared to do. His struggles as a second-language learner stayed with him throughout high school. In ninth grade, he described himself as "lost" in regard to his English comprehension. In tenth grade, however, he began to feel more comfortable, though his studies improved quite slowly. He definitely remembered being able to understand much more of what he read.

Kaying's reading experiences were quite varied. From a Hmong tutor at intermediate school he learned to read a little in Hmong and write a little bit, too, in his first language. He stated that he knew the alphabet and "some words" when he saw them written. Mostly at home he would read Thai books, Hmong folk stories in Thai, although he surprised himself by buying John Steinbeck's *Of Mice and Men*. He said that he liked the story because it was about friendship. Sometimes when he was bored, he read the dictionary at home, but he could not understand much. "I always read my school books at home, the novels," he reported. Kaying also said that he viewed reading in Thai as recreational and reading in English as "school work."

While reflecting on his writing development, Kaying criticized himself for his spelling and saw this as a major problem in his writing. He knew that the time he had spent writing did improve his writing skills, "but it took a lot of time to think," he stated. He saw tutoring as the best way for him to learn. Kaying's extreme shyness magnified his need for tutoring and small group instruction.

> When somebody sit with me and points to my mistake, I can fix it. I like small group, because I can look around and pick-up information. It depends on the activity but small group is easier to talk. This is how I learn best, I think. This is how I pass the writing test to graduate. The teacher talk to me about my essay and ask me questions to get ideas to write.

Kaying was rescheduled into a tutoring period during the spring semester of his senior year. He along with another student named Jesus reported to their senior English teacher during a time when her student-teacher was teaching her class. About this experience, Kaying said:

> I sit with my friend Jesus and listen when she talk with him on his paper, too. I like to write my papers over to make the writing better and to fix the grammar mistakes. Now I know better how to write my papers over and fix the thinking.

Because Kaying's senior English teacher was also his tenth grade English teacher, he felt less anxious in her classroom. As a senior, Kaying saw himself becoming more independent and less afraid. "I ask more questions now. I raise my hand sometimes." He raised his hand for the first time in April of his senior year. "I like better to stay after school to talk to the teacher." In retrospect, Kaying wished he had had more teaching of grammar and more tutoring to "point out" his mistakes. He felt that rewriting his essays was very important. "It helps me think of what to say." But he needed someone to talk with him about his writing, to ask him questions, to make him think more about what he was trying to say. About his future schooling he said, "School is very hard for me. I think I will go to City College. I hope, if I can get in."

KAYING'S ACTIONS TOWARD LEARNING

School was very hard for Kaying. Learning English was very hard. Every summer he went to summer school, and in addition to taking courses such as algebra and art, Kaying also took English. He felt as if he was doing all that he could to improve. However, it was not until his sophomore year that Kaying actively sought any help. He said that he spent several lunch times with his English teacher to get help with his papers. He also remembered spending a lot of time rewriting so that his "sentences would make sense." Yet his cousin Mua, who accompanied Kaying to the classroom and stayed with him, always initiated the lunchtime visits. Kaying never asked for help on his own that year. But, the following year, he braved going alone to his junior English teacher for help. He confessed that he was beginning to worry about failing English and not graduating.

> When I was in English 11, I stay after class to ask questions. We read novels and did group discussions. I always listen. The vocabulary is very hard but I try. I want to graduate with Mua [his cousin].

Many of the words in the vocabulary book, such as "dichotomy," "effusive," "fractiousness," and so on, were difficult and foreign to all of the students. One fall day in his senior year, after the teacher pointed to and pronounced all of the words she had written on the board, Kaying buried his head in his book, flipping the pages back and forth, trying to identify synonyms, find definitions, and fill in the appropriate words in the given sentences. Having little luck guessing, he turned to the large dictionary lying on his desk. He looked up the first word, which took about a minute, and then placed his finger under the text as he carefully read the definition. He appeared to be rereading several times, moving his index finger as he did so. Then he looked back at his vocabulary book to find a matching definition or synonym.

The teacher walked around the room, asking students if they needed any help. Kaying said no by shaking his head when she approached him. When she walked away, Jeff, who sat next to Kaying, leaned over towards Kaying's vocabulary book, looking as if he were comparing answers. He pointed at the page, said something, and then watched as Kaying erased and then rewrote one of his answers. Periodically, Jeff looked over Kaying's book to check on his progress. Kaying continued to change answers at Jeff's prompting; however, he never directly asked Jeff for help. Nor did he look at Jeff's book to check his answers. Kaying seemed to play a waiting game, yet he turned down the teacher's offer to help. He later explained, "I don't know where to start with her because I need help on all of the words." Except for his resistance to asking questions, Kaying was a very good student. Throughout the year he remained attentive, concentrated hard when working, followed directions as best he could, and so on. His diligence seemed to convey his belief that if he continued to try, if he continued to work hard, he would improve in his English language skills. It also showed his determination and perseverance. He exhibited no signs of hopelessness.

Finally in April, Kaying raised his hand and asked for further explanation about how to proceed in preparing to write an argument paper. Kaying had listened intently as students discussed the issue. His eyes followed whoever was speaking, trying to comprehend. Finally he asked, "Can you show some example?" In response to his question, the teacher lifted a point from a newspaper article they had just read together and asked the class which side it should go on, pro or con. Several students responded that the author's point made an argument "for" the issue. "That means it is pro. Do you understand, Kaying?" she asked. He shook his head affirmatively. It should be noted that the teacher laughed in a delighted way when Kaying raised his hand. "Is this really you?" she asked, teasing him. He simply smiled a very wide smile before asking his question.

For the rest of the period, Kaying worked the entire time, writing slowly, hesitantly, continually referring to his notes on the instruction guide-sheet. He asked no questions of the teacher, though she checked with him three times, reading over his shoulder and correcting his language use as he wrote. Instead, he depended on his neighbors, Sarah and Jeff, for help with establishing his pro and con arguments. The fact that Kaying dared to ask a question showed him to be more comfortable in the classroom. He even raised his hand in response to the teacher's question: "Who wants to go to college after high school graduation?" He was involved in the lesson, and he focused on what he wanted to say in his argument rather than being concerned about correct language use, with which the teacher would later help. The task at hand was academic in nature and cognitively demanding. Yet Kaying was thinking in English, not translating from his native Hmong. His question about listing pros and cons from the article testified to this. Furthermore, he had developed a working relationship with Sarah and Jeff.

Kaying's lack of confidence and his need for specific direction had been holding him back. In class he took notes only when told to do so. He resisted asking questions while he wrote, even when the teacher tried to make herself available. He realized he was too shy to call attention to himself. However, in June of his senior year he showed himself as having become an active learner.

On Senior Showcase Portfolio Presentation Day, Kaying sat quietly in his group
with three other seniors, two juniors, and a parent volunteer—all strangers to
Kaying. While he waited, he looked through his portfolio, reviewing the pieces
he would read aloud. He kept his head down, eyes fastened on his portfolio,
until the first student started to read. Kaying listened intently to the essays and
to the discussions that followed. When Kaying's turn arrived, he spoke so quietly that the parent volunteer signaled for the students to lean in to hear him. After
the reading, the students asked questions, forcing Kaying to discuss his writing.
The parent who sat next to him encouraged him with pats on the arm and the
group's applause brought a smile to Kaying's serious face.

Although Kaying was not visibly nervous, he confessed to having "flies" in
his stomach. To read his work aloud to strangers was an incredible statement
about how far Kaying had come in his growth as a writer and communicator in
English. He could have stayed home that day to avoid reading his work in public. Instead, he came to school and participated, his action being typical of the
determination he had exhibited the whole year.

KAYING'S SCHOOL ENVIRONMENT
AND THE TEACHING

Kaying was the only Hmong student in a class of mostly white students except
for three Hispanic boys, one of whom, Jesus, had limited English proficiency
akin to Kaying's. In creating a seating chart, the teacher had allowed the students to remain in the seats they had initially selected. Kaying seemed comfortable in his seat, although he did not join Jeff and Sarah in their conversation.
Other students were busy chatting with friends, gossiping, complaining, and
generally being noisy, even after the tardy bell, until the teacher called for attention. Kaying sat quietly as he waited for class to start, but he did seem to be listening to Jeff and Sarah as they leaned backward, talking behind him. A sudden
smile gave away his eavesdropping.

The first lesson for the year involved learning techniques for writing an
abstract from a magazine article. The teacher began by explaining the meaning
of the word "abstract" as taking something out, such as extracting a tooth. She
related the term to a type of writing where "the writer takes out important parts
of something he or she has read and then writes a new piece that contains those
important parts. The new piece is considered an abstract of the original." Then,
to each student she passed out a copy of an article about banking trends in the
1990s from *Business Week* along with a colored highlighter. Slowly reading the
article aloud, she encouraged students to highlight words, sentences, and even
paragraphs they thought to be important.

Kaying went to work, intently listening to the oral reading, highlighting as directed. Later when the teacher discussed what might have been good to highlight as key ideas to be abstracted from the article, Kaying had highlighted these, as well as other parts. The teacher called on students to read aloud their highlighted sentences, asking questions when students highlighted what appeared to be superfluous information. She did not call on Kaying, and he gave no indication of being overly anxious that she would. Her next directions were for the students to write an abstract of the article by connecting their highlighted key ideas, adding words and sentences as necessary.

Again, Kaying went right to work, copying the main ideas he had marked. As his eyes moved from the article to his own paper, he carefully moved his finger along the highlighted text so as not to lose his place. He copied word for word, adding no connectors of his own. Occasionally the teacher glanced over her shoulder to check his progress, moved past several other students, then reminded them all to paragraph as they wrote. Kaying continued copying the words above his index finger, concentrating on correctly spelling each word, oblivious to the teacher's reminder. The comment about paragraphing was for Kaying's benefit, yet the teacher had not considered the level of concentration necessary for Kaying to complete the copying task at hand. Banking language in the article was unfamiliar and difficult. Paragraphing would seem to be at a higher level, to be dealt with only after the students' ideas were collected and connected. Kaying, intent on his copying, missed the teacher's indirect help.

By April the students in Kaying's class were being challenged with higher level thinking and argument writing. A discussion on remedial courses at the college level led to controversial issue essay writing. The teacher had passed out an article from the local newspaper about the concern with so many remedial courses at college campuses. As she read aloud, the students were to highlight the key ideas, which Kaying did. A discussion followed in the form of directed questions from the teacher to help clarify the problem and identify the arguments on both sides. The teacher did not call on Kaying to respond to any of her questions.

Next the teacher gave out a guide-sheet that called for students to write out a definition of remedial classes and also to explain the problem as they saw it. They were allowed either to work together or individually and then compare their responses. Mostly Kaying listened to Jeff and Sarah talk and then wrote what they wrote. The next step was to turn to the large "T" shaped chart on the student's guide sheet and write arguments for remedial classes on one side and arguments against on the other. Students could use information from the article and also think of more arguments on their own. It was at this point that Kaying surprised everyone by asking a question. Later he explained that the topic was important to him because he knew his success as a college student depended on the help he would receive in remedial English classes.

To begin the rough draft, the teacher demonstrated how to write an opening paragraph with a thesis statement that took a clear stand on an issue. She illustrated with topics other than remedial courses at colleges and wrote two paragraphs on the board as models, talking out loud about her thinking process as she wrote the words. Upon completion of their own introductions, students were encouraged to develop as many arguments as they could in the time remaining. (In the next class session the counterargument would be addressed.) For the rest of the period the students composed their first drafts. Kaying wrote two-and-a-half pages!

Although the lesson was difficult, the prewriting activities, including the newspaper article giving both sides of the argument, the discussion that clarified the issue, and the visual/graphic organizer represented by the "T" bar, helped Kaying organize his thoughts. Also, the introduction paragraph models that the teacher provided gave him direction for starting the essay. Perhaps most important was the topic being argued. All students were engaged because the controversy over colleges offering remedial courses directly affected them as potential college students. Kaying successfully completed this assignment. The writing process instructional approach guided him through the first draft and his second draft. Jeff and Sarah tutored him in his use of English as best they could. Each day he came prepared with revisions in hand and for the first time he opened up to other students, allowing Sarah and Jeff to help him.

Kaying spent most of his free time at school with his Hmong cousins. They spoke Hmong together and a little English sometimes, but mostly slang words. He considered his cousins his only friends, and he worried about being alone at the local community college. His Hmong culture strongly influenced his writing, as many of his essays related to the problems of immigrants trying to start a new life in a world of unwelcoming people. He wrote about prejudice, including a letter to school counselors asking that something be done to help people understand their differences. He wrote about the prejudice he observed with the Thai against the Hmong in the camps in Thailand. He wrote about the Vietnam War and the havoc it caused. He wrote an essay on discrimination against Asians in America. One of his senior essays described a combative experience between two Hmong groups that could have been potentially dangerous, and another told of a scary incident in the refugee camp. These personal experiences allowed Kaying to write about what he knew best and what he felt were important issues—being Hmong and trying to adjust to life in America.

KAYING'S WRITING

Although Kaying's ability to construct an acceptable personal experience essay had improved considerably, his expository prose remained problematic for readers. His grammatical and syntactical problems, in particular, frustrated him and limited his ability to express his thoughts. At the same time, this limitation inhibited his ability to work on content development. Yet, his writing had improved over the four years particularly in terms of his intellectual processes, as the examples below illustrate. Kaying's four pieces selected for examination include a personal experience of prejudice, a scary incident when he sneaked out of the refugee camp, a story about a humorous event, and an introduction to his senior portfolio.

Grade 10–Prejudice

Prejudice is a uneducated judgment to other. When I first came to Thailand. I had seen a lots of things that I hadn't been saw before. When we came from Laos the Thai governor have taken us to a little village. They got us some rice, meat and other things.

A few years later, the governor give us independence where we can get out of the city and cut some tree to build our home. That time they have sent some Thai to live with us. When they came to live with us, we started to have problem and we always live under control. We can't do anything about it because we are living in their country so we had to follow their control.

One day they came to our village and made troblem with our peoples, and attack our peoples. Our leader confess about that but their leader doesn't say anything. A few week they still came back to our village again make troblem again we know that four of the Thai have kill after that they never make troblem again.

Grade 11–Sneaking Out of Camp

I remembered one time, my cousin Mua and I sneaked out of the camp, in Ban Vinai. It was the most dangerous time in my life, because the Thai police are very strick and mean.

It was around 12 o'clock in the afternoon. Anyway, I asked Mua to go with me to the creek close to the camp where we stayed. The little creek is on the other side of the street. The police station is inside the camp. Everyone who wants to go out needs to have permission. However, we went to the police station and asked one of the officers for permission. He yelled at us and didn't want us to go near the station. On our way back Mua and I came up with a new idea which is we have to sneak out through the fence. The officer didn't spot us when we sneaked out of camp, because they were too busy playing cards. When Mua and I got to the creek the water was so clean, we can see the fish swimming around. In fact, we even jump in the water and tried to catch them with are hands. Mua got 4 and I got 9 fish, but we let all of them go.

After 1/2 of hour one of the police rode on a motorcycle to patrol the street. He yelled at us because we are outside of the camp. The police in the station all looked at us. Mua and I started running. Mua climbed off the fence. However, my shirt was sticked on the fence. I thought that I were going to be beat up by the police officers. Anyways, the officer ran toward me and I pulled off my shirt hard, and it got tear and I ran fast into the apartment.

Since that happened I never went out the camp. Every time I thought of the issue I got scared and I said to myself that I would not let it happen to me again because the thing I had done would cause me more trouble.

Grade 12 (45 min.)—A Funny Fight

One of the most humorous times in my life was when my cousin Bunlert was going to get into a fight. Everytime I think about what happened I would laugh to myself while everyone else stared at me as if I was insane.

It was the last day of school before Christmas Vacation during my sophomore year. So my friends and I decided to ditch school and go cruising. Our destination for that morning was Avocado Lake. We got there around 8 o'clock in the morning.

It was a bright suning day. Our cars rolled into the parking lots and my friends jumped out like a pack of hungry wolves toward the beach. While we were enjoying ourselves, cars pulled up on the other side of the beach. My cousin Bunlert pointed his finger and said, "Look there, the punk who tried to jump me!" Quickly we jumped in our cars and went to the other side of the beach. Bunlert then jumped out of the car and with his awkward Hmong heart said, "Hey, Man." His enemy confronted him. They were taking turns looking at each other. They got so close to each other I thought they were going to kiss each other. They were so close they looked like they missed each other so *much*.

Then, Bunlert stepped back, took off his shirt, and tied his shirt around his head. The other guy took off his flip flops. They both started to strip one by one, taking off their clothes. It was getting too hilarious so one of the cousin's brother walked in and stopped the whole things. Gosh, I still wonder what would happen if my cousin didn't stop the fight. Would they have taken off each other's clothes?

Grade 12 –Introduction to My Portfolio

During my four yours in high school I have written many papers, and many different articles. The time I spent on the papers I wrote, it improved my writing skills, but it took a lot of time to think. Some of the assignments were easy and some were not. I picked these following essays because it was the best to me. I think that these essays have sample to me every time I thought of the other assignments.

The first piece was the title Dave Thomas, whom dream to have the best restaurant in the world. He worked hard and so that one day his dream of becoming the owner. Just like me, I always dream that one day I'll become a expert of playing soccer no matter how hard I need to practice I won't get up. Thomas is the example for me. I tried hard each day to become successful to near my goal.

The second pieces were titled Interviews. I enjoyed it very much because the assignment was to interviews people that had held their job for three years or more. By getting to know the people and their occupations of teacher, nurse, and social worker I was able to share the information with you. I wanted you, the reader, to learn how people find jobs and why they like the different jobs, so that you and I both can make good decisions after we graduate from high school.

The third pieces is about the Mall Observation. The reason I pick this pieces is because it was the first time in my life I went to observe and wrote it as an assignment in class. I can feel that this paper wasn't hard because I got more information. I read over couple time for myself what needs to be added to make it perfect. After I wrote and received it back from the teacher I can see that my papers was okay, just that I want it more better.

The last piece is Remedial Classes. This assignment was the most frustrate one. When I tried to get information, I have to argue with my partners with con and pro. I haven't find the right ideas to fight with [about] the remedial class. I asked one of the friend how she did and she explained it to me little by little. I never like this essay because I didn't do well on it. However, I was kind of confuse but at least I tried my best to completed it. I worked hard so that the reader would understand my point of view.

After four years in high school, during my freshman and sophomore years, I felt that my spelling have not improve at all. During my junior year, the teacher teaches in class after school help student whose not good in writing. I decided to spend my times after school and attend one class at adult school. Until my senior years I still get help by tutoring and pass all the requirements and to get ready to go to college.

Kaying's most obvious growth is in his fluency development. As his language develops, so does his focus as a writer, as evidenced by his use of details. His description is becoming more concrete, and he is able to create physical context in his narrative writing. He is also in control of time sequence, and he experiments with dialogue. Clearly, the chronology of a narrative guides him as a writer. Expository writing, however, is more difficult, as evidenced by his tangled sentences and convoluted language structures. He is still struggling for words to express his ideas.

MUA'S STORY

A translation of a birth certificate from the Kingdom of Laos indicated that Mua was born on February 5, 1976. His father was a district official, mayor of Nga County, and his mother a housewife. Although neither was formally educated, as an elected governor the father had learned to speak Lao. In Laos, the family was held in high esteem in their village where they farmed rice, bananas, papaya, and vegetables. The father had much help with farming because his wife had given birth to seven boys, but the mother had no daughters to help her. Her eighth child, Mua, was the youngest boy and last child. According to his mother, he was born "in the year of the war." Mua stated that he had no memories of living as a family in the village.

After Mua was born, the family moved from village to village. Then when Mua was two years old, they fled Laos on foot in the night. They changed clothes so as to appear to be Laotian and not be shot. Then they swam across the Mekong River with bamboo poles under their arms to stay afloat. Two-year-old Mua was on his mother's back. His mother told the story of how the water was cold and swift moving; many drowned and some were shot, even another mother with a baby on her back. Mua's mother considered it a miracle that the family made it into Thailand.

Upon reaching the border of Thailand, the family met other relatives, and they rode a bus to a camp called Nongkhai, located at the Thai border, where they stayed for four years. Mua's mother described the prejudice she saw in the eyes of the Thai men who escorted them to the camp. She said that everyone was standing when the bus arrived, eager to get off into a safe environment. When a young boy slipped on the step, an accident that Mua's mother attributed to the "eagle eye" of the Thai man watching him, the man grabbed the boy roughly, pushing him toward those that went ahead, shouting, "You, Moia, watch your step around here!" Mua explained that Moia means a cat in Hmong, "a dirty animal who has no land to live on and no bones to feed on." Mua wrote about this story in his tenth grade English class.

After three years in the camp, Mua's oldest brother left for the United States with his wife, and the remaining family members moved the following year to Camp Ben Vinai in a hilly region close to the Lao border. The year was now 1982. Mua remembered little about the Thai camp except that he played with lots of cousins, particularly his cousin Kaying. Although Mua's official departure date from the refugee camp was listed as June 21, 1988, Mua recalled that his family came to America in 1989 and settled in California. The required transition camp to which all refugees were transported prior to their departure to the United States can explain this gap in time. The transition camp introduced the refugees to American ways to help them better adapt to their new culture. On arrival, Mua was thirteen years old.

MUA'S ATTITUDE TOWARD LEARNING

"I did not give up," Mua stated with his head held high, when asked about his attitude toward learning. He described how much he wanted to be successful in school and how important school was to his future. At the same time he described his isolation in elementary school, his being on the edge of learning by being in the background of the classroom. "Sometimes I felt like I was looking inside a window, and I am on the outside," he said. He admitted that he was no longer afraid to speak up if called on by the teacher or to give an oral report, but after seven years in American schools, he still had not braved raising his hand and volunteering to talk. He hoped to someday overcome this hesitation, for Mua had set high goals for himself that he attributed to keeping him on track in school and never giving up.

> I will go to the State University next year. I study very hard so I can do this. Every day I go home from school and study at the big table all by myself. Nobody helps me. I do my work all by myself. It's okay. I like to work by myself.

Mua expressed that the way he learned best in school was by one-on-one tutoring. He preferred for someone to point out his mistakes so he could correct them, especially in his writing. "I think when I rewrite my essays they always get better. I wish I had more grammar lessons. That help me a lot." Small group learning was "okay" in Mua's opinion, but it depended on the activity and the students with whom he was grouped. Sometimes it helped him to understand the lesson better when he listened to other students discussing it in a small group, but sometimes the kids played around and talked too much and wasted time. "I don't learn anything from this kind of instruction." In regard to his writing, Mua felt confident about what he had learned of his composing process, yet mechanical problems in English continued to plague him.

> I'm writing much better now, but it take a very long time. I think my stories are the best. I know what to think about and how to ask myself questions to make it better. It take me a long time to learn this. I write best about my stories. I like to write about things I remember because then I know what to say next. When I write, it is best for someone else to look at it and to give me idea. In fact I always have to have idea from other students when I write. This helps me very much. My spelling is terrible. However, I have to try to improve. The computer is good because it finds my mistakes and I can fix them. I worry that next year at State College I will fail with my writing, but I hope not. I will try my best.

MUA'S ACTIONS TOWARD LEARNING

Mua can best be described as an active participant in his education. "In high school every year I go to summer school to take reading and writing to improve my English." He said that he was determined to learn English as fast as he could because he knew that school would continue to be difficult for him at each new grade level. He also tried to read as much as he could.

> I read books in English at home sometimes, too. We have a lot of books at home. My brother's college books are in every corner of the house. I go to the bookstore in the mall and sometimes I buy second-hand books.

Mua prided himself on his self-reliance. He did not expect anyone to help him. Instead, every evening he usually sat in the dining room at the large, shiny, cherry wood table to do his homework alone. Mua disciplined himself to do his homework everyday as soon as he arrived home from school.

In his senior year English class in late September Mua listened while the teacher presented a lesson on compare/contrast writing. The teacher was using automobiles as an example of how to develop categories for comparison and contrast. Somewhere between dual airbags and good gas mileage, Mua had begun to sketch a car on the empty page of his open notebook. Occasionally he glanced at the board, and to the unobservant eye, appeared to be taking notes. Instead, he created a sleek automobile, low to the ground and quite sporty looking. When the teacher wrote the assignment on the board for the students to compare and contrast two policemen who had been interviewed by Studs Terkel in his book *Working*, Mua was lost. Nevertheless, he did not raise his hand for help. Instead, he listened to the other students at his table talk about how they were going to write the assignment. And then he began to write. Periodically he continued to pause and listen as the members of his group questioned each other about how they were writing.

Clearly Mua viewed the world in a visual way. His drawing was excellent. The details of the automobile also revealed that he had been listening carefully. When the teacher had discussed tires for the car or a sunroof, Mua sketched them in. However, the problem he encountered was that he did not see the cognitive connection between the car and the policemen in relation to the writing task at hand. He needed clearer instructions of how to go about gathering information from the text to compare and contrast the two men. Yet, he asked no questions. Later he admitted to assuming everyone else understood and hoped that if he listened to the other students talk, he would eventually figure out how to do it. His other option was to stay after class. This was the pattern he had learned—first to try it himself, then ask for help.

In December Mua demonstrated his growing comfort in the class during a series of quickwrites. When the first topic was written on the board, "How we treat the elderly in America," Mua sat for a while, staring at his notebook and scratching his pencil back and forth in the margin of his paper. After a minute or so he began to write something and continued writing until the teacher said, "Stop." At this point several students volunteered to share what they had written. A discussion ensued on stereotyping the elderly, personal stories about grandparents, and the need for convalescent hospitals in our society. Mua listened to the conversations but also sketched a man's head in his notebook. The second topic focused on "The importance of a family." This time Mua wrote quickly and for the entire seven minutes. Again he did not share in the conversation, but he seemed to be listening and smiled at one student's comments. The third topic, "Our educational system," stimulated less writing for Mua, but he seemed to be pausing to think as he wrote. Again he did not volunteer to share, but when the teacher called on him to speak, Mua explained that he had written about how much freedom students had in school to tell how they feel about things. He thought we had a good system, but that some teachers were too easy and did not expect much from the students. The blond girl across from him agreed as did several other students. Mua did not elaborate. He had finished. Although Mua did not volunteer to share his writing, when he was asked to speak, he did not hesitate, nor did he appear uncomfortable. He spoke clearly and loudly, looking directly at the teacher.

In April Mua was observed working on his writing with a response partner. Although he did not initiate a partnership, rather than lowering his eyes shyly, he looked around the table to see who would work with him. The blond girl across from him quickly offered her paper in trade. Mua read slowly, writing comments on her paper during his second reading. When they again exchanged papers, she asked him questions about his comments, on which he elaborated, and she did the same. Mua explained that he enjoyed working with only one person because sometimes more people in a group tended to talk and play instead of doing their work. This made him feel uncomfortable and annoyed.

On the first day of June Mua faced a new challenge, Senior Portfolio Presentation Day. He walked into the library with several of his Hmong friends. When Mua sat at his assigned table, he leaned forward to read the directions taped in the center. As the parent volunteer joined the boys at Mua's table, two girls and another boy also seated themselves. It was difficult to tell how Mua was feeling. A serious-looking boy, he did not smile easily. Yet, he chatted with the parent, answering her questions, appearing to be comfortable but a little unsure by the way he fidgeted with the spine of his portfolio. When it was his turn, Mua spoke without hesitation, looking directly at the person to whom he was speaking, and actually engaged in conversation by asking questions. He appeared comfortable with expressing himself in English.

MUA'S SCHOOL ENVIRONMENT AND TEACHING

Mua described his four years of high school English as encompassing very different experiences. His 9th grade class was very small, 20 students to be exact. He felt that the teacher had time to respond to his writing and to give him individual attention. Also, students did a lot of drawing and illustrating in class, and Mua could express himself through his art. He felt that in a way his art skills gained him respect from the other students as well as from the teacher. His English 10 class was a different story. The class had 39 students in it. Mua felt grateful that the teacher had put him in a writing group with his cousin Kaying and two girls whom he described as helpful and patient. "The teacher put us with two very nice and smart girls, Nina and Rachel. They help us a lot, and I talked a little bit with them. I think my English improved that year." Mua explained that the girls asked them questions and were patient as the boys tried to express their ideas. Nina and Rachel encouraged Mua and his cousin to practice speaking, but the English 11 course put Mua in a slump. The reading was too difficult for him to handle alone so he had to continually stay after class to get help from the teacher. "I did not learn very much this year," he said of his junior year. Although he was in a writing group, the students he was supposed to work with mostly played around. Mua wished the teacher had moved him to another group. For English 12 Mua enrolled in the same course as his cousin Kaying, but with a different teacher.

As a senior, Mua seemed to be working more independently. His teacher often used quickwrites because he believed they reduced anxiety about writing in class. He felt it was important for students to explore their ideas or simply explain what they already thought about a topic before they began to write a first draft. Mua seemed very comfortable with this format. Also, the teacher's casual demeanor created a stress-free environment in the classroom. He moved around as the students wrote and complimented them on their thinking as they spoke. He asked questions to delve deeper into each issue, which prompted a sort of free oral response from the class. No one asked how long an essay should be. This may be evidence of the fact that students in class understood the writing process and that the first draft seldom determined how long the actual essay would be. It may also be that they felt comfortable enough with their topic choices so that length did not pose a problem for them.

Mua complimented his senior English teacher who systematically taught punctuation and grammar lessons on a regular basis with vocabulary words, all during the editing of essays. "That was good for me to learn. I like to learn in school and my English is always getting better." He said that he felt more comfortable in the class as the year progressed and school wasn't so bad. He was also happy that he had finally passed the writing proficiency test for high school graduation at the beginning of his senior year. "That was a big scare that suffocated me."

Mua respected his parents and his culture. He particularly liked Hmong music and in fact was in a band that played Hmong tunes. Mua's tie to his culture was demonstrated by some of the works in his Showcase portfolio. He had written about the difficulties of being a student in a new country, about prejudice against a young Hmong boy, about his favorite subject—the Vietnam War—and even a thank you letter to his parents and brothers for guiding his life and his education. Mua had also written several stories about his experiences in the camp in Thailand and his perceptions upon coming to America.

MUA'S WRITING

Mua's four pieces selected for examination include a personal experience about starting school in America, "I Never Gave Up," a personal experience of prejudice when arriving at the refugee camp, a story about an event that made him feel important, "Buying Vegetables," and the introduction to his portfolio. As with the other student, Mua's development as a writer is evidenced not only by his fluency but also by the growth of intellectual process. Based on Odell's (1977) linguistic cues, the following essays demonstrate this growth (Sahakian, 1997):

1. His skill at using focus helps to guide the reader smoothly through the personal experience essay and captures important aspects of his story;

2. Mua has a solid, steady grasp of the possibilities of developing content through the use of contrast, particularly to create dramatic effect;

3. He seems to use classification well to create vivid images and convey emotion. He uses metaphor almost naturally;

4. In the third essay, "change" signals reflection. This essay illustrates Mua's developing sophistication as he moves from reaction to reflection;

5. Mua has a growing awareness of the importance of using physical context as a way to create images in addition to using classification;

6. His growing sophistication in reference to time sequence gives him control of the personal experience essay and illustrates his awareness of having to guide the reader to create the tension he desires to convey;

7. Using cause-effect sequences in his writing would allow Mua to explore more deeply the important issues he raises, but his writing is limited in this linguistic cue.

Grade 9—I Never Gave Up

I started school at the age of 6 in Thailand. The school there was wonderful but there were a lot of things that left out such as sports, club, art, and the most important and not important thing was that each student only could go to school from first grade to six grade then stopped. No further class or grade to continue. Anyway, in 1986 my family decided to come to America. Before we come to the United States legally, we have to run through every single paper and filled it up correctly.

My family arrived in America a little later because my brother had filled the form correctly and honesty. My very first school in America was intermediate School. As a student there, I have a very hard time that I couldn't saw the light or have any brighter way to continue my education as a student and one day became proud of the word student. Every single homework or assignment that my teacher gave me. It made me headache and like I was closing my eyes and walked into a danse forest that I couldn't find my way out. But anyway, I started seeing the important of myself to be a student in a new country. My first four weeks in school there was so lonely and depressed because I have not known anybody and they all look like strangers.

In the fifth months, my brother dropped me from seventh grade to sixth grade but every time I heard my teacher called upon my name, my heart started pounding and my body started shaking with fear. If the teacher asked me to read or walked up to the board, my whole body was shocked and red started forming in my face [so] that I could feel the heat burned upon my face. This is my weakness that I scared at most.

Above was my weakness quality, but down here was my strength. I knew inside my personal feeling that I would not have the capability to act or do like other person. So my strength was to do my best of what I am now and never gave up no matter how hard or long it is. Becoming a new student in a new country, effort and strength are the two unique qualities that will help bring to the reach of my dream. At high school I see a brighter way. I like all teachers and every classmates that I [am] with.

Grade 10—You, Moia!

Shortly after our bus arrived in a camp called Phanet Nickom, I stood up with my hand still carried a bag beside my leg and also all other family on the bus were stood up ready to walk out. All of us included those that already lived or the one just arrived the first night in this camp were all called "refugee". Now people already started walking out. I saw one dark skin man stood outside the bus door. When the bus was clear, I realized that everybody was prejudice by that Thai man and Thai leader who I later found out he was incharge of this camp.

Walking toward the door of the bus, still there were three young infront of me. When one of them [was] about to walk out, I knew he was looking into that Thai man eagle eyes because he failed one foot from the step that his body fell against the door side and just in time his left hand caught on the door [so] that he didn't fell into that Thai man. With two people infront of me, I saw his dark and dirty looking hand grabed onto that young man collar, pushing him after those that headed toward the line, and he shouted after. "You, moia, watch your step around here." Moia which mean to us as a cat. And when anyone was being called by that term I knew he was consider as a dirty little cat who got no land to live on and no bones to feed on. When my turn, I was carefully walked out from the bus and also the rest of my family.

Fifteen minutes later, we, the refugee people were all sitting inside a house facing the front. With my eyes looking, I saw one fat, heavy, and kind of middle age man stood behind a table. On the table was a small microphone. He started giving his speech about how the rule or system they used in this camp and afterall I remembered he said, "I was [am] the leader of his camp and each everyone of you must perform your action under my rule." The speech over and now every family were to walk pass by him to show their family identification card. Almost all the family had passed by smoothly and without any trouble. Unfortunately, when it came to a family before us. I stirred at the man, the husband who tried to pull out his family identification card with a shaky hand and a tense body stood on the ground like a tree was going to [be] pull out by the turbulent wind. His hand tremble and drop the card under the table where that Thai leader was standing. That moment my eyes was rigidly focus on him when I saw he lift up his club in his right hand about to strike that husband's head as he bent down to pickup the card. To myself, I thought we were suppose to be treated nicely and fairly.

When time passed by and all the family have settled down on the camp with each family a place to stay or live temporary. I have a feeling that time can brings so much good and bad stuffs throughout a person because I could still heard the word "moia" used by that Thai man on that young man. Actually everyone was prejudice that night in the heart of every Thai who presented there.

Grade 12 (45 min.)—Buying Vegetables

In general we sometime experienced something that make us feel good or important. I remember one time, I was helping my mom to get home because she broke her ankle from triping on a rock. I was scare and tense, but after I managed to get her home, I felt special about myself.

The day was cloudy and raining a little. My mom asked me to go to the store with her to buy some vegetables and meat for lunch. We both have boots on. When we got halfway, there was puddle of mud and tiny rocks all over in the middle of the road. I remember telling her "careful mom and watch your step." My mom and I then walk slower. But unfortunately, she trip herself on a rock that was burry with mud soon after I told her to careful. My mom fell down and I look at her, she said "I think I broke my ankle" and her hand was reaching to held it.

I was scare at the moment. I grabbed my mom's shoulder to comfort her and when I look around screaming for help, there were nobody around. I don't know what to do. "I must be quick and think of a way to get her home," I said to myself. I ripped off my T-shirt and wrap it around her ankle. I then put her arm around my shoulder and slowly help my mom to get up on her feet. We headed back home.

The rain has not stopped yet and we got home all wet. Somehow, I didn't feel cold, but I felt a little hot inside, because I was too scared. I help her home safely and my dad had wrapped my mom's ankle with some herbs, she later recovered her broken ankle.

Now when I think of this incident, it makes me feel very special and important, because I had helped someone whose a real special person to me, my mom. Whenever we have vegetable or meat for breakfast, I always teased my mom, "hey, mom, we forgot to buy our vegetables." We would laugh and this is what make me feel important.

Grade 12—Introduction to Portfolio

This is my senior showcase portfolio. This portfolio also include many of my other pieces from Freshman, Sophomore, Junior and currently four pieces from this year. Following will be a description to my senior items; why I pick them, how I feel about each one, and plus a brief compare and contrast among all the works I have done in the last four years. How much I have or have not improved and reveal little bit of myself as a reader, writer, and thinker.

My first piece is the argumentative essay. The paper deals with an issue about whether remedial classes should or should not be offered at a four-year college. I like this essay, because I have the choice to pick a side and able to argue anyway I want with my own point of view. In fact, I argue that it's necessary to offer remedial classes at four-year colleges, because these classes will serve as the basic strength for many minorities and below average students.

In my Contemporary English class, we have to read two books, one is called *Dave's Way* and the other called *Lee Iacocca Talking*

Straight. So my second paper is part of the assignment from the book *Dave's Way.* I have to respond to one of these quote, "There is a lot of opportunity out there and you'll make a lot of money, but you have to set high goal and work hard to achieve them." However, my respond is that this quote is still true today. As a matter of fact, after finishing this essay I become so much motivate and encourage even to work harder.

This third essay is also an assignment from the book called *Lee Iacocca Talking Straight.* Obviously, this paper is kind of interesting and simpler for me to do. I only have to pick one specific word that best describe Lee Iacocca's characteristic and find information from the book to support my point. Although, I say he is a very responsible, loving, and caring person. Lee, indeed, is also a terrific father.

My last piece is title as Freedom of Speech. The information in this essay deals with both the advantage and disadvantage on the First Amendment. Basically, in the essay I create a scenario showing how someone in the media can abuse the Freedom of Speech. I like it because this assignment prove the truth that words are sometime powerful weapon and can cause harm to other.

Within my four years as a Freshman, Sophomore, Junior and currently a Senior, I have done quite a tremendous works especially in writing. Almost in all of my papers I have put a lot of effort such as time, thinking, and searching while I wrote them. Therefore, I believe that every piece is done within the best of my capability. I also sure that I have make some improvement because referring to my works in the past, no doubt, my writing now is a lot better.

After all these years, I still think of myself as a writer as an artist. And that's because almost on all of my papers I work just as hard as an artist who only tries to use the right tools, colors, imagine the greatest scene to compose the greatest possible picture. Unfortunately, I can be sure that my weakness lies under the usage of proper grammar, punctuation, and vocabularies. Yet, my strength prove to be no longer tumbling or troubling to dig out what I write. Last but not least, I believe that my portfolio will best present the strength or weakness of myself as a reader, writer, and thinker. Or else, all the works I have done in each year can indicate steps of my gradual improvement.

As with Kaying, Mua's grammar and syntactical structure remained problematic throughout his senior year, yet he developed his writing skills in many areas. Mua's willingness to experiment with words and his desire to express his ideas sometimes resulted in long, awkwardly constructed sentences. But he was not afraid to take a risk, to use language to explore ideas and truly communicate his thoughts and feelings, even to the point of anticipating a readers needs.

WHAT OUR SECOND LANGUAGE STUDENTS CAN TEACH US ABOUT LEARNING

Knowledge of our students' home culture can tell us much about their attitudes and actions toward learning. Though their hearts might be in the right place, and their desire to learn strong, with no one at home to help with schoolwork, they are at a great disadvantage, as you have seen with Kaying and Mua. Yet, a sense of pride, a need for self-reliance, may cause them to resist intervention if it calls attention to them. What does it take for second-language students to let down their guard? The answer to this question can be seen when both boys finally felt comfortable with the teacher and friendly toward their classmates—when they felt as if they belonged. Only then would they speak out to ask or answer questions. Clearly, feelings of isolation hold students back. They ask no questions, even when they are lost. However, the socialization process can be encouraged with as simple a task as the opportunity to write about and share what they know, what they care about, particularly their cultural experiences. Topic choice provides an avenue to honor their differences as unique and interesting. The more choice students have to select topics to write about, the more ownership they bring to an assignment. In the case of second language students, topic choice allows them to bring their lives into the classroom on equal footing with everyone else.

What else can teachers do? To build a healthy social climate for learning, the teacher can set aside time for one-on-one tutoring or conferencing to develop a relationship of trust with the students. Eventually, teachers must nudge gently to encourage participation. As you saw in Mua's story, a simple nod to invite an oral response or the opportunity to work with partners or in small groups as was Kaying's experience can provide the social interaction students need to improve their language skills and their learning. Extended assignments or activities that require out-of-class meetings can even promote real friendships beyond the classroom.

Instructional sequencing can also make a difference. You have seen the importance of modeling and helping students make cognitive connections when the instruction requires higher-level thinking such as drawing analogies. It is most helpful for second language students to see the assignment in written form, particularly if a teacher is speaking too quickly for them. At the same time, asking students to perform multiple tasks overwhelms second language students. They can't read, write comments, and talk or share at the same time! Such cognitively demanding tasks send them into a silent mode where they don't even know which question to ask. They need help with "all of it!" So, they sit quietly, passively, feeling invisible to the teaching and learning going on in the classroom.

Finally, teaching students the writing process gives them access to thinking and language use in so many ways. Quickwrites, drawing, sharing, and other prewriting strategies promote the thinking, the idea collection, and the banking of language required to communicate effectively in written discourse. But the teaching does not stop here. Of equal importance is the rewriting required in revision. Multiple drafts encourage opportunities to learn on many levels: (a) the thinking level where they examine the content of their writing, (b) the sentence level where they learn to manipulate voice and style, and (c) the word level that often carries the tone of a piece of writing. Rather than writing many first drafts that repeat students' weaknesses in writing and provide no windows for direct instruction, opportunities to rewrite/revise/edit move students from the focus of content to the focus of style and correctness. The focus on thinking about content builds confidence for the writer, and the focus on mechanics improves language correctness.

The writing process is inclusive and generative. The ultimate test for the power of the writing process to improve students' writing, thinking, and language use over time can easily be seen in their portfolio selections. Furthermore, writing response groups can build cross-cultural friendships and create a strong sense of community as is evidenced in the experience of Kaying and Mua. When second-language students are given opportunities to interact in class, to learn about each other as well as from each other and from the teacher's thoughtfully designed lessons, they will achieve.

REFERENCES

Bliatout, B. T., Downing B.T., Lewis, J., & Yang, D. (1988). *Handbook for teaching Hmong speaking students*. Sacramento: Folsom Cordova Unified School District.

Britton, J. (1970). *Language and learning*. Middlesex, England: Penguin.

Britton, J., Burgess, T., Martin, N., McLeod, A., & Rosen, H. (1975). *The development of writing abilities* (pp. 11-18). London: Macmillan Education.

Canale, M., Frenette, N., & Bélanger, M. (1988). Evaluation of minority student writing in first and second languages. In J. Fine (Ed.), *Second language discourse: A textbook of current research*. Norwood, NJ: Ablex.

Collier, V. P. (1990). How long? A synthesis of research on academic achievement in second language. *TESOL Quarterly, 23*(3), 509-531.

Cummins, J. (1981). The role of primary language development in promoting educational success for language minority students. In California Department of Education (Ed.), *Schooling and language minority students*. Los Angeles: California State University.

Cummins, J. (1983). Language proficiency and academic achievement. In J. W. Oller Jr. (Ed.), *Issues in language testing research*. Rowley, MA: Newbury House.

De La Luz Reyes, M. (1992). Challenging venerable assumptions: Literacy instruction for linguistically different students. *Harvard Educational Review, 62*(4), 427-446.

Delgado-Gaitan, C. (1987). Traditions and transitions in the learning process of Mexican children: An ethnographic view. In G. Spindler & L. Spindler (Eds.), *Interpretive ethnography of education at home and abroad.* Hillsdale, NJ: Erlbaum.

Dulay, H., Burt, M. &, Krashen, S. (1982). *Language two.* New York: Oxford University Press.

Elbow, P. (1973). *Writing without teachers.* NY: Oxford University Press.

Ellis, R. (1994). *The study of second language acquisition.* Oxford, England: Oxford University Press.

Flower, L., & Hayes, J. (1977). Problem-solving strategies and the writing process. *College English, 39*, 449-461.

Flower, L., & Hayes, J. (1981). The pregnant pause: An inquiry into the nature of planning. *Research in the Teaching of English, 15*, 229-243.

Freire, P. (1985). *The politics of education: Culture, power, and liberation.* Granby, MA: Bergin & Garvey.

Gardner, R. C. (1985). *Social psychology and second language learning: The role of attitudes and motivation.* Bungay, Suffolk: The Chaucer Press.

Graves, D. H. (1983). *Writing: Teachers and children at work.* Portsmouth, NH: Heinemann.

Krapels, A. R. (1990). An overview of second language writing process research. In B. Kroll (Ed.), *Second language writing: Research insights for the classroom* (pp. 37-56). New York: Cambridge University Press.

Krashen, S. D. (1981). *Second language acquisition and second language learning.* Oxford: Pergamon Press.

Krashen, S. D. (1982). *Principles and practice in second language acquisition.* New York: Pergamon.

Kroll, B. (1990) Introduction. In B. Kroll (Ed.), *Second language writing: Research insights for the classroom* (pp. 1-5). New York: Cambridge University Press.

Long, L. D. (1992). Literacy acquisition of Hmong refugees in Thailand. In F. Dubin & N. A. Kuhlman (Eds.), *Cross-cultural literacy: Global perspectives on reading and writing.* Englewood, NJ: Regents/Prentice-Hall.

Long, M. H., & Richard, J. D. (1990). Series editors' preface. In B. Kroll (Ed.), *Second language writing: Research insights for the classroom.* New York: Cambridge University Press.

Moffett, J. (1968). *Teaching the universe of discourse.* Boston: Houghton Mifflin.

Murray, D. M. (1968). *A writer teaches writing: A practical method of teaching composition.* Boston: Houghton Mifflin.

Odell, L. (1977). Measuring changes in intellectual processes as one dimension of growth in writing. In C. R. Cooper & L. Odell (Eds.), *Evaluating writing: Describing, measuring, judging* (pp. 107-134). Urbana, IL: National Council of Teachers of English.

Ramirez, J. D. (1992). *Executive summary of the final report: Longitudinal study of structured English immersion strategy, early-exit and late-exit transitional bilingual programs for language minority children.* Prepared for the U. S. Department of Education. San Mateo, CA: Aguirre International No. 300-87-0156.

Sahakian, P. (1997). *The writing development of four Hmong high school boys.* Doctoral dissertation. University of California, Davis and California State University, Fresno, Joint Doctoral Program

Schieffelin, B. B., & Cochran-Smith, M. (1984). Learning to read culturally: Literacy before schooling. In H. Godman, A. Oberg, & F. Smith (Eds.), *Awakening to literacy.* Exeter, NH: Heinemann.

Schumann, J. H. (1978). *The pidginization process: A model for second language acquisition.* Rowley, MA: Newbury House.

Smith, F. (1973). *Psycholinguistics and reading.* New York: Holt, Rinehart & Winston.

CHAPTER ELEVEN

Accommodating Under Section 504 of the Rehabilitation Act

A Fair Break for Every Kid

Jane House

California State University, Fresno

Have you ever been at sea in a dense fog, when it seemed as if a tangible white darkness shut you in and the great ship, tense and anxious, groped her way toward shore with plummet and sounding line, and you waited with beating heart for something to happen. I was like that ship before my education began only I was without compass or sounding line, and no way of knowing how near the harbor was. "Light! Give me light," was the wordless cry of my soul, and the light of love shone on me in that very hour.

Helen Keller

For many years, the story of Helen Keller stood alone as one of the canon's few tales of the struggles of the disabled. This engaging story of a blind girl's battle to achieve the recognition and attention she deserved has been widely read. All who come to know Helen Keller understand the conflicting emotions of empa-

179

thy for her circumstance and contempt for a world unprepared to accept her needs. Sadly, before federal laws such as Section 504 of the Rehabilitation Act and the Education for All Handicapped Children Act passed in the 1970s, only one out of every five students with a disability was allowed access to a public school. This practice of exclusion left nearly one million American school children without access to a free and appropriate public education (FAPE). The national denial of the existence of disabilities and the additional affect of this discrimination was that approximately 3.5 million students who were enrolled in public schools did not receive the assistance they needed so that they could benefit from their educational experiences. These students were often counted as failures, suffered retention, and frequently ended up as school dropouts.

Essentially, discrimination against individuals with disabilities was an accepted practice in many school districts. In many instances, states had laws that prevented students with certain kinds of disabilities from attending public school. Specifically, schools were legally exempted from providing educational services for a wide range of disabilities including the blind, the deaf, and students who were labeled "mentally retarded" or "emotionally disturbed." As recently as the early 1970s, approximately 200,000 school-age children with mental retardation or emotional disabilities were housed in state or privately funded institutions. The effect of the disability was further exacerbated when the child was poor, from an ethnic or racial minority group, or lived outside of town in a rural area. There was an even greater likelihood that the child would not be welcome in a public school (National Council on Disability, 2000). These children suffered the dual discrimination of disability and racism. Although it has been 25 years since federal laws were enacted to end the abuse of citizens based upon disabilities and race, in many parts of America discrimination against students with differences continues in our public schools. Discrimination is not only illegal; it is immoral.

President George W. Bush (2001) used his inaugural address to acknowledge that the ambitions of some Americans are, "limited by failing schools, hidden prejudice, and the circumstances of their birth." For kids and their families who deal daily with some kind of disability, condition or impairment, this is a fairly easy concept to grasp, despite the president's affirmation of an "American promise . . . . that everyone deserves a chance." In fact, many parents ask, "Why don't teachers and school administrators get it?" Unfortunately, in large school settings, it is often too easy to avoid putting faces on these students and to eschew reaching out to include them. In a growing number of instances, families feel driven to write a complaint against the school on behalf of their child. As these complaints reach school districts and school boards, the Office of Civil Rights (OCR), and the federal courts, school districts are seldom the winners.

As an educator in a public school, you are entrusted with an enormous task: serving students with an array of diversities and needs. Students come with a variety of learning differences and disabilities, races and cultures, languages, family arrangements, religions, and sexual orientations. Often students demand attention to their competing needs. What can you do when each need is equally important and each child is deserving of his or her share of the school's limited resources? As a teacher or school administrator, you will participate in making critical decisions that benefit these students. To be a successful educator, you must show an interest, take a stand, and make good on the school district's mandate to provide FAPE.

WHAT IS SECTION 504?

Section 504 is a major component of the Rehabilitation Act of 1973 (P. L. 93-112). It is essentially civil rights legislation for persons with disabilities, modeled after the egalitarian legislation of the 1960s. This statute is described as the Bill of Rights for persons with disabilities because it guarantees them the right to be free from discrimination. No federal funding is provided to implement Section 504. The act was amended in 1992 to extend its protections to handicapped students seeking access to federally supported schools. Section 504 states:

> No otherwise qualified handicapped individual . . . shall, solely by reason of his or her handicap, be excluded from the participation in, denied the benefits of, or be subject to discrimination under any program or activity receiving federal assistance. (29 U.S.C. § 794)

Section 504 requires that educational programs for students with disabilities must be equal to those provided to others, and it applies to all persons with disabilities in preschool, elementary, secondary and adult school programs. The essential requirements are to provide equal and accessible school buildings, transportation, educational programs, and extracurricular activities such as, sports, school clubs, and field trips. Graduation requirements, textbooks, and district testing procedures may not discriminate against students. Different treatment is allowed only when it is necessary to provide educational services to persons with disabilities that are as effective as those provided to other students (34 C.F.R. § 104.3 [j][1]).

Section 504 requires that a student with disabilities be provided a free, appropriate public education (FAPE) in the least restrictive setting. Most often this stipulation means that the student will be placed and served in general education (also referred to as regular education). The educational program of a student must be provided in general education settings (classroom or classes) unless it is shown that this cannot be satisfactorily achieved. Section 504 assures the use of individualized interventions or specialized educational services, as needed by the student, as well as access to general education programs and the district's mandated curriculum (34 C.F.R. § 104.33 [a]).

SECTION 504 IS NOT SPECIAL EDUCATION

Section 504 is not an aspect of special education. This is confusing because students who are eligible under the Individuals with Disabilities Education Act (1999) for special education programs and related services are also protected under Section 504 from discrimination because of their disabilities. More specifically, Section 504 is the responsibility of the comprehensive public general education system. In this system, building administrators, superintendents of schools or districts, and school boards are responsible for ensuring the implementation of Section 504 regulations. Special education-funded administrators and staff participate most often in the role of a school-based or district consultant. Consulting school staff includes the school psychologist, special education teacher, speech language specialist and the school nurse. However, because 504 students are not special education students, general education teachers and administrators are ultimately responsible for implementation of the 504 process, writing individualized 504 plans (or accommodation plans), evaluating student progress, and monitoring general education teacher implementation of 504 plans.

WHO IS ELIGIBLE UNDER SECTION 504

A student with a disability under Section 504 is defined as any student who has a physical or mental disability, impairment, or condition. The disability, impairment, or condition must substantially limit a major life activity such as learning, caring for oneself, performing manual tasks, and working. However, learning might not be the major life activity affected. For some students there could be limitations of other major life activities such as walking or breathing. Educational need is not the sole 504 consideration. The educational discrimination issue could be school attendance, participation in extracurricular activities, proximity or location of classes, difficulties with written work, or completion of classroom or standardized tests (Letter to McKethan, 23 IDELR 504 [OCR 1995]).

There is no label, condition, disability, or impairment that automatically qualifies a student under Section 504. There is not an absolute right to a 504 evaluation because a parent demands one. This qualification applies to students with Attention Deficit Disorder (ADD), Attention Deficit Hyperactivity Disorder (ADHD), as well as any other type of disability (Letter to Mentink, 19, IDELR 1127 (OCR 1993)). Schools are required to complete 504 evaluations on any students who are suspected of having a disability that substantially limits a major life activity. A school-based team may feel that it is inappropriate to evaluate a student who is making satisfactory progress and is not in danger of retention. The school-based team must inform the parent in writing of their decision and inform the parents of their right to due process to disagree with and challenge the team's decision (OCR Memorandum, 19 IDELR 879 [1993]).

Section 504 eligibility is not automatically or routinely given when a student who was referred for special education is determined to be not eligible. The disability must substantially limit a major life activity, such as learning, and require accommodations or related services to prevent or eliminate discrimination (Letter to Veir, 20 IDELR 864 [OCR 1993]. What is meant by "substantially limits" can mean different things to parents and teachers. When the school team looks at a child's ability to learn, by definition, a student who is succeeding in general education would not be considered a student with a disability that substantially limits the major life activity of learning. A student who is already succeeding would not require specialized services or accommodations to prevent discrimination because there is no discrimination (Saginaw City [MI] School District, EHLR 352:413 [OCR 1987]).

The school-based team decides what aids, benefits, or services are necessary to prevent discrimination and afford the student an equal opportunity to a free, appropriate public education (FAPE). Equal treatment does not mean the same treatment. It simply means that a standard is set for educational access, which may be different based on the individual needs of the student and individualized by Section 504 procedural safeguards (34 C.F.R. § 104.36).

Section 504 was intended to create a level playing field in general education. It was not created to give an unfair advantage such as providing accommodations to a student who is receiving barely passing grades so that the student can earn higher grades or test scores (Kortering, Julnes, & Edgar, 1990). The purpose of Section 504 is equal opportunity, not a guarantee of success. Accommodations are necessary to prohibit discrimination because of the disability, not to overcome the disability (The Americans with Disabilities Act of 1990 and the Rehabilitation Act Amendments, 1992). Any accommodation above what is needed to prevent discrimination and provide equal opportunity or treatment is not required (Jarrow, 1999; Russo & Morse, 1999). Furthermore, teachers are not required to substantially modify instruction or change the course requirements or standards when accommodating a student who is eligible under Section 504.

HOW SECTION 504 WORKS FOR GARY

Gary is African American and a tenth grade transfer student from a rural high school to a larger high school in the suburbs. He is a good student, friendly, interested in basketball, and he played the trumpet at his previous school. He likes his new high school and is making friends. But there are a few problems.

Gary has spina bifida and uses a nonelectric wheelchair to get from place to place. He can stand independently for short periods, walk very short distances, and climb up a few stairs. Although he can be ambulatory, he really depends on his wheelchair to move at school. Gary was excited to attend his new high school because of the reputation of the school's music department and its first-class band.

Gary is eligible for Adapted Physical Education (APE), but he really wants to participate in the regular physical education (PE) program with modifications. In his neighborhood Gary has always played basketball with other kids, only he was in his wheelchair. The other kids learned to play with Gary and his chair. Gary swims because of strong muscles in his arms and shoulders. His form isn't great, but he makes it from one end of the pool to the other. He enjoys playing basketball at school and hits well enough in baseball, but needs someone to run the bases for him. With the help of the APE teacher, Gary participates in the regular PE program.

Gary enjoys his band class and feels that he will be challenged to improve his skills. However, he is frustrated. Part of the music requirement is participation in the marching band, performing at athletic events, and at band competitions. The band director has agreed that Gary can sit with the band in the stands and play during football and basketball games. The band director has decided that Gary will not perform with the band during half time, in parades, or in competitions. He believes that in his wheelchair Gary will slow down or detract from the band's performance. This is a setback for Gary and he has argued with the band director to change his mind. Gary is angry, and his attitude is becoming negative. The same is true for the band director. Gary feels that the band director's decision is unfair and discriminating against him. Gary's mother calls the school to file a discrimination complaint against the band director (Center for Law and Education, 1994). She is tired of people telling her what her son cannot do.

The band director and assistant band director are notified that they are, in fact, discriminating against Gary, because his physical disability substantially limits a major life activity. In Gary's case, the major life activity affected is walking. Additionally, the band instructors are reminded of the school district's board policy that guarantees that the district will not discriminate against students and employees with disabilities.

A school-based team schedules a problem-solving meeting with Gary, his mother, teachers who know Gary, his counselor, the APE teacher, and the 504 coordinator. The challenge is to come up with solutions that will be mutually agreeable to Gary, his mother, and his teachers, including the band instructors. Gary's mother is informed that she has the right to disagree with the school team's decisions and how to access the process to do so according to parent and student rights under Section 504 (Fairfield-Suisun [CA] Unified School District, OCR 1994). After everyone has had a chance to have his or her say, possible solutions are discussed and agreed upon (Blazer, 1999).

Accommodations were made so that Gary can participate in the half-time performances at athletic events, at competitions, and in parades. At football games, Gary will sit on the field with the marimba players and a student whose job is to hit a huge gong on cue. These performers are stationary but essential participants, as is Gary. Gary will attend away games and competitions. The district will provide a wheelchair bus equipped with a lift. After this agreement was reached, Gary said that he would first like to try getting on the regular band bus on his own if one of his band-mates would bring his chair on board and secure it for him (the bus driver assisted in securing the chair). Finally, arrangements will be made so that Gary can participate in the only parade scheduled for the year. He can choose who he would like to push his wheelchair so he can play his trumpet in the parade. Family members of his band-mates have volunteered as well as his sister. Shirts and slacks in the band colors will be provided.

Once a year, until Gary graduates, a school-based team will get together to review and update the 504 accommodations made for Gary because of his physical disability. At the conclusion of his high school years, Gary plans to attend a four-year college or university.

CECILIA'S STORY ABOUT LEARNING

Cecilia is a Latina fourth grader who was born in Mexico. She is one of the kindest and most well-behaved girls in her class and will do anything to please her teacher. She is considered a fluent English speaker who receives English language assistance in reading and writing from a trained tutor. Despite the additional support, her teacher is beginning to notice a pattern of learning difficulties. Cecilia isn't focusing well and has trouble staying on task with many classroom assignments. She works very hard but does poorly on class tests. Her district and state tests scores are gradually dropping each school year. Cecilia often asks for directions to be repeated. She becomes frustrated and upset when she doesn't understand what the teacher is teaching. She takes longer to complete assignments and becomes angry when she is the last one done. She tells her teacher the she feels stupid and feels that other children are teasing her.

Her teacher is also concerned that Cecilia does not seem to retain information and understand instruction compared to other students in her fourth grade class. The teacher wonders if Cecilia is just another one of those students with Attention-Deficit Hyperactivity Disorder (ADHD), or maybe she has a hearing problem. After a general education student study team conference with her mother, the teacher, the English language tutor, and the school psychologist, Cecilia's hearing was checked at school and by the family pediatrician, who recommended an audiology evaluation. The teacher also tried interventions in the classroom for about six weeks. After a follow-up meeting with the school psychologist and the English language tutor, the teacher decided to contact

Cecilia's mother about completing a Section 504 evaluation. She suspected that there was something more than second language issues involved; perhaps some type of disability might be interfering with Cecilia's learning.

The evaluation results indicated that Cecilia did meet educational eligibility under Section 504 because of an auditory processing disorder in the areas of auditory decoding and memory that substantially limited her learning. Cecilia had the most difficulty attending and staying focused when there was increased background noise. The 504 accommodations that were discussed at the meeting made a lot of sense to both Cecilia's teacher and her mother.

Cecilia's seating in class was changed so that she was close to the teacher in a less distracting area (away from the door, drinking fountain, and pencil sharpener). The teacher provided verbal information with visuals, such as using the overhead projector, writing key points in different colors on the board, and providing pictures or visual models. Cecilia would signal her teacher when she did not understand what was said and the teacher would rephrase instructions keeping them clear and short. The teacher gave Cecilia's mom the spelling and vocabulary lists in advance. Her mom would pretutor Cecilia at home so that she would be familiar with the words when presented in class instruction. Cecilia also was given extra time to complete tests and could take tests in a quiet setting. By the end of the quarter, Cecilia's schoolwork, grades, and social skills were improving.

DELAYS IN READING LIMITED ERIK'S LEARNING

Do you know a student who never raises his hand to read aloud in front of the class? That is Erik. At first his teacher thought he was a slow learner. His teacher from last year commented that she felt that Erik was lazy and unmotivated. A general education student study team meeting was held and suggestions were given to the teacher to assist Erik in reading. Because Erik is of American Indian descent he also receives tutoring from the Indian Education specialist. The specialist is concerned that Erik is not keeping pace with his second grade classmates and is wondering if he has specific problems with reading. The teacher and specialist coordinated their efforts to work with Erik and attempted the same reading strategies for about eight weeks. At that point, they spoke with the school 504 coordinator and requested that a referral for a 504 evaluation be made.

The results of the 504 evaluation indicated a pattern of reading difficulties that indicated dyslexia. If the disability substantially limits the student's learning, the Section 504 team can make recommendations for interventions, accommodations, or services to help the student succeed in school. In Erik's case, he was determined eligible under Section 504 for accommodations and specialized services. Specific strategies were recommended to use with Erik that focused on increasing his word recognition, reading fluency, and comprehension. Erik participated in a reading intervention lab at school, and his Indian Education specialist provided additional tutoring in reading using the same strategies. Whenever possible, the teachers used multisensory techniques or the use of two or more sensory pathways (auditory, visual, kinesthetic, or tactile). With the accommodations and specialized reading services Erik is expected to achieve at a comparable rate to his classmates. Each school year, Erik's progress will be evaluated and his individualized 504 plan will be reviewed and adjusted.

WHEN THE MAJOR LIFE ACTIVITY IS BREATHING

Patricia is of Mexican American heritage, and she is proficient in English and Spanish. Malychan is Laotian American, and she is proficient in English and Laotian. Both young women attend local high schools and do average or better school work when they attend. Both students were referred to the district's Office of Child Welfare and Attendance for poor school attendance, failing grades, and lost credits. Both students experience different disabilities that substantially limit the major life activity of breathing. Patricia has cystic fibrosis and has had one lung removed because of the permanent damage caused by this condition. Malychan has asthma that can become so severe that she is hospitalized once or twice each school year.

The Office of Civil Rights (OCR) monitors compliance with Section 504 and investigates disability discrimination complaints from individuals with disabilities or from parents of children with a disability. An OCR decision in one case (Conejo Valley [CA], OCR 1993) clearly indicates that health services may be required if necessary for the student to effectively participate in school.

School absences for both Patricia and Malychan were related to their medical conditions. Because of the pattern of absences, removing the girls from their high school to an alternative education program located at another site without first attempting to accommodate the students would be considered discrimination under Section 504 (Fossey, Hosie, Soniat, & Zirkel, 1995).

Patricia and Malychan were referred for 504 evaluations. Both girls were determined eligible because of their breathing difficulties and the effect that their medical conditions have on their ability to access their education. The schools' 504 teams created individualized accommodation plans to prevent further discrimination because of their health needs. At school the girls were assigned classes on the ground floor that are in the same general location whenever possible. If this was not possible, the students were given extra passing time between classes. If assigned second floor classes, they used an elevator. The students were not required to carry heavy book bags from class to class. Their books were stored in their assigned classes and an extra set of books was checked out to them to use at home. The students were provided a pass that allowed them to go to the nurse's office to rest for short periods during the school day.

When Patricia and Malychan were absent because of their medical conditions, they were given extra time to complete or make up the missing assignments or tests. When the students returned to school, teachers provided extra help. When the girls were absent, arrangements were made for them to call another a classmate or to log on to their teachers' website from a home computer for the class assignments. At each school, a teacher mentor was assigned to check in with Malychan and Patricia weekly and to assist in communicating each student's needs to her assigned instructor. The extra support and monitoring provided by teachers have made all of the difference (Dagley & Evans, 1995).

Under the guidelines of Section 504, the teachers were notified of Patricia and Malychan's health conditions and their individualized 504 accommodations. As a result, the teachers were more open to problem solving situations as they came up and doing their part to keep these students linked to their schools and their education. In the future, there may be a need to consider a temporary alternative education program that can better pace the instructional program as each student's health needs allow. That would be considered as an option of last resort after the schools had exhausted their attempts to provide for the educational needs of these students.

CASSIE'S BRAIN TUMOR AFFECTED HER VISION

Cassie is a student who required individualized 504 accommodations because of a substantial limitation to the major life activity of seeing. Cassie was a second grader when doctors diagnosed her with a brain tumor. After surgery and chemotherapy Cassie's vision was restricted, as well as the ability of her body to tolerate overheating. Cassie needed adequate lighting when she read. She was provided an adaptive device that enlarges print and lights up each line of print. Longer tests are enlarged for Cassie so that she can complete them independently. Because of her vision difficulties, she may require additional time or a short break as she completes the tests. The progression of Cassie's vision problem is unknown. In the future she may require enlarged print workbook and textbooks in order to read and complete work independently.

The teacher and school nurse assist Cassie to monitor her body temperature and to make sure she is drinking enough fluids at school. Cassie carries a chilled bottle of water wherever she goes. Extra chilled bottles of water are stored for Cassie in the nurse's office and the teachers' lounge. If there is any question or concern over her temperature, Cassie's teacher or nurse will check it. If her temperature is up, she is allowed to drink fluids and rest in the nurse's office until her temperature returns to an acceptable range. If not, a procedure is in place to contact one of her parents or, if necessary, emergency medical assistance.

With Section 504 accommodations, Cassie benefits from being at school and is keeping pace with her peers. Adjustments have been made and monitoring is in place so that Cassie can attend her neighborhood school with her friends instead of staying at home where a home teacher would schedule visits once or twice a week. Being in school with her friends is the least restrictive placement for Cassie. Each school year, the 504 accommodations are reviewed and adjusted as needed. If Cassie's vision and health needs become more complicated, an evaluation will be completed to determine if she is eligible under the Individuals with Disabilities Education Act (1999) for special education services or programs. For now, she is doing well, and she is ready to be promoted to the third grade.

WHAT IF MEDICATION IS NECESSARY AT SCHOOL?

A sampling of OCR letters of finding indicate that the refusal of a school to administer medication during the school day to students with Attention Deficit Disorder (ADD) or Attention Deficit Hyperactivity Disorder (ADHD) violates Section 504 (San Ramon Valley [CA] Unified School District, OCR 1991; Pearl [MS] Public School District, OCR 1991). Additionally, another decision (San Juan [CA] Unified School District, OCR 1993) interprets that Section 504 obligates schools to ensure that ADHD students with a long history of attention problems and impulse control deficits consistently take their medicine. These decisions were critical to know when a school-based team considered interventions for James.

James is a fourth grader diagnosed with ADHD. He has the combined type, with behaviors that include inattentiveness, impulsivity, and hyperactivity. James' problem was that he did not always get his medication at home before he left for school. He sometimes forgot to go to the office at lunchtime to get his medication. A nurse was assigned to the school for two days a week. On those days the nurse would contact James' mother to confirm that he had taken his medication, if not, then give him the prescribed dose. On days when a nurse was not at the school site, there was no follow-up on whether James had received his medication or not. Without medication James was extra talkative and frequently out of his seat, to the point that his teacher would eventually send him to the office. If he continued to be disruptive in the classroom, his parents would be called to pick him up from school. A pattern developed where James' parents would be called to pick him up from school early or he would be suspended for the day because of his disruptive behavior.

At the fall parent-teacher conference, James' parents were informed that he was failing math and written language and was strongly being considered for retention. The teacher's recommendation was totally unexpected and devastating to James and his parents. James's parents became angry and upset with the school's lack of intervention with their son. It wasn't just the ADHD. They felt that James was being picked on because he was the only African American child in the classroom. This added to their feeling that there was an unfair negative focus on their son. After talking to a disability advocate, the parents requested the school to evaluate their son for Section 504 eligibility because of the ADHD. They also requested that the disability advocate attend the 504 meeting at the school.

The school-based team completed the 504 evaluation and determined that James was eligible under Section 504 because of his ADHD. The major life activity affected was his learning and classroom accommodations were written on an Individualized 504 plan. James' parents devised a system where they confirmed that James had received his morning medication. If James did not receive his medication, a parent would call and leave a message for the attendance clerk in the school office. The school nurse, along with the attendance clerk and office manager, devised a system to log in the medication that James received each day at school. The nurse trained and supervised the attendance clerk and the office manager so that every day there would be a staff person who would be monitoring the use of medications at school. If James did not come in at lunch to receive his medication, the lunch supervisor would be contacted and remind James to go to the nurse's office. This would be handled in a way that did not call undue attention to James, and his right to confidentiality was maintained at all times.

With input from the parents, their advocate, and the school psychologist, the 504 team also created a behavior support plan with interventions that focused on improving or changing behavior related to the ADHD that was causing James to be sent out of his classroom or suspended. His teacher and parents decided to target James' talking out and being out of his seat in class. A behavior contract was created where James could earn points for special privileges or activities at school and at home when he raised his hand before talking in class and increased the time he stayed in his seat. James and his teacher agreed that special signals would be used to redirect or remind James of his behavior goals. His teacher also planned brief activities where James could be out of his seat for a specific purpose, such as taking the attendance folder to the office, straightening up books on a shelf in the classroom, or collecting materials used in a lesson.

Consequences were outlined in the behavior contract that the teacher would use if James continued to talk out of turn or was out of his seat and his behavior interfered with the instruction of his classmates. James was directed to sit at his "quiet office" (a chair and desk in the least distracting area of class) and complete his assignment. After getting the class started on an assignment, the teacher would check on James. James had the choice to return to his regular seat where he could earn points on his behavior contract or continue to work in the quiet office (a neutral, safe place, but he cannot earn points). If James continued to disrupt the instruction in his class, he was sent to a student assistance counselor who used a strategy to help James think about his behavior and problem solve what he could do instead.

With teacher and parent monitoring of the behavior support plan, James' behavior improved in his classroom. Weekly progress reports sent home indicated that James was completing a higher percentage of assignments with better accuracy. Currently, he is earning passing grades in all subjects and is on target for promotion to the fifth grade. James' parents have requested a 504 transition meeting before the start of school in the fall with his fourth grade and fifth grade teachers. The purpose of a transition meeting is to share the 504 accommodations and the interventions that assisted James in the classroom, what worked and what he accomplished. This information will be very valuable to the fifth grade teacher who will be receiving James.

CONCLUSION

In this chapter, the children were the center of the stage, not the educators. As educators and practitioners, our primary role and responsibility are to support the learning of the child. To do this, we must stretch beyond our own experiences and conditioned certainties and enter into honest, nonjudgmental, and open dialogue that values each child in the diverse multicultural learning communities within the school. It is important that teachers are stakeholders in the process and are involved in planning and implementing accommodations for students with differences or disabilities in their classes. Furthermore, when teachers are involved, it is more likely that innovative ways of understanding student needs and solving problems will arise (Sarason, 1996).

Using a school-based team model, which includes student and parent participation, the barriers that were considered potential discrimination issues were reviewed while keeping the focus on the child and his or her individual needs and circumstances. Solutions for problems were created and accommodations were put in place that enabled each student to continue to benefit from participating in the general education program. The Section 504 process avoided the need to pursue evaluations for special education and avoided needlessly removing or segregating a child from learning opportunities in the least restrictive educational setting. Each time the school-based team met, the level of consciousness for equity issues was challenged and in most cases, was resolved at the school site by people who were the most familiar with the student and his or her family.

In the 21st century, the children who are our students come to us with an array of diversities: learning differences, disabilities, races and cultures, languages, family arrangements, religious affiliations, and sexual orientation. As educators, we must leave behind the historical model of thinking that focuses on our perception of deficits and the exclusion of students who are different from the best opportunities for learning. This will require going against conventional practice and accepting the challenge of educating each and every student who walks through the classroom door. This requires a focus on student strengths as well as individual needs. Educators must persist to discover the capabilities and possibilities within each child. Educators will need to join together to support their own learning in identifying the resources and support systems available to assist their students. As an educator new to the field, you will have the power to implement bold services for these children, not just because your action is federally mandated, but because it is the right thing to do.

REFERENCES

Americans with Disabilities Act of 1990, P. L. 101-336, 42 U.S.C.A. § 12101 *et seq.* (West 1993).

Blazer, B. (1999). Developing 504 classroom accommodation plans: A collaborative, systematic parent-student-teacher approach. *Teaching Exceptional Children, 32*(2), 28-33.

Bush, G. W. (President). (2001). *Inaugural address.* Washington, DC.

Center for Law and Education (1994, May). *Overview: Education rights of children with disabilities under the Individuals with Disabilities Education Act and Section 504 of the Rehabilitation Act of 1973.* Washington, DC: Author.

Conejo Valley (CA) Unified School District, 20 IDELR 1276 (OCR 1993).

Dagley, D. L., & Evans, C. W. (1995). The reasonable accommodation standard for Section 504 eligible students. *West's Education Law Quarterly, 4*(3), 370-382.

Fairfield-Suisun (CA) Unified School District, 21 IDELR 1007 (OCR 1994).

Fossey, R., Hosie, T., Soniat, K., & Zirkel, P. (1995). Section 504 and "front line" educators: An expanded obligation to serve children with disabilities. *Preventing School Failure, 39*(2), 10-14.

Individuals with Disabilities Education Act, 20 U.S.C. §§ 1400 *et seq.* (1999). Formerly known as the Education for All Handicapped Children Act of 1975. Current IDEA regulations appear at 34. C.F.R. §§ 300 *et seq.* (1999).

Jarrow, J. (1999). *Understanding the law to give students with disabilities full potential.* Washington, DC: National TRIO Clearinghouse, Washington, DC: Adjunct ERIC Clearinghouse on Educational Opportunity, & Washington, DC: Center for Study of Opportunity in Higher Education. (ERIC Reproduction Service No. ED 432 196).

Kortering, L., Julnes, R., & Edgar, E. (1990). An instructive view of law pertaining to the graduation of special education students. *Remedial and Special Education, 11*, 7-13.

McKethan, Letter to, 23 IDELR 504 (OCR 1995), 1:2, 3, 18; 2:17, 18; 4:2.

Mentink, Letter to, 19 IDELR 1127 (OCR 1993), 3:18; 4:3, 11,

National Council on Disability. (2000). *Back to school on civil rights.* Washington, DC: U.S. Government Printing Office.

OCR Memorandum (ADD), 19 IDELR 876 (OCR 1993), 1:7; 2:17; 3:18.

Pearl (MS) Public School District, 17 IDELR 1004 (OCR 1991).

Rehabilitation Act Amendments of 1992, P. L. 102-569 (Federal Register). United States Department of Education. Washington DC: U.S. Government Printing Office.

Russo, C. J., & Morse, T. E. (1999). Update on Section 504: How much will schools pay for compliance? *School Business Affairs, 65*(5), 50-53.

Saginaw City (MI) Sch. Dist., EHLR 352:413 (OCR 1987).

Sarason, S. (1996). *Revisiting "the culture of school and problem of change."* New York: Teachers College Press.

San Juan (CA) Unified School District, 20 IDELR 549 (OCR 1993).

San Ramon Valley (CA) Unified School District, 18 IDELR 465 (OCR 1991).

Section 504 of the Rehabilitation Act of 1973, P. L. 93-112, 29 U.S.C. § 794 *et seq.* (West, 1977).

Veir, Letter to, 20 IDELR 864 (OCR 1993), 1:16, 19; 2:19; 3:12, 4:4, 11, 14, 9:7, 8; 11:15.

CHAPTER TWELVE

It's Not About Laptops, It's About Kids!

Bernice Stone and Robin Chiero

California State University, Fresno

GARBAGEMAN:THE MAN WITH THE ORDERLY MIND

What do you think of us in fuzzy endeavor, you whose directions are sterling, whose lunge is straight?
Can you make a reason, how can you pardon us who memorize the rules and never score?

Who memorize the rules from your own text but never quite transfer them to the game,
Who never quite receive the whistling ball, who gawk, begin to absorb the crowd's own roar.

Is earnest enough, may earnest attract or lead to light;
Is light enough, if hands in clumbsy frendzy, flimsy whimsically, enlist;
Is light enough when this bewilderment crying against the dark shuts down the shades?
Dilute confusion. Find and explode our mist.

Gwendolyn Brooks

Reprinted By Consent of Brooks Permissions.

WHAT'S GOING ON HERE?

Striding briskly into the classroom I found myself in the midst of students hustling about, running in and out of the room, typing furiously on computers. I felt like a bewildered child lost in the mall. "What's going on here?" The room had most of the usual classroom stuff but instead of desks there were laptop computers on tables.

"Where's the teacher?" I finally spotted him in the corner, preoccupied with his computer. "Mr. Woods, I presume?" He stood up, a tall, hefty man in his late forties, short blonde hair, blue eyes. "What's happening here?," I asked. "They're working on the school newsletter." He then proceeded to explain the process. His broad smile and warm, friendly, welcoming, voice made me feel at ease and comfortable as if I'd known him a long time. It seemed like a chaotic mess to me and as a university supervisor I wondered if this was an appropriate place for my student teacher.

Fascinated by this classroom and Bob Woods, I was determined to find out what was happening here. Students were working hard, focused on their tasks and obviously enjoying themselves working with their buddies. So I assigned my student teacher to this classroom and returned many times to watch and listen to this amazing teacher in his laptop class. Bob Woods was excited that I was there and wanted to tell his story. He told me he came to teaching late in life after working in construction for many years. He took a large drop in salary but loved working with children and truly enjoyed his job. He believed that he could make a difference for these children and he believed in project-based learning. A newsletter was the current project. The students wandering in and out of the classroom were producing a quarterly school newsletter; conducting interviews, reporting on events, writing stories, taking pictures, and using their computers to produce the newsletter, which was then distributed throughout the school.

Although the classroom appeared disorganized to the eye, it was the result of a carefully carried out teaching philosophy and plan. His goal for the year was not to get through the textbook but to raise the level of the students' skills, to empower them to achieve. Woods came to Rosedale School in a low socioeconomic neighborhood, primarily Hispanic and Southeast Asian, to teach a sixth grade laptop class. This was a pilot program for the district aimed at "leveling the playing field" for these poorly performing students. The district saw the need to increase test scores of this underachieving population, and technology was their answer. Woods did more than that, he produced data that showed his students made huge gains on their standardized test scores, some as much as 50 percentile points.

I was skeptical; I wanted to know what he did to achieve these tremendous gains and how did this increase learning for these students? Other teachers do project-based learning, develop newsletters, and use laptops, but their student achievement is not as great. This man had a magic formula that I was resolved to expose so all teachers could learn.

DO YOU WANT TO BE EXTRAORDINARY?

Fortunately for me, Bob Woods loved to talk about his class, his kids, and what he was trying to accomplish. As he talked, it became obvious to me he had a strong positive vision of himself; he was very clear about his beliefs and where he was going. At the beginning of the year, Woods prepared his class to become learners. Authority was established in the first weeks of school by setting down the rules, procedures, and routines. But most important was developing trust between teacher and students. Mutual respect, structure, and team building was key. His relationship began with kids knowing that he cared about them. "If the kids don't know you care about them, they won't work for you. So that's where you start. I trust them, I believe in them and I believe kids can do remarkable things."

The family atmosphere provided a sense of comfort and acceptance. He told students he had high expectations for their accomplishments, but, they would be held accountable for their behavior. "Do you want to be ordinary or extraordinary? If you want to be extraordinary it takes a lot of work." Most important, he specifically taught them appropriate behavior and what values were expected in his class. Woods was strict but fair and provided a positive, encouraging classroom atmosphere. Students were expected to be responsible for their learning and behavior. "You're smart—you can do better." He strongly believed that sixth grade is critical. "You need to teach them behavior, that's why they get in trouble." Study skills were another important aspect. They must read one half hour every night and parents need to sign a reading log. But he did not expect parents to help, because many of them could not. "I'm not here to beat up parents, just to teach kids. Don't blame parents, the responsibility belongs to the kids."

ARE COMPUTERS THE ANSWER?

Although the district sees computers as the answer to the problem of low-performing students, I discovered this class was not about computers. Rosedale had a sixth grade laptop class for two years run by Woods. Computers were purchased by the district from a state grant in addition to technology funds. Sixth graders used the computers during the day and their parents used them in the evening in an adult education class. Often, the students came in the evening to assist their parents as they learned to use computers. The objective was to "level the playing field" for both students and parents in this low socioeconomic neighborhood. But even with the best up-to-date materials and equipment students are not guaranteed to learn. About using computers, Woods says, "I'm passionate about this! I believe this is where it's at. But people are not getting it. I'm an old construction guy. I know you can build a house with a handsaw or you can use a power saw. They have this power tool and they're building birdhouses with it instead of building homes. Need to get kids engaged. It's not about the product it's about the process, children learning and growing. What they're doing, what they're learning, what we do to help them achieve."

WHAT CAN I DO TO MAKE THEM SUCCESSFUL?

But Woods was not simply a cheerleader. "What can I do to make them successful and how does this relate to the real world?" was his focus. He taught specific skills early in the semester. Communication skills were his major objective; both writing and speaking were taught. Math skills were taught using meaningful activities, and problem solving was stressed in all areas, including working with computers. Students were encouraged to figure things out for themselves, to think. Peer teaching and cooperative learning were used extensively. He taught students directly how to work in a cooperative setting and how to stay on task, always reinforcing good behavior. Gradually, the teacher became a facilitator, providing constant encouragement and reinforcement and more freedom. On the computer he only taught word processing and later on spread sheets; the rest they worked out for themselves as needed. "It's not about goofy things you can do on a computer. They need skills of communication." Students were taught to read their work aloud and have five other students read it as well, constantly making changes as needed. He believed they need to learn to do a number of drafts and make improvements as they go along. Lower achievers accessed and understood good writing by reading others' work. Students served as models for each other in peer teaching and collaborative learning, and projects allowed for more collaboration. Everything has relation to the real world. The newsletter project integrated all the language-arts state standards for sixth grade.

THEY DON'T WANT TO DISAPPOINT ME!

But none of this can happen without effective classroom management, Woods emphasized.

"It starts with good classroom management. Once you've got that then you can move onto a higher level. My kids have, I like to think, a healthy fear of me, it's a fear of authority, I think it's a good thing. They don't want to disappoint me. One kid sent me a letter. He wrote, 'Why are you so strict? Do you really care for us? I want to be just like you when I grow up.' Every day I struggle, I hurt. There are kids that make poor choices—in their behavior. One of the kids I'm struggling with right now said in a letter to me that this is his best year of school. He's still not where I wanted him to be, but he's learning."

Wood stressed, "You have to be strong enough where you are willing to accept kids where they're at. When I say, I know you can, I believe it and they know it."

"Every day I question, how did it go? Good teachers do it automatically every day, just reflect." [Self-reflection was an important aspect of this outstanding teacher.]

"To write lesson plans is difficult for me because I'm changing what I do every day, all the time. Especially with these kinds of kids. I run across situations that I've never experienced like, 'I was woke up by gunshots this morning.' 'My dad was hitting my mom last night.' You must be sympathetic to where kids are, you must listen to them."

Being able to reflect on the day and make the changes based on the needs of the students is the difference between an accomplished and a less accomplished teacher

Clearly, Woods is expert at motivation, setting expectations and reinforcing achievement. He believes that you can intervene and make a difference in any kid's life.

"I truly believe there is no such thing as a bad kid. I never met a bad kid, I have met a bad adult. There's a point in the life of any kid when they become a young adult and it's harder to make change for them, sophomore year in high school. Once they get to middle school it's more difficult to influence kids. Their friends are more important then their teacher."

A classroom can be a nurturing home or a scene of personal destruction—depending on that one significant fixture who can make a difference for kids—the teacher. Woods' classroom was a place that made students feel they could achieve, a place of creative energy and spirit.

Here was a dynamic, effective teacher, but how much did computer training and how much did teacher strategies affect student achievement? Was it only the teacher or was it the ability to use a computer effectively that influenced student growth? To verify Woods' philosophy and teaching strategies, my colleague and I decided to initiate a study of this teacher and one of his classes to see if there was long-term growth. We selected fifteen students who had made the greatest gains in the sixth grade to compare their seventh grade achievement, using their Stanford Achievement Test scores. Current academic achievement scores of Woods' first laptop class at the completion of seventh grade were obtained and compared with their achievement scores at the end of the sixth grade. Students were interviewed about their feelings about school in both sixth and seventh grades and what changes, if any, computer skills had made for them. Parents were interviewed as well for their perceptions of the impact of computers on their children's achievement in school. Middle school laptop teachers and administrators were also interviewed for their views of the abilities of these students. This study would provide both quantitative and qualitative data and give us information on the results of Bob Woods' teaching. The specific questions we were seeking to answer were:

1. Did access to laptop computers in the sixth grade lead to greater academic achievement in the seventh grade for ethnically diverse, low socioeconomic, underachieving middle school students?

2. What were the perceptions of teachers, students, and parents concerning the contributions of laptops to students' academic progress?

3. Did students perceive the portability of the laptop as an advantage to them?

We believed these were important questions to be answered.

WHAT DOES THE RESEARCH SAY?

First we looked at the research in the area of the contribution of computers to student learning and achievement as well as technology in the schools. Most business, government, and educational leaders strongly support the need for computer training and access for all students to provide the skilled workforce needed for the economy's growing dependence on technology. Currently, the cost of technology in our schools is about $3 billion, just over 1 percent of total education spending. Estimates indicate that it will cost about $15 billion to make all of our schools "technology rich," 5 percent of total education spending (Coley, Cradler, & Engel, 1997). Although educational leaders agree that technology should play a major role in 21st-century schools, there are many who question the "return on the investment" in the form of increased student achievement that technology provides. Some authors assert that schools may be overly eager to acquire technology without adequate knowledge of its effect on children.

Among the many spending decisions facing schools is whether to purchase desktop computers or laptops. School laptop programs, sometimes referred to as "anytime, anywhere learning," are designed to have the advantage of blurring the traditional learning boundaries of classroom walls. All students in a laptop program, which typically begins in the seventh grade, have their own computers and therefore have access both at school and at home. The portability of laptops also provides the potential benefit of an additional connection between parents and school. They are also envisioned to help to bridge the gap, or "digital divide," between students with access to technology and those without it by providing equitable access to, and experiences with, computers to all students. What about bridging the "digital divide?" Research has shown that income predicts access to computers at home (Jerald & Orlofsky, 1999) and that the ways computers are used often varies by student race and income (Coley et al., 1997). A recent study also suggests such inequities can have serious consequences for the future of individuals (Roblyer, 2000).

What are the contributions of computers to student learning and achievement? Technology researchers suggest that computers can support authentic tasks using "real world" tools and that they enable students to more fully utilize collaboration. Because of the many claims about the positive impact on learning that will result from computer use, there has been some disappointment in the results of research on the relationship between computers and learning. Past studies have yielded somewhat mixed results. Two major meta-analyses of this research (Kulik, 1994; Sivin-Kachala, 1998) indicated that positive learning gains were made in some academic areas when computers were used and that attitudes toward school are generally improved. Apple Classrooms of Tomorrow (ACOT) evaluations (Baker, Gearhart, & Herman, 1993) showed that students generally improved in critical thinking and problem solving, although these improvements were not particularly reflected in improved achievement scores. Math achievement, as measured by National Assessment of Educational Progress (NAEP) scores, increased for eighth graders when computers were used for problem solving and critical thinking activities (Weglinsky, 1998). Among the findings of a two-year study of laptop programs in seventh, tenth, and eleventh grades by Rockman (1998) were that laptops improved research and analysis skills; that students used computers to find, organize, analyze, and communicate information; and that teachers believed laptops benefited all students' learning. A two-year study of middle school students in South Carolina (Stevenson, 1999) found that use of laptops was associated with a sustained level of academic achievement over time and with sustaining and improving academic achievement among groups of students who historically have not been successful in school.

Investigating the contributions of computers to student achievement is a complex process. Honey, McMillan, Culp, and Carrigg (1999) assert that many factors need to be considered, including the quality of instructional delivery, student attitudes, time spent on computers, and teacher training. According to these authors, a deficiency in many studies is that they did not address more complex issues; they treated technology as discrete rather than studying its use in a social context. The authors asserted that technology should be viewed not as an isolated solution, but as one of many components to address key educational challenges.

THE STUDY

In order to explain whether the increased opportunity to use laptops in sixth grade was related to sustained gains in achievement in seventh grade, we obtained test scores from Stanford Achievement Test, Form 9 (SAT 9), for our quantitative data. Qualitative data included questionnaires and audio-taped interviews of students, parents, middle school teachers, and administrators. Extensive interviews were held with Bob Woods, the sixth grade teacher. Results of questionnaires and interviews were analyzed using both quantitative and qualitative methods.

This study took place in a city in California's Central Valley, which has an extremely diverse and large immigrant population, primarily of Mexican descent, who come here to work as farm laborers and remain permanently. There is also a large group of Hmong, Southeast Asian mountain people, who were brought from Laos because they assisted the Americans during the Vietnam War and were in danger if they remained there. Rosedale, the elementary school that was the site of Woods' sixth grade class, is in a neighborhood made up primarily of low socioeconomic Hispanics and Hmong. When they enter seventh grade Rosedale students are bused to Lincoln Middle School, located in an upper-middle-class neighborhood. Laptop classes have been in existence at the middle school for five years, but students are required to purchase their own computers if they choose to be in these classes. The school's goal was to have all students (seventh and eighth grades) in a laptop program in three years. District and grant funds provided laptops for low socioeconomic students, but a few students managed to buy their own (two students in the study had their own laptop computers). All teachers of laptop classes received extensive training from the district as well as from college courses and had from one to five years experience with laptop classes.

DO LAPTOPS CONTRIBUTE TO HIGHER ACHIEVEMENT?

Did access to laptops in the sixth grade lead to greater academic achievement in the seventh grade for this group of students? Results of the quantitative data analysis found that there were no large changes in achievement at the end of seventh grade. In the sixth grade, all of this group of students scored above the 76th percentile in language (range 76 to 90). By the end of the seventh grade their language scores ranked lower on the whole (range 20 to 73). All students but one ranked lower than their sixth grade scores. One student ranked at the 96th percentile, up from 82 in the sixth grade. In middle school students were using their computers for traditional academic tasks such as papers and reports. Internet access was not available for research at the school.

In reading most were above the 50th percentile (range 49-76) in the sixth grade. At the end of the seventh grade all students but two ranked lower than their sixth grade ranking (range 19 to 45). One student remained the same at 76 and one student ranked higher, going from 74 to 88. Overall, in the district, 60 percent of the sixth grade students were at the 50th percentile in reading and 68 percent of the seventh grade students were at the 50th percentile in reading on the SAT 9. Although we were unable to obtain the data, a Rosedale administrator stated that the sixth grade Rosedale students tended to have lower scores on the SAT 9 when they moved to Lincoln Middle School. This was the major reason for establishing the laptop class at Rosedale.

The test format for the SAT 9 does not differ from sixth to seventh grade, only the level of difficulty is changed. There are no known psychometric reasons for drops between sixth and seventh grade. However, there is a large standard error of measurement, the estimate of the size of the error to be expected in an individual's test score. Students ranking from 26 to 70 percentile are considered average. Therefore, it appears that most students were within average range. From this data it seems that the use of laptops in seventh grade did not contribute to greater student achievement as measured by the SAT 9, although all of them had very positive attitudes about school and their achievement.

Another study completed at Lincoln during the same school year (1999-2000) looked at the effects of computer use on student achievement in seventh grade language arts classrooms and reached a different conclusion. Students also used computers for traditional academic tasks such as writing papers and reports. Those with Internet access could use them for research. But this was not always available at Lincoln.

WHY DID ROSEDALE FALL BEHIND?

Why didn't the Rosedale students also share in this level of achievement? Although the students said they liked being in middle school, liked their teachers, and had a generally positive attitude about the school and their achievement, there could have been problems in adjusting to multiple teachers and a primarily middle-class, Anglo environment. Their self-contained sixth grade class had an extremely encouraging and nurturing atmosphere because the teacher was exceptional in providing support and a "you can do it" approach. His constructivist, project-based curriculum allowed students to work out problems on their own and helped to build confidence in their abilities. Woods stressed that his relationship with the students was most important. In the first two weeks he established his authority as well as built a team. He set up a trusting environment as well as a well-structured classroom. Students knew his expectations, policies, and procedures. He was strict but caring, firm, and understanding. Students knew what he would not tolerate, what the consequences were, and they were held accountable. A mutual respect developed. He clearly believed in their ability to do good work and he valued them as well as their work. Consequently, the students sought his approval and worked very hard to achieve excellence in both their work and their character. Entering middle school they would have a different experience.

TRANSITION INTO MIDDLE SCHOOL

Interviews with administrators and teachers provided evidence that Rosedale students have difficulty making the transition to Lincoln Middle School. Low socioeconomic, ethnically diverse students make up only 15 percent of the total student body at Lincoln and tend to be socially isolated where the majority of students are white and middle class. It was doubly difficult for them to make the transition into a new culture as well as adjust to middle school as self-conscious adolescents. Teachers found it difficult to connect to these students. Teacher expectations, sensitivity to their needs, and helping students become part of the student body were essential for their academic and social development. Although computer expertise was a distinct advantage for these students, to level the playing field for low-income, ethnically diverse, and underachieving middle school students, it was important to provide more than just a laptop computer. The social context, teachers, school environment, and family support were equally important.

IMPORTANCE OF SOCIAL INTEGRATION AND TEACHER RELATIONSHIPS

At both elementary and middle school it is important for teachers to help students become less socially isolated by integrating them into all class and school activities. Rosedale students and their teachers reported that they tend to "hang out" with their elementary school friends and do not feel comfortable with the white, middle-class students who make up the majority of students in the school. Teachers and administrators need to be aware of their special needs. A rally held at Lincoln at the beginning of the school year seated students by elementary schools. Rosedale students were clearly identified and, of course, they were the only students of color. A better plan would have been to allow these students to mix socially at the rally. In one case, a Hmong girl was the only

Rosedale student and the only Hmong placed in an academic block class. She did not communicate or relate to the rest of the white, middle-class students. Although the teacher was Asian, this girl did not communicate with her. The teacher commented that she thought she probably needed to make an effort to spend time talking with this girl particularly since she was failing the class. Another problem reported by the students and the parents was that the Rosedale students had to take a very crowded bus to school, were being harassed by older boys, and couldn't find a place to sit down. Consequently, they had a difficult time transporting their laptops back and forth to school, considering the conditions on the bus. Most of the students said they did not have a printer to use at home and had to pay for the use of the school printer that was expensive for them. In addition, computers would break down and the students did not have the money to have them fixed. This was a hardship for them as well. One of the teachers of a laptop class complained that the Rosedale students didn't bring their laptops to class. He was completely unaware of the problems his students were having, nor did he take the time or effort to ask them why they didn't have their computers. By making an effort to personally relate to and communicate with these students, teachers would be aware of some of these problems and could help to solve them. Instead, some of the students in the study decided to exit from the laptop program and others decided to move to a different school where they felt more welcome.

Bob Woods was aware of these problems because his former students would return to Rosedale to visit and talk to him and he passed on this information to us. They knew he cared about them and could trust and confide in him. He decided to apply to teach at Lincoln in order to mentor the Rosedale students, but he did not get the job.

PERCEPTIONS OF STUDENTS, PARENTS, AND TEACHERS

Perceptions of the contributions of laptops to student academic performance were generally very positive. Comments from interviews fell into the following categories:

"Faster, Easier, Better"

Students, teachers, and parents agreed school work was done better, easier, and "looked nicer." Students with sixth grade laptop experience were "very experienced with the basics and get through lessons quicker," a teacher commented.

"Everyone Learned to Help Each Other"

Collaboration was an important part of the sixth grade. Students worked with partners and helped each other. They continued to work with partners and groups in seventh grade. Helping others was also a source of self-esteem because they were often the computer experts in the class in middle school.

"Empowers Them to Do Things on their Own"

Student centered, active learning—a constructivist approach—enhances learning. One teacher said, "I pushed them to problem solve." Students were challenged and encouraged to figure things out for themselves, both in sixth and seventh grades. Three students with learning problems who were struggling in school previously were making good progress now because of the benefits of visual, hands-on learning, according to their parents.

"School Is Funner," "I Feel Better About Myself"

Students frequently commented that working on laptops was more fun and they felt better at school. Teachers and parents stated students were excited about school, more motivated, and had improved self-esteem.

"Will Benefit Them Professionally," Family Support and Involvement

The assumption cannot be made that low socioeconomic students universally lack access to computers. Some students had computers at home and older brothers and sisters or mothers and fathers who used them at work or school. All parents were supportive and encouraging. They viewed computer skills as preparation for the future. Typical comments were "children do better if taught computer," "I wanted Jorge to have a good career and future," "a better job, better pay."

"Makes Me More Equal With the Other Kids"

Moving from a low socioeconomic, ethnically diverse school to a primarily middle-class Anglo environment is difficult. The sixth grade laptop class helped to level the playing field for these students. All of the students and teachers reported that they were able to work effectively on the computers, could keep up with the class, and even assist others who were having problems.

PORTABILITY

Students definitely saw the portability of the laptop as an advantage because they didn't have to share them. Homework and assignments could be completed at home or at school more easily and in a timely manner. However, most felt the laptop was heavy and hard to carry around without dropping it. No printer at home and breaking down were some problems experienced. The money was not available to repair the computer as needed or to pay for printing. Middle-class kids had computers and printers at home, so they didn't have to carry their laptops back and forth to school. Also, they had parents who could help them with computer glitches and could more easily pay for repairs.

"It's Not About Laptops–It's About Kids"

This statement was made by the director of the Lincoln Middle School technology program, who added, "laptops are just a tool." A teacher commented that laptops are "not a magic pencil," they can't make a difference alone.

WHAT WE LEARNED FROM THIS STUDY

How did Bob Woods' class make a difference for these students? His focus was not on laptops but on the students and his relationship with them. The process began in the first weeks of school. He established his authority by setting down class policy, procedures, and routines. He developed trust between teacher and students, stressing respect, structure, and team building. Primarily, he communicated to the students that he cared for them and had high expectations for them. They were held accountable for their behavior. Most important, he specifically taught them appropriate behavior and what values were expected in his classroom. He was strict but provided a positive classroom atmosphere. Students learned to be responsible for their learning and behavior. All of this is what any good teacher does at the beginning of the year. Where it differs is that he continually communicated his belief in their ability to do well and he sincerely believed in them. He did not blame their environment or their parents and families for their failure. He put the responsibility to succeed with each student, and the students worked hard to win his approval.

The school newsletter was the culmination of his work with the students. To reach this goal students first developed the skills they needed; reading, language, and problem solving. Computers were not the focus, but only the powerful tool that supported learning. Word processing and formatting were taught.

Students learned the rest on their own by problem solving. In this classroom the process was more important than the product. Students working on the newsletter made decisions on their own, deciding who to interview, what pictures to take, and making all necessary arrangements. They were expected to take on the full responsibility.

A recent study by Wenglinsky (2000) for Educational Testing Service analyzed data from the National Assessment of Educational Progress (NAEP) and linked classroom practices to student academic performance. Students whose teachers emphasize higher-order thinking skills and hands-on learning activities outperform their peers significantly. When teachers focus on conveying higher-order thinking skills, particularly those involving the development of strategies to solve different types of problems, students perform better on math assessments. The study reveals the overwhelming importance of teacher quality to student academic performance. According to Wenglinsky, it appears that classroom practices have a larger impact than any other measure of teacher quality, and teacher quality has an impact on student test scores that is comparable in degree to that of student socioeconomic status.

The importance of interpersonal and relational communication in teaching cannot be overemphasized. McCroskey and Richmond (1993) in a review of communication in teaching state:

> Positive teacher-student relationships, particularly in the early grades are critical to student learning. In large measure, students learn what they want to learn, and if they have a positive relationship with a teacher they are more likely to want to learn from the teacher. Research has indicated that when student/teacher relationships are positive, there is a substantial reduction in student misbehaviors and a much greater likelihood of student compliance with teacher requests. (p. 168)

Another aspect is "teacher-student affinity." "Affinity" is the student's liking for the teacher, the rapport the teacher has with the student. Research supports that the higher the student's affinity for the teacher, the more likely it is that the student will engage in behaviors recommended by the teacher, that the student will like the subject matter the teacher teaches, and that the student will learn that subject matter (Daly & Kreiser, 1992). This appears to be the case in Woods' classroom.

By demonstrating that you care and are concerned, are aware of their problems and needs, you will be able to connect to your students in a positive manner. Unless you are communicating, you cannot be there to provide the support and encouragement they need. Just providing laptop computers will not make a difference for underachieving students. Providing opportunities for students to use their capabilities to the fullest in a supportive, nurturing classroom environment will make a difference.

CULTURE AND WHITE MIDDLE-CLASS TEACHERS

Although there is a rapidly growing minority population in the United States, the teacher workforce is primarily white and middle class. Motivational strategies, classroom management routines, and teaching styles, once effective with most students, are failing (Abi-Nader, 1993). The literature suggests that teachers daily enter a culture they admit is foreign to them and practice a pedagogy just as foreign to their students. An example would be the concept of familia, which is central to cultural descriptions of Hispanic people. In a study of 85 Hispanic families living in the United States, Cintron de Esteves and Spicola (1982) found family to be the "first priority in life." The characteristics of "family" that surface in this and other studies include a sense of acceptance and belonging that extends beyond the nuclear family to embrace grandparents, cousins, aunts, uncles, and in-laws. Studies show that culture deeply affects the cognitive development and achievement motivation of minority students and does so in a familial mode that differs from the mainstream American emphasis on individualism (Suarez-Orozco, 1989).

CULTURE, COGNITIVE DEVELOPMENT AND MOTIVATION

Vygotsky, in his theory of cognitive development, emphasizes the importance of social interaction and language (Cole, 1985). By using language in social situations, more knowledgeable partners share their expertise about the world. Instructional strategies based on Vygotsky's theory place students in situations where topics and skills discussed are within the developmental grasp of the learner. This area is called the zone of proximal development; tasks that a child cannot do alone can be accomplished when assisted by a more skilled partner. Collaborative learning and peer teaching are examples of this type of teaching strategy. In Abi-Nader's (1993) study of Hispanic high school students in a successful college prep program, the concept of "family" was the means for achieving motivational objectives, and use of this concept of "family" united the students and gave them a sense of belonging. The motivational model developed by Ryan, Connell, and Deci (1985) proposes that intrinsic motivation results from the satisfaction of basic psychological needs for competence, autonomy, and relatedness. When provided with support and involvement in an educational environment, the student experiences engagement and success. Thus, motivation requires teachers be aware of the students' frame of reference. In middle school, Rosedale students moved from class to class and found "family" only with others from their own community. Diaz, Moll, and Mehan (1986) state:

> It is possible to capitalize on children's social, linguistic and academic strengths to change teaching and learning situations. To do so we need to view students' backgrounds and life styles, not as a hindrance to educational advancement that must be corrected or circumvented, but as legitimate and powerful resources for improving students' performance in schools, and as a consequence, improving the process of schooling itself. (p. 225)

Woods effectively used knowledge of his students, motivation strategies, and his own personality to develop a sense of family in his classroom.

CULTURE AND TEACHING

Liston and Zeichner (1996), in their book *Culture and Teaching,* raise two important questions, "How does one create more equitable and just educational settings in a society that is essentially inequitable and unjust?" and "How does one utilize the dynamics of culture when those dynamics seem to put students of color at a disadvantage?" (p. 84). Their response was, "In schools we must do what we can, we must make every effort possible to offer students an education that is meaningful and empowering" (p. 85). In addition, they state that it is important for teachers to be sensitive to the cultural assumptions in schools and the cultural baggage that we all carry into schools. When teachers face diverse classrooms, made up of many cultural backgrounds, this task is even more complex. Woods made the effort to empower his students as well as provide meaningful activities for them.

Another important response by Liston and Zeichner (1996) is "Schools and teachers can *build character*" (p. 86). This can happen through honest, caring, and nurturing interpersonal interactions and through the creation of classrooms that affirm each student. Teachers need to model this.

> Students need to see examples of adults before them who care deeply and act carefully in the schools and the surrounding neighborhoods. They need to hear adults voice their concerns and affirm their beliefs in others. . . . Teachers must live a life that cares for and sustains others. Teachers need to be the kind of individuals that they want their students to become. (p. 86)

Deborah Meier (1995) of the Central Park East Secondary Schools in Manhattan, New York, writes:

> Caring and compassion are not soft, mushy goals. They are part of the hard core of subjects we are responsible for teaching. Informed and skillful care is learned. Caring is as much cognitive as affective. (p. 63)

Bob Woods was an excellent example of a caring adult and a model for his students. Building character, sensitivity to students' needs, and caring were central to Wood's classroom environment. Students worked together, helped each other, and responded positively to their teachers' expectations.

MULTICULTURAL EDUCATION AND THE GOOD TEACHER

Multicultural education is synonymous with effective teaching (Hernandez, 1989). Good teachers have a deeper and broader understanding of students as learners and an expanded repertoire of strategies and techniques. Multicultural education emphasizes high expectations, adaptation to accommodate individual learner differences, and presentation of all subjects to all students. Bob Woods provided all of the above.

Next to parents, teachers are the single most important factor in the lives of children (Baker, 1983). Individual teachers can and do make a difference in student learning and to a great extent they determine the degree to which education is truly multicultural. Classroom interaction between teachers and students constitutes the major part of the educational process for most students, and "the manner in which the teacher interacts with the student is a major determinant of the quality of education they receive."

What is a good teacher? Clark (1995) reports on his survey of teachers in his book, *Thoughtful Teaching:*

> To teachers, the heart of good teaching is not in management or decision-making or pedagogical content knowledge. No, the essence of good teaching, for teachers, is in the area of human relationships. Teaching is good when a class becomes a community of honest, nurturant and mutually respectful people. (p. 14)

Clark describes two aspects of "thoughtful teaching":

> "Thoughtful teaching" highlights two important aspects of the lives and work of teachers. The first is that teaching is an intellectual enterprise. Teaching demands a great deal of thought in the classic forms of study, problem solving and decision-making. The second sense of thoughtful is to be considerate of another, particularly of the feelings of another. A thoughtful person is empathic. He or she knows how I feel and responds to me in ways that comfort, reassure and encourage. A thoughtful person is able to do two things well: see and feel life from the perspective of another and say and do the right things when we most need that help and support. Thoughtful teaching as being genuinely considerate of children and col-

leagues is less well documented than the intellectual mission of schooling. The intellectual and the relational aspects of teaching are both vital. But being a thoughtful teacher in the second sense often requires teaching against the grain. (p. 15)

Bob Woods was a thoughtful teacher, concerned with the welfare and development of his students, positive, encouraging, and sympathetic to their feelings and needs. He supported the learning of his students with effective teaching strategies and then supported their developing independence.

PERSONAL TRAITS

Reflecting on a study of urban education, Haberman (1993) comments that teaching skills can be taught in the University or through field experiences in the classroom, but personal traits (empathetic, open-minded, positive, dedicated, patient, loving, flexible, and self-confident) are much more likely to be developed in places other than university classes. The obvious implication for Haberman was that these traits are truly crucial, and the selection of teachers for minority children is far more important than training. Believing that all children can learn, being committed to knowing children, and enjoying, caring for, and respecting them, seems to transcend teacher training. The need is to prepare culturally aware, sensitive individuals to operate on these principles.

Bob Woods was obviously an intelligent, thoughtful teacher with all the appropriate personal traits, character, and empathy needed to work with these children. However, his character and personal traits are not easily copied by others and it is these traits that made the difference in his classroom. Although technology provides support and motivation for students in the classroom, it is the teacher and the relationship with the student that truly influences student outcomes and school success. In the end, it's not about computers, it's about the kids!

REFERENCES

Abi-Nader, J. (1993). Meeting the needs of multicultural classrooms: Family values and the motivation of minority students. In J. O'Hair & S. Odell (Eds), *Diversity and teaching*. Fort Worth, TX: Harcourt Brace Jovanovich.

Baker, E. L., Gearhart, M., & Herman, J. L. (1993). *The Apple Classrooms of Tomorrow: The UCLA evaluation studies* (CSE Technical Report No. 353). Los Angeles: Center for the Study of Evaluation, Graduate School of Education, University of California, Los Angeles.

Baker, G. C. (1983). *Planning and organizing for multicultural instruction.* Reading, MA: Addison-Wesley.

Cintron de Esteves, C., & Spicola, R. F. (1982). *Four Hispanic groups: Oral and social traditions, education and play implications for educators* (Report No. RC 013 872). Chicago: International Reading Association. (ERIC Documentary Reproduction Services ED 226 897).

Clark, C. M. (1995). *Thoughtful teaching.* New York: Teachers College Press.

Cole, M. (1985). The zone of proximal development: Where culture and cognition create each other. In J.V. Wertsch (Ed), *Culture, communication and cognition: Vygotskian perspectives* (pp. 146-161). New York: Cambridge University Press.

Coley, R., Cradler, J., & Engel, P. (1997). *Computers and classrooms: The status of technology in U. S. schools.* Princeton, NJ: Educational Testing Service. Available online at www.ets.org/research/pic/compclass.html

Daly, J. A., & Kreiser, P. O. (1992). Affinity in the classroom. In V. P. Richmond & J. C. McCroskey (Eds.). *Power in the classroom: Communication, control and concern* (pp. 121-143). Hillsdale, NJ: Erlbaum.

Diaz, S., Moll, L. C., & Mehan, H. (1986). Sociocultual resources in instruction: A context-specific approach. In *Beyond language: Social and cultural factors in schooling language minority students* (pp. 187-230). Los Angeles: Evaluation, Dissemination and Assessment Center.

Haberman, M. (1993). Contexts: Implications and reflections. In M. J. O'Hair & S. J. Odell (Eds.), *Diversity and teaching, Teacher education yearbook I.* Fort Worth, TX: Harcourt Brace Jovanovich.

Hernandez, H. (1989). *Multicultural education: A teacher's guide to content and process.* Columbus, OH: Merrill Publishing Company.

Honey, M., McMillan, F., Culp, K., & Carrigg, F. *Perspectives on technology and education research: Lessons from the past and present.* The Secretary's Conference on Educational Technology, U.S. Department of Education. Available online at: http://www.edc.org/LNT/news/issue12/feature1.htm

Jerald, C. D., & Orlofsky, G. F. (1999). Raising the bar on technology. *Technology Counts.*

Kulik, J. A. (1994). Meta-analytic studies of findings on computer-based instruction. In E.L. Baker & H.F. O'Neil, Jr. (Eds.), *Technology assessment in education and training.* Hillsdale, NJ: Erlbaum.

Liston, D. P., & Zeichner, K. M. (1996). *Culture and teaching.* Mahwah, NJ: Erlbaum.

McCroskey, J. C., & Richmond, V. P. (1993). Communication: Implications and reflections. In M. J. O'Hair, & S. J. Odell (Eds.) *Diversity and teaching: Teacher education yearbook I.* Fort Worth, TX: Harcourt Brace Jovanovich.

Meier, D. (1995). *The power of their ideas.* Boston: Beacon Press.

Roblyer, M. D. (2000). Digital desperation: Reports on a growing technology and equity crisis. *Learning & Leading with Technology, 27*(8), 50-53, 61.

Rockman, S. (1998, September). *Powerful tools for schooling: Second year study of the laptop program.* San Francisco, CA: Microsoft Corporation, Toshiba America Information Systems.

Ryan, R. M., Connell, J. P., & Deci, E. L. (1985). A motivational analysis of self-determination and self-regulation in education. In C. Ames & R. E. Ames (Eds.), *Research on motivation in education: The classroom milieu (*Vol. 2, pp. 13-52). New York:Academic Press.

Sivin-Kachala, J. (1998). *Report on the effectiveness of technology in schools, 1990-1997.* Software Publisher's Association.

Stevenson, K. (1999, April). Learning by laptop. *School Administrator,* pp. 18-21.

Suarez-Orozco, M. M. (1989). *Central American refugees and U.S. high schools: A psychosocial study of motivation and achievement.* Stanford, CA: Stanford University Press.

Wenglinsky, H. (1998). *Does it compute? The relationship between educational technology and student achievement in mathematics.* Educational Testing Service Policy Information Center.

Wenglinsky, H. (2000). *How teaching matters: Bringing the classroom back into discussions of teacher quality.* Educational Testing Service Policy Information Center.

CHAPTER THIRTEEN

School Leadership and Diverse Student Populations

Naftaly S. Glasman

University of California, Santa Barbara

A day in early July, perfect for climbing. From the mesas above Boulder, Colorado, a heat-cutting breeze drove the smell of the pines up onto the great tilting slabs of the Flatirons.

It was 1961; I was eighteen, had been climbing about a year, Gabe even less. We were about 600 feet up, three quarters of the way to the summit of the First Flatiron. There wasn't a guidebook in those days, so we didn't know how difficult our route was supposed to be or who had previously done it. But it had gone all right, despite the scarcity of places to bang our Austrian soft-iron pitons; sometimes we'd just wedge our bodies in a crack and yell, 'On belay!'

It was a joy to be climbing. Climbing was one of the best things—maybe the best thing—in life, given that one would never play shortstop for the Dodgers. There was a risk, as my parents and friends kept pointing out; but I knew the risk was worth it.

David Roberts (1986, p. 195)

BACKGROUND

Multifaceted Leadership

Schools are about imparting and acquiring knowledge and skills, and in such a high stakes game, the risk of failure is omnipresent. In schools, individuals may wear "a leader's hat" and/or "a follower's hat" depending on their involvement in a particular activity. Teachers, for example, act as leaders when they guide students' learning. Teachers also act as leaders when they inform program specialists or school principals what additional material they need for their teaching. Students also lead. This happens, for example, when students identify situations in which they transcend the need for the teachers' help. Other examples include program specialists or school principals who act as leaders when they guide teachers in the development of instructional plans, particularly those that will enhance students' ability to meet state-mandated curriculum standards. As the leader, being out in front has both the advantage of prestige and risk of failure.

The interdependence among individuals in schools and the interchangeability of leader and follower roles reflect what Spillane, Halverson, and Diamond (2001) label "distributed human activities." These authors see leadership in schools as spanning over an "interactive web of actors and situations." As such, the enactment of leadership tasks in schools becomes distributed across multiple leaders–from students to teachers, counselors, program specialists, assistant principals, and principals. Most importantly, multicultural educators view leadership democratically. This view is well articulated by Steinberg and Kincheloe (1999):

> One of the most important ways (educators can act as a countervailing force) involves challenging conceptually the administrative structures of schools. It is interesting that administration is taught only to people who serve at the head of the administrative structure and not to people who are to be administered. Ideas about democratic forms of management are not concepts that are typically discussed between principals and teachers or teachers and student. As Henry Giroux (1997) argues, critical multiculturalists want to engage students and teachers in an analysis of what is involved in becoming a critical citizen capable of governing instead of merely being governed. (pp. 68-69)

Whereas the distributed leadership framework addresses the practice of school leadership in general, this chapter concerns leadership in relation to the diversity of the student population in particular. Also, although there are multiple leaders in each school and even more than one in a school's central office, the focus of this chapter is on the leadership of the principal. The operating assumption here is that nothing that is attributed to the principal in this chapter could have been conceptualized or occurred in practice without the consideration of the assistance and support of the other leaders in the school's central office (Ubben, Hughes, & Norris, 2001).

The Issue of Limited Control

Any work on the school leader's specific duties and creative activities, especially if described to readers who are not intimately acquainted with the subject, needs to be preempted by a brief discussion of the limited control of the principal. Such preempting is not designed as a disclaimer but rather as a parameter within which the subject should be understood. It is interesting to note that this parameter has been talked about in specific terms primarily in private. In public, and thus also in print, one detects only concepts. It may be that to admit in public to having insufficient control is to admit to achieving less than expected. The latter is often uncomfortable to do (Langer, 1983).

In private one hears, for example, that public school leaders have no control over who enrolls in their schools. Too, leaders receive only minimal discretionary dollars. Despite having formal responsibilities to guide, supervise, and evaluate teachers, principals' influence about what happens in classrooms (once the doors are closed) is minimal and, at least, indirect. Yet, especially in recent years, when demands for accountability in education have intensified, principals' responsibilities increased substantially while their authorities remained the same and in some cases even decreased (Goertz & Duffy, 2000). Rendering judgment about the extent to which principals' accountability is achieved has become a function largely of scores on standardized tests and of the comparison of these scores with state-mandated minimum standards. Principals have had almost no direct input in the determination of the tests or the standards. To a large extent teachers and program specialists are operating within the same parameters.

The increased imbalance between the school leader's authorities and responsibilities has been a major factor in the increased insufficiency of the control that the leader needs to have in order to remain effective (DePasquale, 1996; Glasman, 1994; Rosenholtz, 1985; Sergiovanni, 2000). Another factor contributing to this insufficiency has been the uncertainty associated with the principal's work (Kahneman, Slovic, & Tversky, 1982; Pounder, Ogawa, & Adams, 1997). Other, somewhat more specific factors include the following: (a) the complexity of the school leadership, an ongoing process, (b) the often unpredictable mixing of assigned tasks, learned behaviors and attitudes, and discretionary acts, (c) the production of as many unintentional outcomes as intentional ones, and (d) the need to fulfill expectations of multiple and varied stakeholders (Glasman & Biniaminov, 1981; Gorton & Snowdon, 1999; Hoy & Miskel, 2001; Murphy & Seashore-Louis, 1999).

Compare, for example, a high school principal's level of control to that of his/her basketball coach. The coach can substitute players during a game. The principal cannot replace teachers or students in the same manner. Or consider a school's choir director who can schedule or cancel a concert at will, whereas the principal cannot schedule or cancel student attendance, or even dates for cutting the grass in school. Also, every teacher can call at will a student to order, if needed, but a principal cannot call a parent to order.

It goes on: the school's mean test scores are student-derived and not directly based on efforts extended by the principal. Likewise, the state financial allocation is based on average daily attendance, the grass grows as a function of its health, and the parent's rights are anchored in law. Many of the principals' actions are less predetermined.

The insufficient control problem has been exacerbated with the increase in the student linguistic and cultural diversity. For example, debates have intensified about what individual differences mean in student school readiness, learning styles, developmental processes, and achievement. Efficacy of known teaching strategies has also been questioned. Even the day-to-day related managerial duties of principals have been reexamined (Rosenbach & Taylor, 1999). Although some principals report that increased diversity is a "nonissue" (Riehl, 2000), recent reports (Blackman & Fenwick, 2000) indicate that principal shortages are becoming acute due to several factors, including existing frustrations with, or refusal to enter a profession where one cannot sufficiently control that for which the one is responsible.

Selected Components

I report here data about only two components of leadership. I do so because of two reasons. First, these are the only components about which evidence has been gathered recently and reliably. Second, I am able to frame the available evidence about these components in the context of concepts that have been found to be dependable and useful in the literature on educational leadership.

One of these components involves the development and nurturing of a variety of school visions, each of which embraces student diversity. The other includes the use of all available means to actually incorporate student diversity. By "embracing" diversity I mean "accepting it readily." By "incorporating" I mean "embodying it" and merging it with the school identity. I see the developing and nurturing of the vision as walking in front of followers. The use of means to implement the vision is like walking along with followers. I view both as happening simultaneously. The next two sections describe the recent findings in some detail.

LEADERSHIP: DEVELOPING AND NURTURING VISIONS THAT EMBRACE DIVERSITY

The development and nurturing of visions for schools have always been included among the tasks of school leaders (Cunningham & Cordiero, 2000). The specifics of a vision as a leadership function has not been studied much, perhaps because the efficacy of setting specifics for a vision has been questioned. Nonetheless, mental images of aspects of leadership as vision "setting" have been looked at. For example, educational visions as paths that schools should follow have been found to relate to school leaders' value-driven belief systems (Glasman & Sell, 1972; Lakowski, 1987). Other determinants of visions have been found to include the leaders' attitudes about education that have become solidified so as to constitute their "unalterable educational ideologies" (Bista, 1994; Gardner, 1995; Glasman, 1986).

The process of developing a vision, in essence, seems to begin when the leader activates an ideology-based-and-shaped set of perceptions about the need for a vision and about his/her own role in its development. Guiding concepts about the directions and paths in which the school might go are formed. Depending on the leadership style of the school leader (Bista & Glasman, 1998), various kinds of influence are exerted (e.g., referent-based, expertise-based, role-based), designed to have these concepts accepted. Once the vision is formally accepted, the nurturing process begins, as guiding policies are developed for the implementation of the vision and for monitoring the implementation (Pounder, Ogawa, & Adams, 1997; Razik & Swanson, 2000).

Developing and nurturing visions in schools with linguistic and cultural diversity have not been studied extensively at all (Sergiovanni, 2000). Some writers noted that such functions ought to be integral parts of the principal leadership (Riehl, 2000). Two "oughts" have been studied and, in theory, defended. One is that the vision of the principal in response to diversity ought to be to achieve "inclusiveness" (Riehl, 2000). The other (Drake & Roe, 1999) is that the schools ought to have several visions that should reflect the array of visions found in the society as a whole.

To support multiculturalism I suggest three subcomponents of "leadership as embracing diversity." I also suggest three requirements that school leaders need to fulfill so as to be effective in pursuing each of these leadership subcomponents. The three subcomponents include a vision of "academic" embracing of diversity (Glasman & Fuller, in press), a vision of "internal sociocultural embracing" (Riehl, 2000), and a vision of "external sociocultural" embracing (Crowson & Boyd, in press). I suggest that academic embracing requires the leader to be "evaluation" minded (Ardovino, Hollingsworth, & Ybarra, 2000; Glasman & Nevo, 1988); internal sociocultural embracing—"political" and "symbolic" mindedness (Bista & Glasman, 1998; Bolman & Deal, 1993); and external sociocultural embracing—"communication" mindedness (Crowson & Boyd, in press; Razik & Swanson, 2000).

Academic Embracing

One possible vision that California voters had when they approved Proposition 227 in 1998 was that children of immigrant families would learn to read in English as soon as they started school. The proposition called for the elimination of the dual linguistic track for Limited English Program (LEP) students. As expected, several parents applied for waivers that permitted the continuation of their children's study in bilingual classes and for the postponement of their being mainstreamed into English-only classes.

School district superintendents and school principals in California were mandated to carry out this vision. The state had no plan of its own for the actual implementation (Glasman & Fuller, in press). It was up to the local educational authorities to decide how to abide by the state mandate. Issues such as the following emerged: (a) to what extent does the politically derived academic vision of English-only instruction make academic sense pedagogically? (learning to read English early versus learning to understand cognitive concepts in one's native language); (b) what effects would the new mandate have on teacher recruitment (finding teachers who can teach English to non-English speakers), teaching processes (material covered), and instructional and administrative leadership of the principal's school-wide academic embracing of diversity?; and (c) how do school district leaders develop a plan to implement the new mandate that takes into consideration the existence of value-driven beliefs of those stakeholders who wish to continue the status quo regardless of the new mandate (continued bilingual instruction)?

In one large elementary school district in California (K-8, close to 30,000 students), a conscious decision was made to deal with these issues by transforming the political vision into academic embracing of student diversity. A two-pronged plan was developed with a focus on academics and an overarching thrust of the intensification of the teaching of English. One dimension was to focus the academic embracing of individual differences in the earliest possible grade level: kindergarten. Each principal was charged with developing a specific plan that was designed to improve the learning of low achievers in reading and language arts. Most low achievers were "diverse" students. This effort was labeled "group reading readiness" in which all kindergartners in a given class would share what they learn with everyone else. The specifics were prepared with the help of teachers and specialists and also with assistance from the district's central office.

The second dimension of the vision of academic embracing was to focus on the student population that was the furthest behind in reading: the seventh and eighth graders. Each principal of a middle school in the district was charged with developing, with the help of teachers and specialists, a specific plan of reading instruction. This dimension was labeled "reading instruction only." It amounted to a pilot program of a separate class in simply learning how to read in English for low-achieving seventh and eighth graders.

A major similarity existed in the objectives of the two dimensions in this school district. It was the emphasis on improving reading ability for its own sake as well as to enable diverse students to benefit from other subjects and classes offered in their schools (Glasman & Fuller, in press).

In order to achieve the objectives, school principals acquired additional knowledge and skills in evaluation. Diagnosis of student products and test scores was needed. Principals were also coached in becoming evaluation-minded. This meant having awareness that facts (about the use of curriculum, teaching process, and student learning and achievement) must be continuously gathered and judgment must be rendered on an ongoing basis as to the merit of these facts. Adjustments had to be made on the basis of these periodic evaluations (Glasman, 1986). The plan included guidance in acting the role of an administrator-evaluator (Glasman, 1979; Glasman & Nevo, 1988). The key assumption underpinning the execution of this role was the adoption of the assumption that "diverse" students are "different" rather than "deficient" (Cunningham & Cordiero, 2000). This approach impacted the entire evaluation designs.

Academic embracing included planning, implementing, and evaluating in both projects (kindergarten and grades seven and eight). The projects were first implemented in a few schools only. Teachers were trained in special aspects of academic embracing "strategies" in the classrooms (attending to differences rather than deficiencies) as well as in evaluating their own efforts. Overall, the vision included actions designed to attract and gain teacher acceptance. Once they "bought in," teachers acquired a strong stake in the projects. They even made modifications in the vision itself as it was being implemented, and they did so on the basis of student test scores on benchmarks throughout the year. With regard to these modifications, the teachers' trust that principals would back them up also figured into the vision (DePasquale, 1996). In their contacts with district officials, principals defended and even advocated the position of the teachers in their schools.

Internal Sociocultural Embracing

The concept of sociocultural embracing has its roots (in America) in the political vision of "unifying the vision as a whole." The first advocates among educators of this vision were the missionaries of the mid-nineteenth century. These missionaries traveled from village to village and from town to town seeking to help develop a school system that was governed by the public. The missionaries believed that only through such schools could a unified nation be established. The latter was their ultimate goal (Tyack & Hansot, 1982). It took about 100 additional years before it became clear that sociocultural embracing of diversity in public schools is not only a needed vision for the schools but also for the nation as a whole (Coleman, 1966).

In recent years, immigration has intensified. Several problems also remain in association with the attempts to integrate and acculturate children of second- and third-generation immigrants. Some school leaders are reported to have fared poorly in this regard. Riehl (2000), for example, found that some principals do not even acknowledge the existence of problems associated with children of immigrants and their sociocultural acculturation. These principals do not acknowledge the existence of problems such as hate and stereotyping, either. Sarason (1996) suggests that several principals are actually committed to legitimizing and even valuing existing orders and are against change. Wolcott (1973) asserts that some principals are often involved much more with "continuities" than with reexaminations and adjustments. Riehl (2000) cites examples where principals have not made even minor efforts toward achieving some degree of sociocultural inclusiveness.

On the other hand, some studies identify the occurrences of partial efforts extended by school principals in this regard. One of the early studies that detected significant principal responses was that by Rosenholtz (1985). She identified several routes by which principals try to achieve sociocultural inclusiveness. Her findings amounted to phenomena whereby principals work directly with teachers on sociocultural issues. For example, she found principals who helped teachers decrease their own uncertainties about what they should adopt as instructional and social goals. Rosenholtz also found several cases in which principals were actually guiding teachers in choosing "student inclusiveness" as a primary general goal to attain via classroom activities.

Other studies found additional information. Newmann (1992) and Banks and McGee-Banks (1993) summarized evidence about principals who helped establish "professional" communities of teachers who work with diverse students on both academic and social goals. Such communities seem to help reduce teachers' dissatisfaction and frustrations. Herrity (1997) and Riehl (2000) report about additional studies that suggest that principals work on even broader sociocultural goals.

On the basis of her detailed examination of the literature, Riehl (2000) suggests that sociocultural inclusiveness in the school requires the following:

1. Working with teachers on adopting personalized approaches to students,

2. Working with teachers on appreciating cultural knowledge displayed by students,

3. Creating a caring environment,

4. De-tracking to ensure students' equal and effective access to instruction,

5. Encouraging teachers to continuously examine their academic institution and social coaching (see Herrity, 1997),

6. Having teachers hold high expectations for all students,

7. Taking personally an advocacy approach regarding various forms of discrimination,

8. Taking personally strong steps to meet with all parents (see Smrekar, 1996), and

9. Using interethnic conflicts as opportunities for making changes.

According to Bista (1994), these kinds of inclusiveness efforts require a style of school leadership that is both political and symbolic in nature (Bolman & Deal, 1993). The political style is needed because internal coalitions have to be formed among the school personnel who maybe driven by different ideologies and, thus, hold different opinions on what has to be done. Developing tolerance of ideological differences of opinions is one political strategy. Give and take is another. Symbolic leadership is necessary because without it, leaders cannot foster changes in the meaning of "diversity," or "inclusiveness," or "sociocultural embracing" (Riehl, 2000). Perhaps nothing invokes shared meaning in education more effectively and efficiently than symbols do.

External Sociocultural Embracing

Schools with diverse student populations often need to rely on "mediating institutions" (Berger & Neuhaus, 1997) if their vision to embrace diversity includes student socialization not only to the school but also to the society at large. Such institutions are voluntary associations that work along with parents to socialize youngsters into a variety of processes in the society. Schools capitalize on this work to enhance their own efforts to achieve internal sociocultural inclusiveness. Often, such efforts can help individuals "cross the boundaries," a feat that is quite difficult to accomplish (Sarason & Lorentz, 1998). The physical sites outside the schools become the important components in the development of entire communities (Crowson & Boyd, in press).

It is the school itself that must be the central participating institution if this endeavor is to succeed (Rossi, 1994). There simply is no other institution that touches as many households in a given neighborhood as the school does. The school is recognized as a central institution in the neighborhood and any attempt to work on the "development" of the entire community requires the school's participation. In this model, mutual interdependence develops between the school and the neighborhood. The leader of the centrally participating institution (the school) by nature becomes the "bridge builder" among institutions, the "buffer constructor," and the "political negotiator" (Crowson & Boyd, in press).

Communication mindedness is one of the most important requirements that the school leader must possess for accomplishing these tasks effectively (Glasman, 1994; Razik & Swanson, 2000). The nature of the communication channels between collaborating leaders of the different organizations is important here, as is the nature of the communication channels between their respective leaders and the followers within each organization. School principals typically work with leaders of other organizations in the neighborhood to identify mutually beneficial organizational interests. Communication is key to the understanding and appreciating of the vested interests of "other" organizations. School leaders also work with their own people. Here, communication is central to the conveyance to followers in one's own organization of what the nature of the interorganizational benefits might be (Hoy & Miskel, 2001). Proposals to adopt ways of meeting the mutually beneficial organizational interests heavily depend on effectively articulating both the interests themselves and the ways to meet them (Driscoll & Kerchner, 1999; Etzioni, 1993; Morgan, 1986).

LEADERSHIP: USING ALL AVAILABLE MEANS TO ACTUALLY INCORPORATE DIVERSITY

The discussion of school leadership as a collection of methods that embrace diversity could clearly have been extended to include the ways in which leaders may communicate and embody their vision (Gardner, 1995). I do partial justice to this omission by discussing two practical sets of concerns. One relates to the actual implementation of visions. The other has to do with keeping the diverse people "together" while a vision is being implemented (Rosenbach & Taylor, 1999). Messages about visions must be continuously and repeatedly communicated because new students enroll every year. Embodying visions is also a continuous and a repeated process.

In this regard, the literature suggests the relevance of three sets of activities: the leader's deployment of problem-finding tools, the leader's actual engagement in problem solving, and the leader's interactions with teachers as a specific focus. Problem finding is crucial in schools with diverse populations because of the vulnerability of these schools and because problems are often not easily discovered until it is too late. Actual problem solving needs no justification other than suggesting that unsolved "small" problems may lead to bigger ones. As to teachers, often what they receive in the form of preservice or inservice training in working with diverse student populations is insufficient. Teachers need guidance while on the job.

Using Problem Finding Tools

School leadership as problem finding (Immegart & Boyd, 1979) has been emphasized in the general school leadership literature as well as in related sociological literature. In school leadership, a key assumption is that active problem finding requires knowledge about what constitutes a problem or an unsettled question (Bridges & Hallinger, 1995). Another key assumption is that active problem finding is helpful in identifying the problems and the overall effects of their existence

(Banks & McGee-Banks, 1993; Glasman, 1994). How central problem finding is to leadership effectiveness is unknown. In response to diversity one should assume that problem finding is central (Banks & Mcgee-Banks, 1993).

Herrity (1997) studied 27 principals of elementary, middle, and high schools in California about their problem-finding efforts. Each of her principals was nominated as an expert in leading his/her school all of which had a diverse student population. The nominations were made independently by each principal's own superintendent and by the director of the district's LEP program. Herrity chose eighteen school districts (in Los Angeles, San Diego, Santa Barbara, and Ventura counties) which, in 1995-96, had the highest number of LEP students (percentage of the district's enrollment). She interviewed each of the 27 principals about the problem-finding activities.

Herrity (1997) detected 21 "major problems" that expert principals perceived as associated with student diversity. These problems relate to students, staff, parents, and/or programs. Below is a list of these problems and the respective range of percentages of principals in the sample who mentioned each one of the problems. Forty to 45 percent of the principals mentioned (1) lack of sensitivity to cultural differences among the students, and (2) unprioritized curriculum needs as central problems. Thirty to 35 percent of the principals mentioned problems of (3) lack of sensitivity to cultural differences among teachers, (4) insufficient staff development and subsequent empowerment, and (5) inadequate class scheduling and student placement in classes. And 20 to 29 percent of the principals mentioned as significant problems the following: (6) insufficient staff integration, (7) issues associated with hiring bilingual teachers and aides, (8) unsatisfactory academic progress of students, (9) unsatisfactory progress in keeping student discipline and safety in check, (10) unsatisfactory relations with parents, and (11) unsatisfactory parental involvement.

Other problems were mentioned by a smaller number of principals. These were problems related to (12) lack of acceptance of LEP special education students by peers, (13) lack of student integration, (14) lack of student pride, (15) language barriers among students, (16) displacing English-only teachers, (17) insufficient success in educating parents about educational programs, (18) bilingual students' transition, (19) conflicts between students and staff, (20) lack of student empowerment, and (21) racial tensions among staff.

Problem numbers 7, 16, 17, and 18 need clarification. They all deal with bilingual instruction directly. As was mentioned earlier, California mandated in 1998 to replace bilingual education with English-only instruction. This was done after Herrity had completed her study. Thus, it is possible that her principals could have provided different examples here, had they been asked after 1998 rather than in 1996. But this conjecture is incomplete because, as was noted earlier, waivers were granted to families who applied to have their children continue to study in bilingual classes.

Much knowledge and experience are required in order to be in a position to identify such significant problems. Herrity found that these principals possessed both. They also were sensitive to the issues. In addition, Herrity's leaders reported having acquired specific knowledge in a number of areas. Among them are legal and compliance requirements, language and culture diversity in the society at large and the community, and parental concerns and needs. These leaders seem to also be aware of the numbers of classes needed in the various cases to ensure student access to the core curriculum, the material support required for such classes, the desired supportive climate, and the necessary categorical funding and grant writing. Several of them also knew quite a bit about theories of second language acquisition, student grouping practices, and evaluation strategies and instruments.

Actual Problem Solving

School leadership as problem solving is discussed in the literature often (Cunningham & Cordiero, 2000; Glasman, 1994; Hoy & Miskel, 2001). Problem solving is often viewed as the main function of school leadership, an even more central component than decision making (Bossert, Dwyer, Brown, & Lee, 1982; Bridges & Hallinger, 1995; Cuban, 1988; Drake & Roe, 1999; Herrity & Glasman, 1999; Oaks, 1985; Sergiovanni, 2000). In schools with diverse student populations, the centrality of problem solving in school leadership is especially pronounced because of the school's vulnerability to problems of all kinds (Riehl, 2000).

"Expert" principals in schools with diverse populations report working with teachers on several of the problems they face (Herrity, 1997, pp. 130-131). They first try to match student needs and teachers' strength in their assignments of teachers to classrooms. They also use specific input to solve problems associated with Title I students. Some problems are at least partially solved with the use of resource teachers.

Herrity (1997) reports that such problem solving requires, on the part of the principal, a strong commitment to a vision for educating LEP students; guiding the instruction they receive; serving as the ultimate decision maker; being highly persuasive; scheduling appropriate classes; and communicating to their parents the value of what the students learn. Herrity cites statements from expert principals about other needed requirements. Among them are possessing recent experience in dealing with parents of LEP students and with diverse cultural populations; becoming sensitive to cultural norms including language differences and cultural understanding by reaching out; communicating well, frequently, and meaningfully with key people with LEP families; and becoming personally involved with LEP programs and students.

Herrity also writes about goals that expert principals set for themselves in this regard (1997, pp. 210-220). One problem solving-related goal is bringing homogeneity across a given grade level. Another may be clarifying to parents exactly what the school and the teachers actually do. The setting of such goals is based on guiding principles. A guiding principle for the former, for example, is "equal access to a core subject." A guiding principle for the latter may be "describing specifics in Spanish."

INTERACTIONS WITH TEACHERS

Education is a labor-intensive industry. Personnel is crucial, and teachers most of all. Working with teachers is a central "personnel administration" function, and it is central to the principalship (Castetter, 1992; Fawcett, 1979; Seyfarth, 1991; Webb, Greer, Montello, & Norton, 1987). Principals in Herrity's study mentioned the importance of interacting with teachers in relation to several problems that they identified (numbers 3, 4, 6, and 7, for example, mentioned earlier). The following are some details.

Twenty-three of the 27 principals described and explained how they solicit and utilize specific input from their teachers about student progress and about the instructional process. Twenty of these 23 said that they have strong trust in their teachers' knowledge and judgment to make important classroom decisions.

Twenty-two of the 27 principals described in detail the value of teacher inservice in working with diverse students in particular. The principals emphasized their personal involvement in facilitating and enhancing the development of their teachers in this regard. In particular, principals mentioned their involvement in recruiting teachers, making employment decisions, integrating the teachers into the school family, "teaching" them, and "empowering" them.

Altogether, Herrity (1997) found ten categories of activities that expert principals reported as using in relation to their work with teachers. Eighteen of the 27 principals expressed a strong commitment to all ten categories of activities. These categories literally cover all dimensions of the principal's role and, thus, also all aspects of needed leadership responses to diversity.

A RESTATEMENT AND SELECTED IMPLICATIONS

Summary

The last two sections of this chapter have touched upon what are and what might be effective school-wide responses to increased student diversity. The centerpiece of these responses is a commitment to a vision to embrace and incorporate diversity. Figure 13.1 displays these two components of leadership along with subcomponents (selected on the basis of available data) and requirements needed on the part of leaders as they attempt to pursue these tasks effectively.

Leadership as the Development and the Continuous Nurturing of a Vision to Embrace Diversity	Leadership as the Use of All Available Means to Actually Incorporate Diversity
1. **Leadership:** **Academic Embracing** *Requirement:* Evaluation Mindedness	1. **Leadership:** **Using Problem-finding Tools**
2. **Internal Sociocultural Embracing** Requirements: Political Mindedness and Symbolic Mindedness	2. **Actual Problem Solving**
3. **Contextual Sociocultural Embracing** Requirements: Communication Mindedness	3. **Interactions with Teachers** Requirements: Knowledge, Sensitivity, and Personal Involvement

FIGURE 13.1 A Conceptual Framework for Leadership in Schools with Diverse Student Populations

Figure 13.1 is an outgrowth of the definition of leadership offered earlier in the chapter. The figure is also anchored in selected examples of this leadership as they occur in practice.

The subcomponents outlined in Figure 13.1 are certainly interdependent. For example, one principal who participated in the study of "embracing the vision of academic diversity" said: ". . . without the teacher buy-in we would never have had the degree of success (in academic embracing) which we actually achieved . . . it could have failed altogether . . .".

Or as one principal who participated in the study of "incorporating diversity" said: ". . . you cannot effectively identify problems unless you start getting to know the students' homes and with whom they spend their afternoons (internal and external sociocultural embracing) . . ."

The findings described in this study cover only a small area of leadership in schools with growing diverse student populations. Nonetheless, some preliminary implications may be derived for the findings. The implications selected for this final section of the chapter are in the domain of school-wide leadership.

Implications for Practice

Because of the interdependency between the subcomponents of leadership described here, the first implication for practice might be that an effective response to diversity means an effective integration of all or some of these components as a function of specific situations. For example, a school-wide response of academic embracing of diversity probably should follow the deployment of tools to find academic problems rather than precede it. In this case, the establishment of a database of student ability and potential is crucial, so that an effective problem-finding effort can enable the leaders to decide what kinds of academic embracing should be pursued. That is why the leader must be equipped to effectively assemble and diagnose data about student achievement.

Another example might be associated with the actual implementation of academic embracing of students. Academic embracing is put into practice by actually solving pertinent pedagogic problems. In the event that solutions do not seem to meet the expectations, additional problem finding may uncover the need to augment the acts of academic embracing with sociocultural embracing. The implication for practice suggested here, then, is that a school-wide response to increased student diversity may be enhanced by effectively "packaging" of all or some of the six leadership components at any given period of time, depending on needs and the assessed probability of meeting them.

This implication has to be examined, however, in juxtaposition to the suggestion offered earlier that the school principal possesses only limited control. Within such a context, one possible option is to suggest a restructuring of the authority layout in the school district as a whole, so as to empower principals to deal with increased diversity with additional discretion. Pertinent examples include more say over finances, complete authority over hiring teachers, and heavy input into the development of specific curricula and tests of student achievement. Charter schools have followed this model, but data are unavailable about their success in responding specifically to increased student diversity. A serious obstacle to pursuing this option is the increased centralization of decision making in several states (Sergiovanni, 2000). As state educational mandates increase, the relative authority of local school superintendents decreases, thereby limiting that which might be delegated to school principals.

Another possible option is to suggest a restructuring of the authority layout within the school itself. By delegating authority to, say, grade level teachers or department chairs, school principals may encourage creativity and accompanied commitment on the part of the staff to respond to diversity in effective ways. In such an event principals must remain accountable for the staff's actions and the corresponding results. This is a risky move, indeed. But as Figure 13.1 depicts, interaction with teachers is a pivotal subcomponent of school-wide leadership that responds to increased diversity.

Implied New Concepts

Increased diversity in public education calls for amending some conceptual dimensions of school-wide leadership. As this chapter suggests, there is a need for a total re-visioning of the school. This amounts to nothing less than restructuring our interests in the concepts of diversity and to modifying the ways we think about linguistic and culturally diverse students. In the academic domain this concept means not only helping the "different" students become proficient in what the "nondifferent" students are, but also encouraging the "different" students to pursue learning with the aid of their native tongue in areas where their individual cognitive potential may carry them. The principal's vision, if it includes such a restructuring of interests, may play a pivotal role in modifying the way diversity is perceived and even capitalized on.

The same holds for visions of the internal and external sociocultural domains. Principals may lead the way in constructing and displaying symbols or tools with which we think about diversity. Principals also may lead the way in the process of learning about the community, the arena in which our thoughts develop.

Some new concepts might be useful with regard to using all the means available to leaders to incorporate diversity. Using tools to find problems becomes a matter of actively searching and identifying the essence of diversity-driven phenomena, which might have the potential of clashing with existing realities experienced in the school. In such events, school leadership requires preemptive work. Effective leadership in this area may ease the burden of the never-ending actual problem solving. That is where the newly perceived concept of interaction with teachers comes in. Preemptive leadership can be viewed as a shared responsibility.

Implications for Further Research

There may be interest in continuing research about the interrelationships among the various leadership elements discussed here. This interest can lead to further work on the effects that different "packages" of these elements may have on the perceived overall effectiveness of the principal. This could include the creativity of the principal in vision and in deed, the creativity and commitment of the staff, the classroom climates, and the achievement of students.

Another line of research may be derived from the conceptual implications of this study. For example, a general research question associated with re-visioning might be focused on identifying the kinds of specific leadership attitudes, behaviors, and actions needed to enable "different" students to study in the two concurrent paths described earlier. One such question might be: what would it take to identify the highly motivated "different" students, to equip the school with means to teach them, and to communicate to stakeholders about such activities?

With regard to the concept of preemptive shared work mentioned earlier, a different general research question may be pertinent. Here the issues are related to leaders' skills in problem finding and the cost benefit of such endeavors. Research could focus on actual skills needed by leaders to find problems, ways in which to acquire such skills in preparation programs (Glasman, 1997) and/or on the job, and the use of these skills. As to cost benefit, research could involve the identification of cost and benefit variables (Alexander & Salman, 1995) pertinent to the school as a unit of analysis, the development of measures for each one of these variables, and the examination of relations among the variables.

These kinds of studies could improve our awareness and understanding about today's needed school leadership which we believe ought to be committed to respond effectively to increased diversity in the schools. Before long, such new knowledge may be an absolute requirement. It may become the very essence of all of school leadership rather than about school leadership's response to diversity. As we continue to work to meet the challenges of the 21st century, we may find that diversity itself becomes the integral part, the core, rather than a marginalized dimension within American public schools.

REFERENCES

Alexander, K., & Salman, R. G. (1995). *Public school finance.* Boston: Allyn & Bacon.

Ardovino, J., Hollingsworth, J., & Ybarra, S. (2000). *Multiple measures.* Newbury Park, CA: Corwin.

Banks, J. A., & McGee-Banks, C. A. (Eds.). (1993). *Handbook of research on multicultural education.* New York: Macmillan.

Berger, P. L., & Neuhaus, R. J. (1997). *To empower people.* Washington, DC: American Enterprise Institute.

Bista, M. B. (1994). *Determinants and effects of the structural, human resource, political and symbolic leadership styles of school principals.* Unpublished doctoral dissertation, University of California, Santa Barbara.

Bista, M. B., & Glasman, N. S. (1998). Principals' perceptions of their approaches to organizational leadership: Revisiting Bolman and Deal. *Journal of School Leadership, 8,* 26-47.

Blackman, M. C., & Fenwick, L. T. (2000, March 29). Looking for leaders in a time of change. *Education Week*, pp. 44-46, 68.

Bolman, L. G., & Deal, T. E. (1993). *The path to school leadership.* Newbury Park, CA: Corwin.

Bossert, S., Dwyer, D. C., Brown, B., & Lee, G. (1982). The institutional management role of the principal. *Educational Administration Quarterly, 18*(3), 34-64.

Bridges, E. M., & Hallinger, P. (1995). *Implementing problem-based learning in leadership development.* Eugene, OR: ERIC Clearinghouse on Educational Management.

Castetter, W. B. (1992). *The human resource function in educational administration.* Englewood Cliffs, NJ: Merrill.

Coleman, J. S. (1966). *Equality of educational opportunity.* Washington, DC: U.S. Government Printing Office.

Crowson, R. L., & Boyd, W. L. (in press). The new role of community development in educational reform. In N. S. Glasman, & R. L. Crowson (Eds.), Reexamining relations between schools and their constituents. *Peabody Journal of Education.*

Cuban, L. (1988). Why do some reforms persist? *Education Administration Quarterly, 24*(3), 329-335.

Cunningham, W. G., & Cordiero, P. A. (2000). *Educational administration: A problem-based approach.* Boston: Allyn & Bacon.

De Pasquale, F. (1996). *Principal leadership behavior and faculty trust: Is there a connection.* Unpublished doctoral dissertation, University of California, Santa Barbara.

Drake, T. L., & Roe, W. H. (1999). *The principalship.* New York: MacMillan.

Driscoll, M. E., & Kerchner, C. T. (1999). The implications of social capital for schools, communities, and cities. In J. Murphy & K. S. Louis (Eds.), *Handbook of research in educational administration* (pp. 385-404). San Francisco: Jossey-Bass.

Etzioni, A. (1993). *The spirit of community: The reinvention of American society.* New York: Simon & Schuster.

Fawcett, C. W. (1979). *School personnel systems.* Lexington, MA: Lexington.

Gardner, M. (1995). *Leading minds.* Boston: Basic Books.

Glasman, N. S. (1979). A perspective of education as an administrative function in education. *Educational Evaluation and Poling Analysis, 1*(5), 39-44.

Glasman, N. S. (1986). *Evaluation-based leadership.* Albany: SUNY Press.

Glasman, N. S. (1994). *Making better decisions about school problems.* Newbury Park, CA: Corwin.

Glasman, N. S. (Ed.). (1997). *New ways of training for school leadership.* Mahwah, NJ: Erlbaum.

Glasman, N. S., & Biniaminov, I. (1981). Input-output analysis of schools. *Review of Educational Research, 51*(4), 509-239.

Glasman, N. S., & Fuller, J. (in press). Superintendent evaluation: Concepts, practices, and an outcome related case. In B. S. Cooper & L. Fusarelli (Eds.), The school superintendency at the crossroads: Executive leadership for the 21st century. *Peabody Journal of Education.*

Glasman, N. S., & Nevo, D. (1988). *Evaluation and decision making.* Boston: Kluwer.

Glasman, N. S., & Sell, R. (1972). Values and facts in educational administrative decisions. *Journal of Educational Administration, 10*(2), 142-163.

Goertz, M., & Duffy, M. (2000). *Variations on a theme: What is performance-based accountability.* Paper presented at the annual meeting of the American Educational Research Association. New Orleans, LA.

Gorton, R. A., & Snowdon, P. E. (1999). *School leadership and administration.* Madison, WI: Brown & Benchmark.

Herrity, V. A. (1997). *An exploratory study of the knowledge, practices, cognitive processes and perceptions of expert principals relative to the administration of educational programs for linguistically and culturally diverse students.* Unpublished doctoral dissertation, University of California, Santa Barbara.

Herrity, V. A., & Glasman, N. S. (1999). Training administrators for culturally and linguistically diverse school populations: Opinions of expert practitioners. *Journal of School Leadership, 9,* 235-253.

Hoy, W. K., & Miskel, C. G. (2001). *Educational administration.* Boston: McGraw-Hill.

Immegart, G. L., & Boyd, W. L. (1979). *Problem-finding in educational administration.* Boston: Lexington.

Kahneman, D., Slovic, P., & Tversky, A. (Eds.). (1982). *Judgement under uncertainty.* Cambridge, MA: Cambridge University Press.

Lakowski, G. (1987). Values and decision making in educational administration. *Educational Administration Quarterly, 23*(3), 70-82.

Langer, E. J. (1983). *The psychology of control.* Newbury Park, CA: Sage.

Morgan, G. (1986). *Images of organization.* Newbury Park, CA: Corwin.

Murphy, J., & Seashore Louis, K. (Eds.). (1999). *Handbook of research on educational administration.* San Francisco: Jossey-Bass.

Newmann, F. N. (Ed.). (1992). *Student engagement and achievement in American secondary schools.* New York: Teachers College Press.

Oaks, J. (1985). *Keeping track: How schools restructure inequities.* New Haven, CT: Yale University Press.

Pounder, D. G., Ogawa, R. T., & Adams, E. A. (1997). Leadership as an organization-wide phenomena: Its impact on schools performance. *Educational Administration Quarterly, 31*(4), 564-588.

Razik, T. A., & Swanson, A. D. (2000). *Fundamental concepts of educational leadership.* Columbus, OH: Merrill.

Riehl, C. J. (2000). The principal's role in creating inclusive schools for diverse students: A review of normative, empirical, and critical literature on the practice of educational administration. *Review of Educational Research, 70*(1), 55-81.

Roberts, D. (1986). *Moments of doubt and other mountaineering writings.* Seattle: The Mountaineers.

Rosenbach, W. E., & Taylor, R. L. (Eds.). (1999). *Contemporary issues in leadership.* Boulder, CO: Westview.

Rosenholtz, S. J. (1985). Effective schools: Interpreting the evidence. *American Journal of Education, 93*(3), 352-388.

Rossi, R. J. (Ed.). (1994). *Schools and students as risk: Context and framework for positive change.* New York: Teachers College Press.

Sarason, S.B. (1996). *Revisiting the culture of the school and the problem of change.* New York: Teachers College Press.

Sarason, S. B., & Lorentz, E. M. (1998). *Crossing boundaries: Collaboration, coordination, and the redefinition of resources.* San Francisco: Jossey-Bass.

Sergiovanni, T. J. (2000). *The principalship.* Boston: Allyn & Bacon.

Seyfarth, J. T. (1991). *Personnel management for effective schools.* Boston: Allyn & Bacon.

Smreker, C. (1996). *The impact of school choice and community.* Albany: State University of New York Press.

Spillane, J. P., Halverson, R., & Diamond, J. B. (2001, April). Investigating school leadership practice: A distributed perspective. *Educational Researcher, 30*(3), 23-28.

Steinberg, S., & Kincheloe, J. L. (1999). *Changing multiculturalism.* Buckingham, England: Open University Press.

Tyack, D., & Hansot, E. (1982). *Managers of virtue.* New York: Basic Books.

Ubben, G. C., Hughes, L. W., & Norris, C. J. (2001). *The principalship: Creative leadership for effective schools.* Boston: Allyn & Bacon.

Webb, L. D., Greer, J. T., Montello, P. A., & Norton, M.S. (1987). *Personnel management in education.* Columbus, OH: Merrill.

Wolcott, H. F. (1973). *The man in the principal's office: An ethnography.* New York: Holt, Rinehart & Winston.

CHAPTER FOURTEEN

Deep Culture

Pushing the Epistemological Boundaries of Multicultural Education

Karen Ann Watson–Gegeo
University of California, Davis

David Welchman Gegeo
California State University, Monterey Bay

My daily meditations take me to a center where the rhythmic flow of tides and predictable morning showers feed my spirit. My heart touches the soft melodies of Hawaiian style music and the honest tongue of my mother language. This land of towering peaks, green valleys, warm beaches, and mighty ocean embraces and comforts me . . . Wherever I might be, my heart and commitment is to the āina (land) of my kūpuna (ancestors).

Maenette Kape'ahiokalani Padeken Ah Nee Benham
(quoted in Benham & Heck, 1998, p. 135)

[M]any white educators have pulled multicultural education away from social struggles and redefined it to mean the celebration of eth- nic foods and festivals; the field is sometimes criticized as having turned away from its initial critique of racism in education.

(Sleeter & McLaren, 1995, p. 12)

Multicultural education has undergone evolution since its early beginnings in the Civil Rights and political liberation movements of the 1960s and 1970s (Banks, 1992; Gay, 1983; McLaughlin & Tierney, 1993). The recent move to integrate multicultural education with critical pedagogy (see the essays in Sleeter & McLaren, 1995) promises to push multiculturalism beyond its reductionistic treatment of culture as the celebration of ethnic foods and "colorful customs." Critical pedagogy reinstates the political voice that was lost in multicultural education because of white America's assimilationist demands and often overt hostility to cultural, ethnic, and racial difference (Mattai, 1992; San Juan, 1992). We completely support the political project argued in contemporary multiculturalism by radical feminists, postmodernists, and ethnic political leaders from a variety of cultural communities.

However, we do not accept Sleeter and McLaren's implied dichotomy between an interest in culture, on the one hand, and a realistic understanding of the politics of race and ethnicity, on the other. We will argue that one of the most politically radical and meaningful transformations that needs to occur in multicultural education is to take the term "culture" seriously. That means going beyond even seemingly informed but actually superficial notions of "other people's" cultures, to what we are calling *deep culture*.

Our purpose in writing this chapter is somewhat different from that of authors who are focusing on interventions that work in classrooms. Although we will briefly examine successful interventions, our primary goal is to interrogate the term "culture" in "multicultural education" by examining those levels of culture that, although ignored in schools, are absolutely central to people's culture(s) and to (re)creating cultural meaning. The argument we make is congruent with and supported by research over the past fifteen years in several disciplines and fields just now coming together in highly significant ways, but that has yet to work its way down to schools: research in cognitive science, cognitive anthropology, and the critical social sciences, including cultural and cross-cultural psychology, critical sociolinguistics, feminist and gender studies, and ethnic studies. Our argument is also informed by our combined experiences over the past two decades conducting sociocultural and sociolinguistic research in communities and schools in rural and urban areas of the Solomon Islands (southwest Pacific), Hawai'i, and the United States (Massachusetts and California). Moreover, our position is grounded in our experiences as teachers of culturally diverse students at the university level, and our own lives in school as nonmainstream students who succeeded in the educational system, though not without struggle and not without developing an acute awareness of the politically and culturally biased nature of mainstream education and schools.[1]

---

[1]Karen is of German, English, and Cherokee/French ethnicity and working-class background, grew up in a rural agricultural area, and was bused to a middle-class town school during elementary school. In first grade she was told by her teacher that she did not speak "good English" because she spoke a rural nonstandard dialect of English; and she

CULTURE IN A POSTMODERN, HYBRID WORLD

Currently, there is debate regarding whether or not Native American religion should be taught by non-Native people. Some contention has been made that precepts of religion are universal and that the process of describing Indian spirituality is no different from describing other religious beliefs and practices. The notion that religion has universal precepts comes from the philosophical underpinnings of Western culture. Those very ideas imbue those teachings of Western univeralism with power. . . . Without an understanding of what it means to live a spiritual life very opposed to Eurocentric individuality, non-Natives attempting to teach Indian religion are merely talking to themselves. Their talk, however, has lasting implications for Native Americans as we are overcoming issues of identity imposed by centuries of outside definition. (Ritchie, 1995, p. 312)

Feeling masked because of ethnic and racial differences is directly linked to the process of cultural assimilation, and to the pervasive Latina/o resistance against assimilation. . . . Assimilation has become yet another mask for the Latina/o to hide behind. I have a clay mask made by Mexican artisans that captures this idea but from a different perspective. The outermost mask is a white skeleton face wearing a grimace. The second layer shows a face with an aquiline nose and a goatee suggesting the face of the Spaniard, the colonizer of indigenous Mexico. This second mask parts to show the face of a pensive Aztec. This clay sculpture suggests the indigenous Indian preserved behind the false masks, the death mask, the conquistador mask. [It] represents all of us who have been colononized and acculturated—who have succeeded in withholding a precious part of our past behind our constructed public personas. (Montoya, 1994, pp. 193-194)

---

failed fourth grade, although she was passed because of an understanding teacher. In teenage years, she worked summers hand-cutting apricots alongside Mexican immigrant farmworkers in the Central Valley of California to earn money for school clothes. These experiences were what drew her originally to issues in minority education. David grew up bicultural (Kwara'ae/Lau) and trilingual (Kwara'ae, Lau, Solomon Islands Pijin) in a poor rural village in the Solomon Islands under colonialism, where he experienced and observed many examples of colonial oppression and racism. He learned English in school, attending senior primary and secondary schools off-island that drew students from all of the 70 different languages/cultures in the Solomons. The ethnic, cultural, and linguistic diversity of the Solomons increased his interest in cultural diversity generally. After four years as a radio broadcaster in the Solomons, he came to America where he pursued a higher education. In California, he has worked as a volunteer in an elementary classroom in Chula (Central Valley), assisting Mexican immigrant children of farmworker families to learn literacy in English.

Cultural frameworks for thinking, speaking, and acting are often subsumed under the term "worldview," which has been defined by anthropologists as a cultural group's "way of looking at reality" consisting of "basic assumptions and images" (Kearney, 1984, p. 41) "implicit in almost every act" (Wallace, 1970, p. 143). Older notions of "worldview," which have been imported into education, are subject to criticism and "idealist" because they focus on the ideas people have in their heads (Bowlin & Stromberg, 1997; Kearney, 1984) at the expense of examining the sociopolitical contexts and interactions through which concepts and patterns of thinking and behavior are created, develop, and change.

Even in anthropological research, the representation of the world's cultures has often been superficial, and has contributed to the "Othering" of non-Anglo-Euro-American peoples. "Othering" refers to the process of turning people who are the subjects of research into objects and distancing them from nonmainstream selves (Yeatman, 1994). In this process, "Others" are defined as inherently different from the observer and the observer's culture. Rather than embracing the creative and positive possibilities of cultural diversity, "Othering" is concerned with ruling in certain kinds of human being-ness and ruling out other kinds, so as to narrow what is socially acceptable. Typically those who are "Othered" are people of color, immigrants from the Third World, or people who have been marginalized by sexual identity or orientation, gender, or disability. "Othering" is accomplished by those who position themselves as white (essentially male) middle-class mainstream persons. Mainstreet cultural patterns constitute the Dominant Interpretive Framework (Ulichny & Watson-Gegeo, 1989) that controls and guides socialization, language and discourse, information flow, the representation and creation of knowledge, expected behavior and self-presentation, and procedures for interpreting meaning in the classroom. Teachers and mainstream students collaborate in (re)creating and maintaining the Dominant Interpretive Framework that is part of the process of "Othering" and disenfranchising nonmainstream students, and which leaves little or no room for the expression of non-mainstream interpretive frameworks.

"Cultural difference" studies of the 1960s and 1970s located the causes of ethnic minority children's poor school performance in contrasting rules, expectations, and practices between children's home cultures and mainstream classroom culture. Some "cultural difference" research uncovered important differences between home and school that led to highly successful classroom interventions. One such example was the Kamehameha Early Education Program in Hawai'i, in which Native Hawaiian children's reading skills were dramatically increased by redesigning literacy instruction around the discourse routines of "talk-story," a local oral narrative and conversational discourse event (Au & Jordan, 1981; Boggs, 1985; Watson, 1975). However, many cultural difference studies were superficial in their treatment of culture, focusing primarily on interactional behavior (e.g., do you show respect by lowering your eyes, or by eye contact?) rather than on complex cultural patterns. As critics (e.g., Foley, 1991) pointed out, although expectations for appropriate classroom behavior may initially create barriers for students unfamiliar with mainstream behavioral expectations, most students learn to negotiate their way through them fairly quickly.

Ogbu's (1978, 1987) structural analysis of the job barriers caste-like involuntary minorities face strongly challenged cultural difference assumptions. Ogbu argued that involuntary minorities (such as African and Native Americans) develop "secondary" cultural characteristics in opposition to the racist barriers they experience, and that these are the problematic cultural patterns often identified by cultural difference and sociolinguistic analysis. Secondary cultural characteristics are forms of resistance: they are acts against oppression. In general, resistance theory (e.g., Giroux, 1983) holds that ethnic minority children's problems in school stem from sociopolitical and historical causes rather than contrasting cultural characteristics or values. Not only does this argument undermine the notion that culture is important in learning, but if carried to its logical conclusion it would mean that multicultural education would not even be necessary if we seriously addressed political and economic inequalities.

The apparent contradiction between cultural analysis and political/structural analysis is resolved, however, when we look at recent research in cognitive science and the critical social sciences. We agree with Ogbu and others that school failure—and it is school rather than student failure—is primarily explained by sociopolitical factors. However, structural analyses underestimate the role of culture and discourse practices in linguistic and cultural minority children's problems in mainstream educational programs. Culture is more than surface developments in opposition to historical and current oppression of minority and immigrant populations, or to an imposed system of education, such as in the Third World. Rather, culture profoundly shapes the way we think and behave.

Today there is much discussion of postmodern, globalizing processes that are undermining and fragmenting people's experience of culture and of themselves. Many earlier formulations of biculturalism, such as the notion of "walking in two worlds," evaporate under the contemporary realities of people's interactions across former cultural boundaries and the emergence of new identities brought about by rapid social change. As Bhaba (1990, p. 207) has pointed out, "all forms of culture are continually in a process of hybridity," that is, in creating a "third space" that enables new cultures and cultural positionings to develop or be constructed (i.e., people's revising and (re)creating culture, making new cultures, or variably and intermittently claiming one or more of the cultural or ethnic identities that they embody). In Chaudhry's (1995, p. 49) phrasing, hybrid individuals "exhibit hybrid identities as well as hybrid world-views deriving from different systems of meaning." Does it make sense, then, to talk about a person's "culture" and the deeper levels that shape thinking and behavior?

This question arises partly because of white America's inability to imagine a genuine cultural diversity within one person, given the socialized notion of "one language, one culture" derived from nationalism. Contemporary anthropology realizes that culture is constantly changing and is a multiplicity of voices and perspectives (Rosaldo, 1993). Diaspora scholar Stuart Hall (a British Jamaican indigenous scholar) has argued that cultural identity involves (at least) two ways of thinking about one's culture. First is that of "one shared culture, a sort of collective 'one true self,' hiding inside the many other, more superficial or artificially imposed 'selves,' which people with a shared history and ancestry hold in common" (Hall, 1991, p. 223). Second is the identity produced by "the ruptures and discontinuities" that result in "critical points of deep and significant difference," especially those differences caused by the traumatic character of "before the colonial experience" as well as current processes of migration, modernization, and globalization (Hall, 1991, p. 233). Beyond these identities, people are increasingly growing up in bicultural or multicultural homes, such that situations or contexts may evoke differing senses of cultural identity or belonging. Each of these may be genuinely and deeply held and experienced, and none of them may resemble the mainstream culture in which a person is currently living.

In laying out the notion of deep culture, we are embracing the complexity of culture(s) within individuals as well as within communities and schools. We agree with Nozaki's (2000) concern about the power of the "essentializing dilemma"—that creating categories at all tends to essentialize differences, but ignoring cultural differences undermines people's identity. Heterogeneity needs to be emphasized, as well as the sociohistorical variations members of a group experience as they grow up, and their individual agency in taking action in the world. Although we will usually refer to "culture" rather than the hybridity of "culture(s)," all that we say is applicable to the multiple and evolving cultural understandings that one person may embody. We understand this because we ourselves come from hybrid cultural backgrounds.

WHAT IS DEEP CULTURE?: LANGUAGE, CULTURAL MODELS, AND INDIGENOUS EPISTEMOLOGY

Language is the means by which people perceive/experience themselves and the world and, thus, is the means by which they exist. It is the embodiment of the very axioms of existence. A non-Arabic-speaking person may learn the Arabic vocabulary and grammar, and may master them even better than most Arabs. Yet he/she would not be able to grasp all the "waves" and "webs" of meaning. [It] is extremely difficult for the non-Western indigenous anthropologist to communicate his/her "implicit" knowledge to his/her Western col-

leagues: Some of this knowledge is very difficult to translate into English-anthropology, some simply resists articulation in writing.

(Kanaaneh, 1997, pp. 9-10)

Here Arab anthropologist Moslih Kanaaneh describes processes of thinking central to cultural identity that discussions of the nature of culture, the role of language in culture, and the need for multicultural education tend to play down. Multilingual and bilingual speakers often report the sensation of becoming a different person with a different understanding of the world when they code-switch from one language to another. This feeling is supported by research showing that speakers respond differently to the same pictures when asked to respond in different languages, and that the differential responses reflect the cultures associated, respectively, with those languages (Chaudhry, 1991; Ervin-Tripp, 1964a, 1964b). The close relationship of language to culture is suggested in anthropologist Michael Agar's (1994) term *languaculture*, that is, the fusing of language with culture.

What, then, is deep culture? Below the surface level of behavior and the linguistic level of morphology and syntax is a deep set of propositions and images that shape perception, information processing, and the assignment of values. It is this deeper level of thinking and understanding that we are calling *deep culture*. Deep culture is at the heart of culture identity, cultural survival, and thinking. It includes ontology, cultural models, and indigenous epistemology.

Ontology refers to the nature of reality (what exists, what there is), and epistemology to the nature of knowledge and knowledge construction (how we know). Work in cognitive anthropology over the past two decades has revisited the idea of linguistic relativity and demonstrated through empirical research that differences in languages do have a significant impact on differences in thinking (e.g., see the papers in Gumperz & Levinson, 1996). This does not imply that such differences involve superiority of one language over another. Rather, our perceptions of reality are affected by the distinctions we make in our language(s), and there is no one correct way of experiencing the world through language.

Research on linguistic relativity is closely related to parallel research on cultural models for thinking and behaving by cognitive anthropologists (D'Andrade & Strauss, 1992; Holland & Quinn, 1987; Shore, 1991) using schema and prototype theory originally developed in cognitive psychology. Cultural models research is also closely related to research by psycholinguists on children's languages and cognitive development. Drawing on schema and script theory, Katherine Nelson (1996, p. 12) states that "Human minds are equipped to construct complicated 'mental models' that represent . . . the complexities of the social and cultural world." These mental models or Mental Event Representations (MERs), are the basic, flexible structures of children's cognitive development and take the form of schemas and scripts that become a mental context for future behavior in similar situations.

Cognitive anthropologists define cultural models as "prototypical event sequences in simplified worlds" (Quinn & Holland, 1987, p. 24). Cultural models frame and interpret experience and guide a variety of cognitive and behavioral tasks, including setting goals, planning, directing action, making sense of action, and verbalization. Analytically, the notion of cultural models is compatible with a neuronal network model of the embodied mind (Lakoff & Johnson, 1999).

Cultural models are usually tacitly understood and often unconscious, but are at the core of a culture's ontology and indigenous epistemology. Until very recently, ontology and epistemology were terms applied only to what Western philosophy and science had invented with regard to understanding reality and creating knowledge about reality. Everybody else was said to have only a "worldview," as defined above. Today scholars from Third World societies, and ethnic minority and oppressed indigenous peoples living under colonial conditions in First and Second World societies are challenging the privileging of Western ontology and scientific epistemology. This challenging has come in the wake of the critique of mainstream ontology and epistemology by the neurosciences (see the review in Lakoff & Johnson, 1999), and by third-wave feminist scholars against the Anglo-Euro-American patriarchal positioning of mainstream epistemology.

Epistemology refers to both the theory of knowledge and theorizing or constructing knowledge (Goldman, 1986, 1999). Feminist and Third World scholars have challenged the taken-for-granted objectivity on which much of Western science depends for its claim that the knowledge it produces is necessarily universal and always superior to all other forms of knowledge. This challenge is incorporated in the notion of standpoint epistemology, which recognizes that "Knowledge claims are always socially situated" (Harding, 1993, p. 54; Alcoff & Potter, 1993). That is, all knowledge is subjective, positioned (from a standpoint, not objective in a final sense), historically variable, and specific, even when what is constructed turns out to have universal implications. Moreover, feminists have effectively argued with other postmodern writers that knowledge is always political as well as cultural. This raises the issue of who gets to represents whom? Typically, it has been white Anglo-Euro-American researchers who study and represent mainly non-European "Others," and these are the representations that are taught in school and often also incorporated into multicultural education. The "Others" are not allowed voice to represent themselves as they wish to be or are positioned. As Yeatman (1994, p. 31) asks, "Who must be silenced in order that these representations prevail?"

We live in exciting times, however, in the early stages of Third World scholars writing about their own cultures, not only their indigenous ontologies (formerly worldviews), but also their indigenous epistemologies. By indigenous epistemology we mean "a cultural group's ways of thinking and of creating, reformulating, and theorizing about knowledge via traditional discourses and media of communication, anchoring the truth of the discourse in culture" (Gegeo & Watson-Gegeo, 2001, p. 58; Gegeo, 1994; Gegeo & Watson-Gegeo, 1999; Gegeo & Watson-Gegeo, 2002; Watson-Gegeo & Gegeo, 1999). As a concept, indigenous epistemology focuses on the process through which knowledge is constructed and validated by a cultural group, and the role of that process in shaping thinking and behavior. The rapidly growing literature on indigenous epistemology continues to expand to involve many indigenous groups (e.g., Chiu, 1991; Diaz-Guerrero, 1993; Enriquez, 1990; Ho, 1981; Imbo, 1998; Keck, 1998; Lambek, 1983; Meyer, 1998a, 1998b; Nsamenang, 1992; Pe-Pua, 1990; Salmond, 1985; Sinha, 1997; Smith, 1999; Yang, 1988).

A major significance of cultural models and indigenous ontology/epistemology for multicultural education lies in the recent recognition by the cognitive and behavioral sciences that cultural and sociopolitical processes are central in rather than incidental to cognitive development. In fact, researchers in the neurosciences, cognitive anthropology, and cultural psychology are increasingly preferring the term "mind" over "cognition" to emphasize the more holistic understanding of human thinking that is evolving from the new research. We now realize from research that we human beings understand the world the way that we do because of the kinds of bodies and the potential for neuronal development that we have (Regier, 1995, 1996). As feminists have also argued (Grosz, 1993), ours is an embodied mind, and therefore the Cartesian split between body and mind constitutes a fundamental error in Western philosophy. The term "cognition" focuses on only some parts of the mind, typically what Vygotsky (1981) called the "higher mental functions" of voluntary memory, logical reasoning, language, metacognitive skills, and some forms of categorization. These are the skills emphasized in schools. Until now it has been assumed that the higher cognitive functions are independent of other mental processes, such as feelings, intuition, and so forth–in fact, that they must be kept separate from the latter, less rational mental processes. However, research has shown that emotion (for instance) is essential to making logical, rational judgments, including moral decisions (Damasio, 1994), and that emotion "links closely with cognition to shape action, thought, and long-term development" (Fischer, Kennedy, & Cheng, 1998, pp. 22-23). Howard Gardner (1983, 1989) has demonstrated that human beings develop "multiple intelligences," including many forms of intelligence and knowing that lie outside the "cognitive skills" emphasized or even recognized in schools as important.

At the same time that our understanding of mind is changing, research is demonstrating that older theories of cognitive development that represented development as more or less an automatic series of stages independent of experience or context are incorrect. As summarized in the recent National Academy of Sciences compendium on the brain and learning, "human development is shaped by a dynamic and continuous interaction between biology and culture" from conception (Shonkoff & Phillips, 2000, p. 3). The national panel's review of research finds that "culture influences every aspect of human development" and is "fundamental" to both child and adult development (Shonkoff & Phillips, 2000, p. 25). Because experience literally shapes human neuronal networks and therefore how human beings perceive and understand the nature of reality, culture combined with family and individual experiences is central to how children learn to think, reason, and express their understandings. Research has seriously challenged the notion that the "stages" of human development are universal in the Piagetian sense, because what is expected of children from an early age and the kinds of sociohistorical processes in which they are undergoing development vary cross-culturally in substantial ways, and also vary across historical time periods (Shonkoff & Phillips, 2000). Again, this is not to suggest that certain cultures therefore provide an inferior set of learning opportunities or developmental paths from others. Rather, as in all other things human, diversity rather than uniformity characterizes human developmental paths. The idea that only some kinds of contexts provide learning opportunities is also an obsolete notion in its more extreme versions. As Lave (1996) and others argue, learning is ubiquitous and is an aspect of all activity, not just certain kinds of contexts and situations (such as school classrooms) (Chaiklin & Lave, 1996; Lave & Wenger, 1991; Resnick, Levine, & Teasley, 1991).

How does deep culture intersect with cognitive processes? First, neuroscience research has demonstrated that 95 percent of all thought is unconscious, referred to by Lakoff and Johnson (1999, p. 13) as the "cognitive unconscious." It is this unconscious thought, lying outside our awareness, that "shapes and structures all conscious thought," and it includes all implicit knowledge that we have learned through socialization, beginning in the prenatal months. Deep culture resides primarily in the cognitive unconscious. It is the neuronal networks of deep culture, in the form of cultural models, premises, and other kinds of unconscious patterns, that shape how we argue, reason, make sense of the world, value or disvalue, create, and judge. Discourse practices are also learned through socialization and are largely unconscious. Discourse practices are the nexus of the formation, transformation, and use of deep cultural knowledge including indigenous epistemology, and for speakers' positioning of themselves with regard to cultural identity. Discourse is action with social consequences. Through discourse people create and reproduce social relations and behavior, enact or resist oppression, and make claims and pursue various goals—all guided by deep culture and other processes in the cognitive unconscious, as well as by conscious-level decision making. Discourse organization shapes and supports thinking and knowledge creation that are rooted in deep culture and the structure and organization of one's language(s).

So far we have "talked theory" in discussing deep culture and related issues. Now we want to illustrate why deep culture is important to multicultural education by briefly examining three cultural situations—two of them educational interventions, one of which involves taking a second look at why the intervention was successful. Due to limitations of space, we are unable to provide transcript examples to support our contentions; however, we provide references where such materials can be readily located.

DEEP CULTURE IN ACTION: CREATING AND INTERPRETING KNOWLEDGE

To me, every American lives in a lot of little worlds, sort of like boxes. The American goes from box to box to do whatever he has to do...church, school, home. They don't mix together very much. You can see the new baby in the glass cage . . . and the dead also go into a box. In Laos it was not that way. Everything was together. Neighbors had a special place. It was one big box instead of many little ones here. It is easy to be very alone here. I don't like this too much. It makes my heart sad. For this thing, I miss my country. . . .

(Young Laotian immigrant man, quoted in Proudfoot, 1990, p. 212)

In the late 1970s and early 1980s, researchers at the Kamehameha Early Education Program developed a "talk-story" method of teaching reading, following the lead of a Hawaiian teacher in whose classroom they observed that "something different" was happening from an ordinary reading lesson. The structure of a "talk-story" literacy event was described as "bridging" (Au & Jordan, 1981) typical classroom communicative routines grounded in the basic IRE (initiation, response, evaluation) structure described by Mehan (1979) and the much differently organized, as well as more open and fluid, talk-story routines in Native Hawaiian children's oral narration described by Watson (1975). In KEEP classrooms, children were allowed to share the Initiation of topics and Response phases of the reading-and-discussing-a-story classroom routine, and sometimes also Evaluation, although the teacher still retained control over the direction of the talk. The talk-story reading lesson was described as "talking story with a book" (Au & Jordan, 1981).

In his analysis of a lengthy talk-story reading lesson transcript, Boggs (1985, p. 140) pointed out that "this method of instruction is effective because it introduced a rich context for the act of reading—a context that integrated immediate, social functions of speech with referential language, both oral and printed." He disagreed with some KEEP researchers' contention that the talk-story method of reading was simply an example of good teaching and of the application of Vygotskian principles, and so could be applied anywhere (Tharp & Gallimore, 1988). Instead, his careful discourse analysis of KEEP reading lesson transcripts revealed that the lessons functioned well because of the virtually egalitarian relationship set up between teacher and students—parallel to egalitarian relationships essential to effective peer interactions in Native Hawaiian culture—and because the discourse of the reading lesson became a joint production among participants, as in co-narration in children and adult's talk-story conversations/narrations in the Native Hawaiian community (Boggs & Watson-Gegeo, 1978; Watson, 1975; Watson-Gegeo & Boggs, 1977). Talk-story is a central cultural event in the Native Hawaiian community, and plays an important role in *hoʻoponopono*, the traditional conflict-resolution speech event (Boggs & Chun, 1990; Ito, 1985; Pukui, Haertig, & Lee, 1972a, 1972b; Shook, 1986).

We agree with Boggs' analysis, and here want to carry it further, deeper into deep culture, so to speak. None of those who have examined the KEEP talk-story reading lesson transcripts have taken into consideration aspects of epistemology central to creating knowledge via talk-story, and with that, the nature of knowledge creation among speakers whose first and primary language variety is Hawaiʻi Creole English (which was the case for Native Hawaiian children in the transcripts analyzed in the published sources). Here is an example where cultural hybridity becomes a necessary and central issue in analysis. Except for upper-middle-class children, the dominant language of Native Hawaiian children on Oʻahu at the time that the KEEP studies were done and the talk-story reading lesson developed was Hawaiʻi Creole English (HCE), locally called "Pidgin." Indeed, HCE was the dominant language variety of all working-class children born in Hawaiʻi among immigrant and Pacific island groups.

HCE was created in the early 20th century by Hawaiian-born children of Hawaiʻi Pidgin English-speaking immigrants from Asia, Europe, and the Pacific Islands, and additionally, Native Hawaiians, all of whom were recruited to work on sugar plantations in colonial Hawaiʻi (Sato, 1985, p. 261). Today speakers can be arranged along a continuum from more basilectal to more acrolectal forms; the Native Hawaiian children studied by Watson (1975) were mesolectal. Basilect, mesolect, and acrolect are approximate positions along a continuum of language varieties from the basic or base-level Creole to the acrolectal or Hawaiʻi Standard English variety (which differs from U.S. Mainland Standard English). Being able to speak HCE fluently, with its many nuances and distinct discourse practices, is essential to claiming and enacting "local" identity in Hawaiʻi—despite the strong pressures of the state educational, political, and business institutions to discredit "Pidgin" and those who speak it, and often the Native Hawaiian community's disavowal of HCE (which Native Hawaiians sometimes argue is a colonial inheritance and a factor inhibiting their community from rising economically) (Sato, 1991; Schmitt, 1982; Watson-Gegeo, 1994).

Talk-story is an oral narration form used throughout the local communities of Hawaiʻi. As in other HCE-dominant cultural communities in Hawaiʻi, for the Native Hawaiian community co-narration in talk-story is an epistemological strategy for (re)creating knowledge about important as well as casual topics. Among important topics, talk-story co-narrations often take on the task of attempting to illuminate mysterious or unexplained happenings or events, or spiritual experiences, whether those of the speakers or of others from whom they have heard accounts. Making sense of the social world in a community in which (as articulated by the Laotian immigrant quoted at the beginning of this section) people are closely connected to each other and joined by multiple overlapping relationships, is an important focus in conversation. So is making sense of the spiritual world that surrounds and infuses the community. Our purpose here is not to detail the complexities of the very rich Native Hawaiian ontology and epistemology described elsewhere with insight, elegance, and sensitivity by Native Hawaiian scholars (e.g., Meyer, 1998a, 1998b, 2001; Pukui, Haertig, & Lee, 1972a, 1972b). Rather, our purpose is to point out that in looking at the talk-story transcripts, the enthusiasm of the students and the ways in which they interact around the story of "Freddie the Frog"[2]

—interaction that involves exploring how frogs look and feel to the touch, how they behave, and in the story, various themes of hiding and threat—parallels the ways in which Native Hawaiian children of the same age enthusiastically pursue issues of ghosts, spirits, and messenger owls in serious conarrated stories collected over a year's time under naturalistic conditions in the children's peer group studied by Watson (1975). The children are not just sharing what they know about frogs in discourse routines with which they are comfortable because of cultural familiarity. Rather, what the white researchers called "speculating" was actually one of Native Hawaiian children's indigenous epistemological strategies for creating knowledge: that is, an example of an epistemological strategy, based on child culture and on the adult culture they are learning, to investigate ontology and to create new knowledge in an epistemological process. And we need to interrogate "speculating" a bit further: would much of what these Hawaiian children do in trying to make sense of their experience with frogs and what might happen in the story be called "hypothesizing" or applying "heuristics" if it were being done by white children or adults? (Issues of children's ontology and epistemology have been examined in the research literature on play; see Watson-Gegeo, 2001).

Our second example relates the KEEP intervention to work on HCE specifically. In a preliminary study of information structure in Hawai'i Creole English discourse events, Sato and Watson-Gegeo (1992) were able to show that the way that knowledge is represented in HCE discourse, especially the way that *explanation* is constructed discoursally in HCE, differs substantially from how knowledge is constructed discoursally in Standard English. They demonstrated that an HCE speaker first elaborates a topic and/or comment on the topic with additional material that itself consists of a series of entailed topics and comments. Elaborated topics and comments often turn into a series of mini-narratives. The impression given to white Anglo-Euro-American listeners (including

---

[2]We refer to the "Freddie the Frog" lesson because it is the one analyzed by Boggs (1985) and also made available to non-KEEP researchers to view and study.

teachers) is that the speaker is talking via a chain of associations and moving "off topic," not "sticking to the point," moving too slowly to the point, or including extraneous detail (i.e., is unable to distinguish between what is important and what is not important). But interactions in the HCE-speaking community are often organized via a network of elaborated topics, and the structure of the interaction may be recursive, looping back through topics to clarify points or relationships among points. Within the complex, extended kin lines of many local people in Hawai'i, kin relationships and family history are learned and reinforced via these discourse practices, which constitute what is meant by "talking story" (Watson-Gegeo & Gegeo, 1999a). However, many other kinds of knowledge about the world are also articulated and shared through such epistemological practices.

Sato and Watson-Gegeo (1992) suggested that the seemingly meandering way in which explanations are offered in HCE, in which talk folds back on itself and progresses incrementally, would be unacceptable in, for instance, a high school science classroom, and may be at the root of why so many "local" students do not do well in secondary school science. Sato and Watson-Gegeo "hypothesized that the range or scope of expected answers to given types of questions—the issue of what a question is really asking, and what would constitute an appropriate answer or account—differs substantially in HCE and SE," and that "the differences reflect more general preferences for discourse form and content, and underlying cultural models/indigenous epistemology" (Watson-Gegeo & Gegeo, 1999a, p. 109). Because for HCE speakers their discourse structures and style are part of their deep culture, the difference is not just a matter of students who "can't think;" or are "limited" in their linguistic skills because they speak primarily HCE. Nor are the features of HCE discourse merely explained as an example of "resistance" discourse, as Ogbu might argue–that is, the development of a set of secondary features to express opposition to a dominant culture. Rather, the differences are part of deep culture in the hybrid local community of Hawai'i.

For our third example, we draw on research we have carried out in Kwara'ae villages and schools in the Solomon Islands (Watson-Gegeo & Gegeo, 1986a, 1986b, 1990, 1992, 1994, 1999a, 1999b; Watson-Gegeo, 1996, 2001). As one trajectory in Kwara'ae rural villagers' revitalization of their traditional culture beginning in the late 1970s and continuing through the 1990s, a few teachers in local schools have begun incorporating Kwara'ae language, discourse practices, and speech events into their classrooms, especially the teaching of English. We observed two such teachers in the early 1990s who were regarded as model teachers in the local district: Lindsay (teaching both kindergarten and Standard One [first grade] in different years) and Rebekah (teaching "prep," equivalent to kindergarten in the United States) (Gegeo & Watson-Gegeo, 2002; Watson-Gegeo & Gegeo, 1994). These two teachers used Kwara'ae indigenous epistemological strategies in two ways: to assist their students to understand English grammar and literacy materials (including textbook narratives in English), and to teach Kwara'ae values within the context of classroom lessons and materials.

In reasoning, planning, debate, and philosophical discussion, the Kwara'ae use a variety of epistemological strategies that are named and recognized (several of which we describe and illustrate in Gegeo & Watson-Gegeo, 2001). In one English lesson, for instance, Lindsay used the epistemological strategy called *'ini te'ete'e suli ru'anga* (literally, "inching with the fingers along it"). This strategy, a metaphor from gardening, refers to careful, step-by-step systematic reasoning well supported with evidence, involving a set of clearly marked discourse routines. Among the concepts Lindsay was teaching in the lesson was the meaning of the English word "and," which requires considerable explanation in translation, because Kwara'ae has more than one term for "and" depending on syntax and various shades of meaning being communicated. Similar to the painstaking and complexly entailed way that topics are taken up in Hawaiian talk-story, *'ini te'ete'e suli ru'anga* probably would be considered by Anglo-Euro-American teachers to be a "boring" way to present information and stimulate student discussion because it moves relatively slowly and incrementally in laying out what it is to be understood. But the children in the class were intensely engaged in Lindsay's lesson, and highly interactive with him, including the co-construction of meaning—in contrast to nearby classrooms using a colonial style of teaching where students were silent, sometimes appeared to be frightened, and showed disinterest. We also observed Rebekah using the same strategy even when she was conducting her lessons in Solomon Islands Pijin, the lingua franca of the Solomons in which she often taught.

The two teachers' valuing of the children's culture was particularly shown in their incorporating *fa'amanata'anga*, the traditional Kwara'ae equivalent of formal schooling, into their classrooms. *Fa'amanata'anga* is a general term in Kwara'ae for "teaching," and literally means "shaping the mind." It also has a specialized meaning referring to a formal, serious-to-sacred event in which direct teaching and interpersonal counseling are undertaken in high rhetoric, the formal discourse register in Kwara'ae (Watson-Gegeo & Gegeo, 1990). *Fa'amanata'anga* is a fundamental speech event for the application of indigenous epistemology in analyzing and (re)constructing sociocultural understandings and meanings. In Kwara'ae families, *fa'amanata'anga* begins in early childhood, when children are as young as 18 months of age, and continues throughout life. Families' use of this set of socially emphasized epistemological discourse practices is a measure of the degree to which they are committed to traditional culture and values. It is also an indication of the degree to which their children are learning how to engage in indigenous epistemological strategies from a very young age.

Both Rebekah and Lindsay use strategies from *fa'amanata'anga* in some kinds of lessons related to village life, health, and related topics, and in doing so, legitimatize for the children the value of their indigenous culture. Lindsay, however, goes further to employ *fa'amanata'anga* in a more profound way. In an example lesson we recorded in 1990, Lindsay's class was visited by a young local villager (Robinson) who was then studying at a foreign university, had come home on holiday, and decided to visit the primary school he attended as a child. In using *fa'amanata'anga* to talk about what Robinson had accomplished as the young man sat with the students in the classroom, Lindsay emphasized that when Robinson finished his education, he would "teach white people"—an inversion of the status relationship that Lindsay's students had already been socialized to expect. Lindsay also emphasized that despite his foreign education, Robinson is "still one of us" because he comes home to the village, speaks Kwara'ae, and associates with everyone. Then Lindsay argued that Robinson's success illustrates how "knowledge is knowledge" (that is, to be equally valued) whether it is from school or from the village. He emphasized that it is possible to succeed in school without abandoning one's culture and community. Lindsay's students were listening intensely and respectfully throughout this *fa'amanata'anga* session, and assumed the body positioning and facial expression appropriate to *fa'amanata'anga* events just as they would at home. Although we cannot prove that Lindsay's use of *fa'amanata'anga* was essential to his students' success in school, it is nevertheless true that the students in his classes went on to produce the best record for passing the national exams to transition into secondary school. The provincial authorities recognized Lindsay's success by making him headmaster of the school despite his having only a Standard Seven education himself and virtually no formal teacher training (for more analysis of Lindsay and other teachers' teaching styles, including lesson transcripts, see Watson-Gegeo & Gegeo, 1994).

MULTICULTURAL EDUCATION FOR THE FUTURE: MOVING FROM HOPE TO ACTION

> I believe that . . . all genuine hope has to go through the fire of despair. . . . How do we reconstruct our families and communities and churches and mosques and synagogues in such a way that we [who learned struggle through the Civil Rights movement] are more in the lives of young people as exemplars of the struggle that we know brought us as far as we are? . . . Because once it becomes hip to be a Freedom Fighter among young people, it's a new world. It's a new world. (Cornel West, quoted in West and Sealey, 1997, pp. 57, 61)

With Sleeter and McLaren (1995), we believe that teachers and other educational practitioners need to rise to the challenge of reinstating the political voice into multicultural education. We have tried to show in this chapter, however, that a focus on deep culture is part of that reinstatement of voice—that the voice needed is both political and cultural. Such a voice speaks holistically to children and youth, it speaks to their complex identities-in-the-making, and it values the home communities of which they are members even as they are facing the demands, frustrations, challenges, and completion with other cultural patterns and values with which they must contend to achieve an education in school.

A teacher is likely to ask, "How can I possible learn about the deep culture of my students when my classroom may include children from several different cultural groups?" Our experience has been that awareness of the profound implications of deep culture as a concept that is real and operating in the world, not just an academic construction, is a starting point. As teachers ourselves in diverse cultural situations, we recognize that we are asking a great deal of our educational system and of dedicated teachers to genuinely meet each child where the child is. However, there is little choice but to do so in our increasingly diverse society, if unity within diversity is going to be more than mere rhetoric and if we want to move beyond racism to understanding. Thanks to the work of Howard Gardner, we have recently come to understand that there are multiple intelligences, even though we have only started on the path towards valuing them equally. Our next challenge is an old challenge that we have yet to meet in this country: to recognize that there are multiple ways of knowing and being that strengthen and enrich us.

REFERENCES

Agar, M. (1994). *Language shock: Understanding the culture of communication.* New York: William Morrow.

Alcoff, L., & Potter, E. (Eds.). (1993). *Feminist epistemologies.* New York: Routledge.

Au, K. H-P., & Jordan, C. (1981). Teaching reading to Hawaiian children: Finding a culturally appropriate solution. In H. T. Trueba, G.P. Guthrie, & K. H-P. Au (Eds.), *Culture and the bilingual classroom: Studies in classroom ethnography* (pp. 139-152). Rowley, MA: Newbury House.

Banks, J. A. (1992). African American scholarship and the evolution of multicultural education. *Journal of Negro Education, 61*(3), 273-286.

Benham, M. K. P., & Heck, R. H. (1998). *Culture and educational policy in Hawai'i: The silencing of native voices.* Mahwah, NJ: Erlbaum.

Bhaba, H. (1990). The third space: Interview with Homi Bhaba. In J. Rutherford (Ed.), *Identity* (pp. 206-211). London: Lawrence Wishart.

Boggs, S. T. (1985). *Speaking, relating and learning: A study of Hawaiian children at home and at school* (with the assistance of K. A. Watson-Gegeo & G. McMillan.) Norwood, NJ: Ablex.

Boggs, S. T., & Chun, M. N. (1990). Ho'oponopono: A Hawaiian method of solving interpersonal problems. In K. A. Watson-Gegeo & G. M. White (Eds.), *Disentangling: Conflict discourse in pacific societies* (pp. 122-160). Stanford, CA: Stanford University Press.

Boggs, S. T., & Watson-Gegeo, K. A. (1978). Interweaving routines: Strategies for encompassing a social situation. *Language in Society, 7,* 375-392.

Bowlin, J. R., & Stromberg, P. G. (1997). Representation and reality in the study of culture. *American Anthropologist, 89,* 123-134.

Chaiklin, S., & Lave, J. (1996). *Understanding practice: Perspectives on activity and context.* New York: Cambridge University Press.

Chaudhry, L. N. (1991). *Portraits of South Asia bilingualism: Multiple measures of dominance, interference, and the bilingual imagination.* Master's thesis, University of Hawai'i, Mānoa.

Chaudhry, L. N. (1995). *Marginality, hybridity, empowerment: A critical feminist ethnography of the resistance of Pakistani Muslim immigrant women in community and educational contexts.* Doctoral dissertation, University of California, Davis.

Chiu, C. (1991). Righteousness: The notion of justice in Chinese societies. In C. F. Yang & H. S. R. Kao (Eds.), *Chinese people and Chinese society* (pp. 261-285). Taipei: Yuen Liao.

Damasio, A. (1994). *Descartes' error: Emotion, reason, and the human brain.* New York: Grosset/Putnam.

D'Andrade, R., & Strauss, C. (Eds.). (1992). *Human motives and cultural models.* New York: Cambridge University Press.

Diaz-Guerrero, R. (1993). Mexican ethnopsychology. In U. Kim & J. W. Berry (Eds.), *Indigenous psychologies: Research and experience in cultural context* (pp. 44-55). Newbury Park, CA: Sage.

Enriquez, V. G. (Ed.). (1990). *Indigenous psychologies.* Quezon City: Psychological Research and Training House.

Ervin-Tripp, S. (1964a). An analysis of the interaction of language, topic, and listener. *American Anthropologist, 62,* 86-102.

Ervin-Tripp, S. (1964b). Language and TAT content in bilinguals. *Journal of Abnormal and Social Psychology, 68,* 500-507.

Fischer, K. W., Kennedy, B., & Cheng, C-L. (1998). Culture and biology in emotional development. In D. Sharma & K. W. Fischer (Eds.), Socioemotional development across cultures. *New Directions for Child Development, 81,* 21-43

Foley, D. E. (1991). Reconsidering anthropological explanations of ethnic school failure. *Anthropology and Education Quarterly, 22,* 60-86.

Gardner, H. (1983). *Frames of mind: The theory of multiple intelligences.* New York: Basic Books.

Gardner, H. (1989). *To open minds: Chinese clues to the dilemma of contemporary education.* New York: Basic Books.

Gay, G. (1983). Multiethnic education: Historical developments and future prospects. *Phi Delta Kappan, 64,* 560-563.

Gegeo, D. W. (1994). *Kastom and bisnis: Toward integrating cultural knowledge into rural development in the Solomon Islands.* Doctoral dissertation, University of Hawai'i, Manoa.

Gegeo, D. W., & Watson-Gegeo, K. A. (1999). Adult education, language change, and issues of identity and authenticity in Kwara'ae (Solomon Islands*). Anthropology and Education Quarterly, 30,* 22-36.

Gegeo, D. W., & Watson-Gegeo, K. A. (2001). "How we know": Kwara'ae rural villagers doing indigenous epistemology. *The Contemporary Pacific, 13,* 55-88.

Gegeo, D. W., & Watson-Gegeo, K. A. (2002). The critical villager: Transforming language and education in Solomon Islands. In J. W. Tollefson (Ed.), *Language policies in education: Critical issues* (pp. 309-325). Mahwah, NJ: Erlbaum.

Giroux, H. A. (1983). *Theory and resistance in education.* London: Heinemann.

Goldman, A. I. (1986). *Epistemology and cognition.* Cambridge, MA: Harvard University Press.

Goldman, A. I. (1999). *Knowledge in a social world.* Oxford: Oxford University Press.

Grosz, E. (1993). Bodies and knowledges: Feminism and the crisis of reason. In L. Alcoff & E. Potter (Eds.), *Feminist epistemologies* (pp. 187-216). New York: Routledge.

Gumperz, J. J., & Levinson, S. C. (Eds.). (1996). *Rethinking linguistic relativity.* New York: Cambridge University Press.

Hall, S. (1991). Cultural identity and diaspora. In A. D. King (Ed.), *Culture, globalization and the world system: Contemporary conditions for the representation of identity* (pp. 222-236). Albany: State University of New York Press.

Harding, S. (1993). Rethinking standpoint epistemology: "What is strong objectivity?" In L. Alcoff & E. Potter (Eds.), *Feminist epistemologies* (pp. 49-82). New York: Routledge.

Ho, D. Y. F. (1981). Traditional pattern of socialization in Chinese society. *Acta Psychologica Taiwanica, 23,* 81-95.

Holland, D., & Quinn, N. (Eds.). (1987). *Cultural models in language and thought.* New York: Cambridge University Press.

Imbo, S. E. (1998). *An introduction to African philosophy.* New York: Rowman and Littlefield.

Ito, K. L. (1985). Ho'oponopono, "to make right": Hawaiian conflict resolution and metaphor in the construction of a family therapy. *Culture, Medicine and Psychiatry, 9,* 201-217.

Kanaaneh, M. (1997). The "anthropologicality" of indigenous anthropology. *Dialectical Anthropology, 22,* 1-21.

Kearney, M. (1984). *World view.* Novato, CA: Chandler and Sharp.

Keck, V. (Ed.). (1998). *Common worlds and single lives: Constituting knowledge in Pacific societies.* New York: Berg.

Lakoff, G., & Johnson, M. (1999). *Philosophy in the flesh: The embodied mind and its challenge to Western thought.* New York: Basic Books.

Lambek, M. (1983). *Knowledge and practice in Mayotte: Local discourses of Islam, sorcery, and spirit possession.* Toronto: University of Toronto Press.

Lave, J. (1996). The practice of learning. In S. Chaiklin & J. Lave (Eds.), *Understanding practice: Perspectives on activity and content,* (pp. 3-32). New York: Cambridge University Press.

Lave, J., & Wenger, E. (1991). *Situated cognition: Legitimate peripheral participation.* New York: Cambridge University Press.

Mattai, P. R. (1992). Rethinking multicultural education: Has it lost its focus or is it being misused? *Journal of Negro Education, 61*(1), 65-77.

McLaughlin, D., & Tierney, B. (Eds.). (1993). *Naming silenced lives: Personal narratives and the process of educational change*. London and New York: Routledge.

Mehan, H. (1979). *Learning lessons: Social organization in the classroom*. Cambridge, MA: Harvard University Press.

Meyer, M. A. (1998a). *Native Hawaiian epistemology: Contemporary narratives*. Doctoral dissertation, Harvard Graduate School of Education.

Meyer, M. A. (1998b). Native Hawaiian epistemology: Exploring Hawaiian views of knowledge. *Cultural Survival Quarterly, 22,* 38-40.

Meyer, M. A. (2001). Our own liberation: Reflections on Hawaiian epistemology. *The Contemporary Pacific, 13,* 124-148.

Montoya, M. E. (1994). Mascaras, trenzas, y greñas: Un/masking the self while un/braiding Latina stories and legal discourse. *Harvard Women's Law Journal, 17,* 185-220.

Nelson, K. (1996). *Language in cognitive development: The emergence of the mediated mind*. New York: Cambridge University Press.

Nozaki, Y. (2000). Essentializing dilemma and multicultural pedagogy: An ethnographic study of Japanese children in a U.S. school. *Anthropology and Education Quarterly, 31,* 355-380.

Nsamenang, A. B. (1992). *Human development in cultural context: A third world perspective*. Newbury Park, CA: Sage.

Ogbu, J. (1978). *Minority education and caste: The American system in cross-cultural perspective*. New York: Academic Press.

Ogbu, J. (1987). Variability in minority school performance: A problem in search of an explanation. *Anthropology and Education Quarterly, 18,* 312-334.

Pe-Pua, R. (1990). Pegatatanong-tanong: A method for cross-cultural research. In V. G. Enriquez (Ed.), *Indigenous psychologies* (pp. 231-243). Quezon City: Psychological Research and Training House.

Proudfoot, R. (1990). *Even the birds don't sound the same here: The Laotian refugees' search for heart in American culture*. New York: Peter Lang.

Pukui, M. K., Haertig, E. W., & Lee, C. A. (1972a). *Nānā I ke kumu [Look to the source]*. Vol. 1. Honolulu: Hui Hanai, Queen Lili'uokalani Children's Center.

Pukui, M. K., Haertig, E. W., & Lee, C. A. (1972b). *Nānā I ke kumu [Look to the source]*. Vol. 2. Honolulu: Hui Hanai, Queen Lili'uokalani Children's Center.

Quinn, N., & Holland, D. (1987). Introduction. In D. Holland & N. Quinn (Eds.), *Cultural models in lanuage and thought* (pp. 3-40). New York: Cambridge University Press.

Regier, T. (1995). A model of the human capacity for categorizing spatial relations. *Cognitive Linguistics, 6,* 63-88.

Regier, T. (1996). *The human semantic potential: Spatial language and constrained connectionism*. Cambridge, MA: MIT Press.

Resnick, L. B., Levine, J. M., & Teasley, S. D. (Eds.). (1991). *Perspectives on socially shared cognition*. Washington, DC: American Psychological Association.

Ritchie, M. (1995). Whose voice is it anyway?: Vocalizing multicultural analysis. In C. Sleeter & P. McLaren (Eds.), *Multicultural education, critical pedagogy, and the politics of difference* (pp. 309-317). Albany: State University of New York Press.

Rosaldo, R. (1993). *Culture and truth: The remaking of social analysis*. Boston: Beacon.

Salmond, A. (1985). Maori epistemologies. In J. Overing (Ed.), *Reason and morality* (pp. 40-70). London: Tavistock.

San Juan, E., Jr. (1992). *Articulations of power in ethnic and racial studies in the United States*. Atlantic Highlands, NJ: Humanities Press.

Sato, C. J. (1985). Linguistic inequality in Hawai'i: The post-creole dilemma. In N. Wolfson & J. Manes (Eds.), *Language of inequality* (pp. 255-272). Berlin: Mouton.

Sato, C. J. (1991). Sociolinguistic variation and language attitudes in Hawai'i. In J. Cheshire (Ed.), *English around the world: Sociolinguistic perspectives* (pp. 647-663). Cambridge: Cambridge University Press.

Sato, C. J., & Watson-Gegeo, K. A. (1992, January). *Information structure in Hawai'i Creole English*. Paper presented at the Society for Pidgin and Creole Linguistics conference, Philadelphia.

Schmitt, R. (1982). Hawai'i's social rating. *Social Process in Hawai'i, 9,* 151-157.

Shonkoff, J. P., & Phillips, D. A. (Eds.). (2000). *From neurons to neighborhoods: The science of early child development*. National Research Council and Institute of Medicine. Washington, DC: National Academy Press.

Shook, E. V. (1986). *Ho'oponopono: Contemporary uses of a Hawaiian problem-solving process*. Honolulu: University of Hawai'i Press.

Shore, B. (1991). *Culture in mind: Meaning construction and cultural cognition*. New York: Oxford University Press.

Sinha, D. (1997). Indigenizing psychology. In J. W. Berry, Y. H. Poortinga, & J. Pandey (Eds.), *Handbook of cross-cultural psychology: Theory and method* (Vol. 1, pp. 131-169). Boston: Allyn & Bacon.

Sleeter, C. E., & McLaren, P. L. (Eds.). (1995). *Multicultural education, critical pedagogy, and the politics of difference*. Albany: State University of New York Press.

Smith, L. T. (1999). *Decolonizing methodologies: Research and indigenous peoples*. New York: Zed Books.

Tharp, R. G., & Gallimore, R. (1988). *Rousing minds to life: Teaching, learning, and schooling in social context*. Cambridge: Cambridge University Press.

Ullichny, P., & Watson-Gegeo, K. A. (1989). Interaction and authority: The Dominant Interpretive Framework in writing conferences. *Discourse Processes, 12,* 309-328.

Vygotsky, L. S. (1981). The genesis of higher mental functions. In J. V. Wertsch (Ed.), *The concept of activity in Soviet psychology* (pp. 144-188). Armonk, NY: M. E. Sharpe.

Wallace, A. F. C. (1970). *Culture and personality* (2nd ed.). New York: Random House.

Watson, K. A. (1975). Transferable communicative routines: Strategies and group identity in two speech events. *Language in Society, 4,* 53-72.

Watson-Gegeo, K. A. (1994). Language and education in Hawai'i: Sociopolitical and economic implications of Hawai'i Creole English. In M. Morgan (Ed.), *Language and the social construction of identity in Creole situations* (pp. 101-120). Los Angeles: Center for Afro-American Studies, UCLA.

Watson-Gegeo, K. A. (1996). Argument as transformation: A Pacific framing of conflict, community, and learning. In D. Berrill (Ed.), *Perspectives on argument* (pp. 189-204). Cresskill, NJ: Hampton Press.

Watson-Gegeo, K. A. (2002). Fantasy and reality: The dialectic of work and play in Kwara'ae children's lives. *Ethos, 29,* 1-26.

Watson-Gegeo, K. A., & Boggs, S. T. (1997). From verbal play to talking story: The role of routines in speech events among Hawaiian children. In S. Ervin-Tripp & C. Mitchell-Kernan (Eds.), *Child discourse.* New York: Academic Press.

Watson-Gegeo, K. A., & Gegeo, D. W. (1986a). Calling-out and repeating routines in Kwara'ae children's language socialization. In B. B. Schieffelin & E. Ochs (Eds.), *Language socialization across cultures* (pp. 17-50). New York: Cambridge University Press.

Watson-Gegeo, K. A., & Gegeo, D. W. (1986b). The social world of Kwara'ae children: Acquisition of language and values. In J. Cook-Gumperz, W. Corsaro, & J. Streeck (Eds.), *Children's worlds and children's language* (pp. 109-138). Berlin: Mouton de Gruyter.

Watson-Gegeo, K. A., & Gegeo, D. W. (1990). Shaping the mind and straightening out conflicts: The discourse of Kwara'ae family counseling. In K. A. Watson-Gegeo & G. M. White (Eds.), *Disentangling: Conflict discourse in Pacific societies* (pp. 161-213). Stanford, CA: Stanford University Press.

Watson-Gegeo, K. A., & Gegeo, D. W. (1992). Schooling, knowledge and power: Social transformation in the Solomon Islands. *Anthropology and Education Quarterly, 23,* 10-29.

Watson-Gegeo, K. A., & Gegeo, D. W. (1994). Keeping culture out of the classroom in rural Solomon Islands schools: A critical analysis. *Educational Foundations, 8,* 27-55.

Watson-Gegeo, K. A., & Gegeo, D. W. (1999a). Culture, discourse, and indigenous epistemology: Transcending current models in language planning and policy. In T. Huebner & K. A. Davis (Eds.), *Sociopolitical perspectives on language policy and planning in the USA* (pp. 99-116). Amsterdam: John Benjamins.

Watson-Gegeo, K. A., & Gegeo, D. W. (1999b). (Re)modeling culture in Kwara'ae: The role of discourse in children's cognitive development. *Discourse Processes, 1,* 227-246.

Watson-Gegeo, K. A., & White, G. M. (1990). *Disentangling: Conflict discourse in Pacific societies.* Stanford, CA: Stanford University Press.

West, C., & Sealey, K. S. (1997). *Restoring hope: Conversations on the future of Black America/Cornel West.* Boston: Beacon Press.

Yang, K. S. (Ed.). (1988). *The psychology of the Chinese people: An indigenous perspective.* Taipei, Taiwan: Keui-Kuan Publishing Company.

Yeatman, A. (1994). *Postmodern revisionings of the political.* New York: Routledge.

CHAPTER FIFTEEN

Standards for Educators

Cultivating the Garden

Greg S. Goodman

Karen T. Carey

California State University, Fresno

"I know too," said Candide, "that we must cultivate our garden."

"You are in the right," said Pangloss, " for when man was put into the Garden of Eden, it was so that he should work in it; and this proves that man was not born to be idle."

"Let us work then without disputing," said Martin. "It is the only way to render life supportable."

The little society, one and all, entered into this laudable design and set themselves to exert their different talents. The little piece of ground yielded them a plentiful crop. Cunegund indeed was very ugly, but she became an excellent hand at pastry work; Pacquette embroidered; the old woman had the care of the linen. There was none, down to Brother Girofle'e, but did some service; he was a very good carpenter and became an honest man. Pangloss used now and then to say to Candide:

"There is a concatenation of all events in the best of all possible worlds; for, in short, had you not been kicked out of a fine castle by

*the backside for the love of Miss Cunegund, had you not been put
into the Inquisition, had you not traveled over America on foot, had
you not run the Baron through the body, and had you not lost all
your sheep which you brought from the good country of El Dorado,
you would not have been here to eat preserved citrons, and pista-
chio nuts."*

*"Excellently observed," answered Candide, "but let us cultivate
our garden."*

Voltaire's *Candide* (pp. 124-125)

Mirroring the diversity within your classroom, the authors of *Critical
Multicultural Conversations* have presented myriad perspectives to the central
and essential question: how can we first reach and then teach within today's
school? As you have gleaned these pages for answers to these essential and critical questions, we are certain that your perspective is influenced by your experience and prior educational process. It should be no surprise that this is true for
your students, as well. We hope you can break with some of the traditional, and
perhaps, imperialistic viewpoints to entertain a more critical, multicultural perspective. Having learned to perceive the world within the tainted lens of tradi-
tionalist thinking, our possession of inadequate tools is understandable.
However, to continue to perpetuate hegemonic relations is to succumb to the rituals of the past and to fail the needs of today. The call is for change and the
opportunity awaits you: the emerging educator.

As Voltaire used irony to mock the simplistic philosophic position of opti-
mism in eighteenth century France ("everything is for the best in the best of all
possible worlds"), he challenged and defied the gulf between blind-faith opti-
mism and the harsh realities of his day. Today's educator is confronted by this
same discrepancy between the need to prepare students for a world that carries
many of the same cruel realities Voltaire experienced and the hope that we can
overcome global differences to build one safe world. If our legacy is to achieve
the "best of all possible worlds" or if we in fact create the worst of all possible
worlds, our children and their children will be the recipients. With these tremendous stakes, we all sense the urgency of our work.

As we conclude our quest for diversity affirmations, we want to review the
standards for teachers in California and to relate those standards to the writing
you have just read. California's standards for teachers are similar to those of
other states, and they can be easily translated to your circumstances. To assist in
the preparation of new teachers, the state of California's Department of
Education provides a set of six standards delineating the path of teacher creden-
tial programs.

The first standard for the teaching profession specifies that teachers will be
"engaging and supporting [of] all students in learning." This first standard
directs teachers to:

- Connect students' prior knowledge, life experience, and interests with learning goals;
- Use a variety of instructional strategies and resources to respond to student's diverse needs;
- Facilitate learning experiences that promote autonomy, interactions, and choice;
- Engage students in problem solving, critical thinking, and other activities that make subject matter meaningful;
- Promote self-directed, reflective learning for all students.

All students have a right to be treated with dignity and respect. Basic human rights fundamentally undergird the operation of a democratic classroom (Kohl, 1994). More important than any other aspect of the pedagogy of your classroom, your affirmation of the diversity represented by each individual within your classroom will determine the outcome for each student (Nieto, 1996). Of the many voices supporting the development of diversity, Sonia Nieto offers some of the best practical advice. Nieto (1996) suggests a model for diversity that begins with tolerance, evolves into acceptance, and is reinforced with respect. The ultimate goal of multicultural education is to achieve affirmation of diversity.

All of the leading spokespersons for multiculturalism share the conclusion that implementation of best practices in the provision of equitable instruction are complex and demanding (Banks, 1994; Freire, 1979; Giroux, 1997; McLaren, 1999; Mouffe, 1988; Steinberg & Kincheloe, 1997). To change yourself and to adapt to the diversity in your classroom requires multiple methodologies and approximations that evolve over long periods of time. As Banks (1994) suggests, moving from simple expressions of the celebration of cultural differences to the assimilation of deep understanding of individual identifications is multifaceted. As educators begin the changes through consciousness raising of both themselves and their students, transformations of a deeply personal nature are required.

The second standard calls for upon teachers to "create and maintain effective environments." The standard seeks to:

- Create a physical environment that engages all students;
- Establish a climate that promotes fairness and respect;
- Promote social development and group responsibility;
- Establish and maintain standards for student behavior;
- Plan and implement classroom procedures and routines that support student learning;
- Use instructional time effectively.

The environment within which the daily practice of instruction takes place sustains the student's motivation and capacity for learning. Both the physical and social atmosphere speak highly of the teachers commitment to multicultural education (Goodman, 1999). Seeing artifacts, realia, and other representations of the cultures and communities around us reinforces those values and identifications of each individual. Posters, photographs, quilts, tapestries, statues, and other symbols of the classroom's multiple cultures enhance the student's connection to the environment. Valuing the cultural capital (Bourdieu, 1993) of every classroom constituent is a fundamental requirement of today's educators.

Creating a spiritual and social climate is also essential to the multicultural classroom. Simply maintaining a safe and protected place for students to learn increases the likelihood that learning can be accomplished (Pianta & Walsh, 1996). Trusting that the teacher will protect every student from put-downs or other humiliations is the largest support a teacher can provide. Without a warm, supportive environment, learning cannot take place (Hart, 1983).

The third standard elicits educators to reflectively consider the domain of "planning instruction and designing learning experiences for all students."

This standard calls for teachers to:

- Draw on and value student's backgrounds, interests, and developmental learning needs;

- Establish and articulate goals for student learning;

- Develop and sequence instructional activities and materials for student learning;

- Design short-term and long-term plans to foster student learning;

- Modify instructional plans to adjust for student needs.

Curriculum and lesson plans vary for every student. Each student has an individual experience, and is therefore, unlike any other student in your class. The advantage for educators is that every student brings something unique to contribute to the classroom and the potential benefit of all (Rury & Mirel, 1997).

Exploring each student's background and interests allows you, the educator, to plan effective and interesting lessons for all of your students. Individualization of instruction not only motivates each student. Individualization of instruction is the number one methodology for the improvement of achievement. In a recent study of California's Central Valley schools, the majority of schools surveyed (84%) said that they were using some form of individualization of instruction to increase student performance (Goodman et al. 2001).

The fourth standard for teaching calls upon teachers to be "understanding and organizing of subject matter." This standard requires teachers to:

- Demonstrate knowledge of subject matter content and student development;

- Organize curriculum to support student understanding of subject matter;

- Interrelate ideas and information within and across subject matter;

- Develop student understanding through instructional strategies that are appropriate to the subject matter;

- Use materials, resources, and technologies to make subject matter accessible to students.

Aligning the curriculum to the state frameworks for subject content is essential for student competency within those specific subject matter rubrics (California State Board of Education, 2000). However, your students cannot know it all, even if the state department expectations specify the outcome. You must draw on all of the resources available to you through the district office, your colleagues, and your students.

Articulating curriculum to state and district standards helps the educator to see their students on a continuum of knowledge and skill development. The strategy of aligning instruction to standards and instructional objectives gives the teacher clear direction and will help the student achieve the greatest level of proficiency within each subject area.

The fifth domain for teacher competency is referred to as "assessing student learning." Within this domain, teachers:

- Establish and communicate learning goals for all students;

- Collect and use multiple sources of information to assess student learning;

- Involve and guide all students in assessing their own learning;

- Use results of assessment to guide instruction;

- Communicate with students, families, and other audiences about student learning.

Assessment is the tool for directing instruction, and it is the primary method of evaluation for the outcome of the learning process. To effectively individualize instruction, you must assess each student's skill and knowledge level. From your assessment of their current status, you may proceed to organize student goals and objectives.

Assessment of student outcomes has become the singular focus of critics of education. In particular, state-mandated tests have made the issue of assessment a "high stakes" enterprise. Using assessment to make judgments about communities, specific schools, or individual teachers can result in significantly deleterious consequences. Although state-mandated assessments will not disappear, these authors hope that more authentic measures of student achievement will become the preferred assessment methodology. Evaluation and assessment of student growth are critical in the quest to show results; however, the assessment instrument must be valid for each individual student. This means that we need to test what is taught, and the test's normative group must match the audience we choose to assess (GoPaul-McNicol & Thomas-Presswood, 1998).

The final domain of teacher competency calls for "developing as a professional educator." This domain guides the teacher to:

- Reflect on teaching practice and plan professional development;
- Establish professional goals and pursue opportunities to grow professionally;
- Works with communities to improve professional practice;
- Works with families to improve professional practice;
- Works with colleagues to improve professional practice;
- Balances professional responsibilities and maintains motivation.

Your development as a professional educator is, potentially, the most rewarding domain for you. Looking at your career as an opportunity for lifelong learning should fill you with joy. As a teacher, you hold the intrinsic values of learning as truth. Seeing how learning has enabled you to achieve success and the reward of living an intelligent life, you understand the reinforcing nature of learning.

Hopefully, you will be a part of a school district that reinforces learning. Senge (1990) describes the value of the learning organization in his work, *The Fifth Discipline*. Being a part of an organization that values learning and development of its staff is very rewarding. The authors of this text represent the values inherent in continued professional growth. Most of the authors in this text have been practitioners and/or continue to function in that role. However, all of the authors have earned doctoral degrees in pursuit of their continuing education. This professional growth has had the effect of reinforcing their quest for developing mastery within their professional experience.

As we have reviewed the six standards, the first standard, "engaging and supporting individuals" corresponds to this entire text. Critical multicultural educators seek to include all students in the process of learning. Leading the way into the 21st century, critical educators believe that success for one cannot occur without success for all. Education is not about the identification and reward of valedictorians; education is about the democratic experience of valuing all of the community. We all have a role as citizens, and that function is to promote the well-being of each of our neighbors (West, 1999).

This book is not a cookbook; there is no recipe for multicultural education. However, there does exist a wealth of knowledge that is available to enhance our understanding, compassion, and commitment to the goal of supporting diversity and realizing the dream of democracy (Mendieta, 1999). Principal to the goal of developing democratic classrooms and societies is the discovery of methods that bring us together (Banks, 1994). We come together by recognizing the ways in which we have been divided in our past. Divisions based upon ethnicity, privilege, intelligence, and other forms of cultural capital have worked to dismantle democracy (Novak, 2002). More than any other time in our history, we need to work to reduce the divisions that separate us (Willinsky, 1998). Modeling ways in which we can achieve one unified world for a diverse population in your classroom or school is the beginning of our being able to extend democratic principles to larger communities.

As you have understood the authors in this book to say, we are one world, one community, and we need to understand the complexity and chaos that surrounds us (Cairns & Cairns, 1994). The never-ending task of pursuing a meaningful and thoughtful present and future existence for all students is the goal of the professional educator. Accomplishing student's success is the work and the reward of a passionate educator (Slavin, 1996). We hope you keep the fire alive and that you find this to be the fulfillment of your life dream as an example of what one can achieve for the betterment of us all!

REFERENCES

Banks, J. A. (1994). *Multiethnic education: Theory and practice* (3rd ed.). Boston: Allyn & Bacon.

Bourdieu, P. (1993). *The field of cultural reproduction.* New York: Columbia University Press.

Cairns, R., & Cairns, B. (1994). *Lifelines and risks: Pathways of youth in our time.* Cambridge, England: Cambridge University Press.

California State Board of Education. (2000). J. Lundin & S. Bruton (Eds.), *Mathematics framework of the California public schools: Kindergarten through grade twelve.* Sacramento, CA: California Department of Education.

Freire, P. (1979). *Pedagogy of the oppressed.* New York: Continuum.

Giroux, H. (1997). *Pedagogy and the politics of hope: Theory, culture, and schooling.* Boulder, CO: Westview.

Goodman, G. S. (1999). *Alternatives in education: Critical pedagogy for disaffected youth.* New York: Peter Lang.

Goodman, G., Brown-Welty, S., Bushman, J., Lomack, G., Garcia, P., Hernandez, P., & Dorn, S. (2001). *Looking for success.* Fresno: California State University, Fresno.

GoPaul-McNicol, S., & Thomas-Presswood, T. (1998). *Working with linguistically and culturally different children.* Needham Heights, MA: Allyn & Bacon.

Hart, L. A. (1983). *Human brain and human learning.* Village of Oak Creek, AZ: Books for Educators.

Kohl, H. (1994). *I won't learn from you: And other thoughts on creative maladjustment.* New York: The New Press.

McLaren, P. (1999). *Schooling as a ritual performance: Toward a political economy of educational symbols and gestures.* New York: Rowman & Littlefield.

Mendieta, E. (1999). Becoming citizens, becoming Hispanics. In D. Batstone & E. Mendieta (Eds.), *The good citizen*. New York: Routledge.

Mouffe, C. (1988). Radical democracy: Modern or postmodern? In A. Ross (Ed.), *Universal abandon? The politics of postmodernism* (pp. 31-45). Minneapolis: The University of Minnesota Press.

Nieto, S. (1996). *Affirming diversity: The sociopolitical context of multicultural education*. White Plains, NY: Longman.

Novak, B. (2002, Fall). Humanizing democracy: Matthew Arnold's nineteenth-century call for a common, higher, educative pursuit of happiness and its relevance to twenty-first century democratic life. *American Educational Research Journal, 39*(3), 593-637.

Pianta, R., & Walsh, D. (1996). *High risk children in schools: Constructing sustaining relationships*. New York: Routledge.

Rury, J., & Mirel, J. (1997). The political economy of urban education. In M. Apple (Ed.), *Review of Research in Education, 22*, 49-110.

Senge, P. M. (1990). *The fifth discipline: The art and practice of the learning organization*. New York: Doubleday.

Slavin R. E. (1996). *Education for all*. Lisse, Netherlands: Swets and Zeitlinger Publishers.

Steinberg, S., & Kincheloe, J. (1997). *Changing multiculturalism*. Buckingham, England: Open University Press.

West, C. (1999). The moral obligations of living in a democratic society. In D. Batstone & E. Mendieta (Eds.), *The good citizen*. New York: Routledge.

Willinsky, J. (1998). *Learning to divide the world: Education at empire's end*. Minneapolis: University of Minnesota Press.

AUTHOR INDEX

SUBJECT INDEX

A

academic achievement, 16, 18, 124, 152
  math, 201
academic embracing, 219–221
acculturation, 151
African-Americans, 93, 108, 190
AIDS, 49, 52, 58
alienation, 13
American Council on Education, 11
American Indian, 186
  Native American, 237
Americans With Disabilities Act, 2
Angelou, Maya, 9
Arab Americans, 79–91
  diversity, 82–83
  language, 82
  values, 82
assessment, 84, 89, 104, 121
  504 evaluation, 187
  IQ tests, 102
  normed reference testing, 94
  Scholastic Aptitude Test, 111
  standards, 103
  standardized tests, 124, 217
  Stanford Achievement Test, 200
  student learning, 261–262
  test scores, 221
assimilation, 10–11, 43, 65, 81, 259
at risk youth, 119–135
Attention Deficit Disorder (ADD), 182, 189

attitudes
  Arab, 89
auditory processing, 186
authentic reading, 31

B

biases, 15, 17, 87
bigotry, 41
bilingual, 154
  Education Act, 12
Brazil, 24
Brown vs. Board of Education, 11, 96
  separate but equal, 100
Brunei, 64
Burma, 64

C

California, 64, 123, 154, 258
  Central Valley, 66, 73, 202, 237
  Department of Education, 258
  Fresno, 68
Cambodia, 64
caring, 210–211
Castro, 52
Character, 210
charter schools, 229
China, 28
  Han Chinese, 150
Christian, 7
civil rights, 85, 236
  Civil Rights Act, 12
  Office of Civil Rights, 180, 187
classroom, 16
  climate, 259

273